SAVAGES
AND
CIVILIZATION

ALSO BY JACK WEATHERFORD

SAVAGES

AND

CIVILIZATION

Who Will Survive?

JACK WEATHERFORD

CROWN PUBLISHERS, INC., NEW YORK

Published by Crown Publishers, Inc., 201 East 50th Street, New York, New York 10022. Member of the Crown Publishing Group.

Random House, Inc. New York, Toronto, London, Sydney, Auckland

CROWN is a trademark of Crown Publishers, Inc.

Manufactured in the United States of America

Design by Leonard Henderson

Library of Congress Cataloging-in-Publication Data

Weatherford, J. McIver.
    Savages and civilization : who will survive? / by Jack Weatherford.
        p.   cm.
    Includes bibliographical references and index.
    1. Ethnic relations.   2. Culture conflict.   3. Civilization.
4. Indigenous peoples.   I. Title.
GN496.W43   1994
305.8—dc20   93-28836
                                                    CIP

ISBN 0-517-58860-9

10   9   8   7   6   5   4   3   2   1

First Edition

Dedicated with appreciation
to
Marnie and Roy Pearce

Contents

Acknowledgments

I thank my wife, Walker Pearce, for accompanying me on the long quest to research and write this book, and I appreciate her thoughtful comments. I appreciate the constant encouragement of our children, Walker Buxton and Roy Maybank, as well as the twenty-five years of support from my wife's parents, Marnie and Roy Pearce, to whom this book is dedicated.

Since 1979 I have worked closely with my editor, James O'Shea Wade, and my agent, Lois Wallace, and I appreciate their years of advice and assistance.

At Macalester College, I thank Robert Gavin, Nancy Gibbons, Betty Ivey, Kathy Hyduke, David McCurdy, Anna Meigs, Anne Sutherland, the staff of the DeWitt Wallace Library, and mostly I thank my students for their many comments, suggestions, and criticisms.

I thank the W. K. Kellogg Foundation, particularly Bobby Austin, Norm Brown, Larraine Matusak, Russ Mawby, Betty J. Overton, Anna Sheppard, Roger Sublett, and the advisors and fellows of Group XI of the Kellogg National Fellowship Program. I appreciate the support of the Fulbright-Hays program at the American University of Cairo and the fellows who shared my experience in Egypt.

For special support along the way, I thank Roger Chilton, Virginia Greene, David de Havilland, Peter Johnson, Phil Lucas, and Stephanie Yoo, all of whom helped to make my travels more enjoyable.

PART I

Tribal Culture and the Origins of Diversity

The savage in man is never quite eradicated.
—HENRY DAVID THOREAU

1

The End of the Modern World

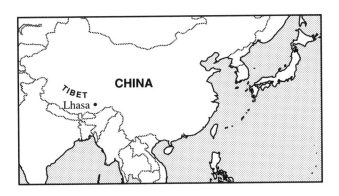

You cannot have both civilization and truth. . . .
—Iris Murdoch

So many broken bones littered the Tibetan field of the dead that I had to dismount from my bicycle to avoid puncturing a tire on one of the sharp, splintered ends sticking up from the dirt and rocks. All around me, strips of worn and faded cloth scattered across the ground in the light breeze; they fluttered like miniature prayer flags from bushes or lay wadded in inert lumps among the rocks. In every direction I saw the broken and shattered remains of human bones that one could barely identify—femur, tibia, rib, and occasionally a smashed skull or jawbone with a few teeth intact.

As I picked my way carefully across the field, I headed for the source of the broken bones and teeth; I moved toward a distant rock that served as the butchering platform where special mourners cut up the corpses and fed the bloody scraps to birds that circled overhead in great numbers. Walking closer to the sky-burial site, I could not avoid the thick, sour odor of death. As I started to climb the rock, I strained to find a firm hold for my hands and feet. Despite the worn grooves for hand- and toeholds in the rock, the boulders had a slippery coating of body fat and other liquids that had dripped from the platform for years and coated everything below it.

I found the sky-burial platform and the adjacent field of bones in the northern outskirts of Tibet's capital city of Lhasa, less than a mile from the Sera Monastery, a major religious center founded at the base of Tatipu Hill in the fifteenth century. For nearly five centuries the Sera Monastery served as a Buddhist university with an unusual mission in a pacifist religion. The monastery trained a special corps of fighting monks whose martial-arts powers made them prized allies of many armies and political causes through the centuries.

The monks do not butcher the bodies of the dead; that task belongs to experienced "body breakers" or *domdens*. Working at dawn, they skin the body and dissect it, then hack it into pieces and crush the bones, which they mix with *tsampa*, the staple Tibetan flour made from roasted barley. The *domdens* then leave the chopped body parts for the hungry vultures, ravens, and kites that live around the field of bones and depend almost exclusively on human flesh for their diets.

Highland Tibet offers few possibilities for the disposal of the dead. Unlike their Hindu neighbors to the south, the Tibetans cannot cremate the dead because most of the country is well above the timberline, and what little wood it possesses has much more important uses. Unlike the Chinese, the Tibetans find it difficult to bury their dead in the ground, because much of the ground is frozen and filled with rocks that make digging extremely difficult.

Even though many traditional cultures around the world once exposed their dead to the elements or to animals, the butchering of the body and sky burial of the Tibetans is unique. Traditionally only wealthier Tibetans or important monks merited burial in a tomb that had to be cut from rock. Sometimes people disposed of the dead by throwing the bodies into the river, but the rivers proved too small, and the bodies floating in them interfered with the daily activities of drinking and bathing. Sky burial proved to be the most efficient way of disposing of the bodies without leaving them to rot or become mummified in the dry, cold wind of the mountains. Tibetans consider sky burial an honorable and generous way for the deceased to perform one more act of earthly good by feeding the birds.

The practice of sky burial over many centuries allowed the development of a sophisticated body of psychological and medical knowledge gleaned from the work of the *domdens*. Long before

Western medicine had sufficient knowledge of the workings of the body, the Tibetans understood such complex phenomena as the operation of the circulatory system and the development of the embryo. This knowledge seems surprisingly akin to modern science in that Tibetans saw the human being as passing through stages as fish and reptiles before becoming human.

Sometimes monks used human bones for other purposes, such as a trumpet used in exorcism, made from the human thigh bone, or a small drum made from a human cranium. Even though these human artifacts had ritual and religious purposes, the monks who used them seemed well aware of their impact to inspire fear in a poorly educated nation of village peasants and nomadic tribes. The Chinese communist government later put these instruments to propaganda purposes and used them to justify their claim of having liberated the Tibetans from their harsh and unjustifiably cruel theocracy.

Religion and politics overlap and intertwine in most societies, but in the history of Tibet, religion and politics have traditionally been the same enterprise. Through the centuries, monks, lamas, and abbots ruled the mountainous nation and guided it through successive religious feuds, purges, revolts, and wars. In the twentieth century, religion has been a major flashpoint in the struggle between the Tibetans and their Chinese rulers.

Religious practices, particularly mortuary rites, have a strong emotional content in most cultures. What we do with our dead constitutes an integral part of our identity as members of a particular cultural and moral group. The act of sky burial became one way in which Tibetans could resist Chinese rule during recent decades. It became a means of emphasizing their Tibetan culture in the face of Chinese culture. Even when the Chinese authorities closed the monasteries, burned the sacred books, destroyed the statues and paintings, razed the buildings, killed the nuns and priests, and forced the people to wear uniformly drab clothes and even made them change their diets, the Tibetans did not surrender their way of disposing of the dead.

Sky burial became a point of great contention between the Tibetans and the Chinese government. The Chinese authorities disapproved of the practice, but, drawn by morbid curiosity, Chinese soldiers and administrators frequently came to watch the butchering of the dead. The Tibetans resented the Chinese for many reasons, but they particularly resented the intrusion on

them during a time of grief. In 1985, as tensions mounted between the native Tibetans and the Han Chinese, repeated skirmishes and fights erupted at the sky-burial rituals. The small
skirmishes finally resulted in a virtual riot when a large group of
mourners raced down the incline from the sky-burial platform
and attacked the Chinese by hurling sticks, stones, and, reportedly, even body parts at them.

At the sky-burial site, the Tibetans had reached a point at
which they fought back against the Chinese-imposed government. The episode seemed to embolden the Tibetan people, and
over the coming months they demonstrated openly in the city,
and eventually provoked a series of major confrontations with
the Chinese authorities. Fighting erupted in central Lhasa and
around the monasteries, leading to another Chinese clamp-down
and to yet additional restrictions on visitors to the area. Because
of the tight communications embargo, no one knows how many
Tibetans were killed or imprisoned during these episodes.

I had come to Tibet for only a few weeks at the end of a
long journey, but I encountered there a raw cultural conflict
of proportions that seemed out of place in the technologically
sophisticated modern world. The Chinese had occupied Tibet
since 1959, when the Dalai Lama fled to India amid fighting
that, according to Chinese sources, killed 87,000 Tibetans; the
Tibetans place the figure at more than one million. In the intervening decades since the 1959 revolt, the Chinese communist
authorities had moved in millions of new administrators, settlers,
and soldiers to solidify their hold on the mountainous land. Still,
the people resisted the central Beijing government in small and
large ways.

In the nervous young recruits of the People's Liberation Army
of China with their array of heavy weapons and armored vehicles,
I saw the brute force of the state. Yet in the eyes of the old
lamas, the pilgrims, and even the children strapped to their
mothers' backs, I saw the resistance of a people to that state, no
matter how large its army or how great its power. I heard the
same resistance in the creaking turn of the prayer wheels in front
of the monasteries, and saw it in the massive embroidered *thanka*s
hanging over the monastery walls, displaying the sacred image
of the Buddha. I saw it in the traditional clothes the women
wore. I smelled it in the fresh juniper and the rancid butter

burning in the temples, and I even tasted it in the salty Tibetan tea made with the same yak butter as that burned in the lamps.

The cultural conflicts that I saw so vividly displayed in Tibet challenged many of my notions about humans and their cultures. How did human groups become so different from one another? Why is there still such tremendous cultural variety in the world, and why does it persist? Are the cultural differences among humans around the world increasing or decreasing?

Compared to such animals as dogs or cats, which show tremendous physical variation, humans around the world show only minor differences in size, color, and features. Humans who live in cold climates have no more hair than people who live in hot climates, and humans run only a modest color variation from dark to light, with none of the vivid blues, purples, yellows, oranges, and greens characteristic of birds and fish. The male and female of the human species differ less than even some of our closest relatives, such as the baboons, in which species the male may be several times the size of the female.

With such marked homogeneity in physical form, it seems all the more surprising that humans vary so much in culture, language, and behavior. Compared with physical variation, cultural variety seems incredibly great. For example, some groups have a relatively unencumbered attitude toward sexuality, whereas for others it is a matter of death if a person has sexual contact with a person of a forbidden category or at a forbidden time in life. Some societies allow multiple spouses; others specify only one. Buddhists and Hindus believe that it is wrong to kill an animal for any reason, while the ancient Greeks and Jews believed that their gods wanted animals killed on the altar as the highest sacrifice humans could make to their deities.

As the modern global culture emerged during the twentieth century, it seemed at first that local variations of culture might disappear. As orthodox communists, the Chinese government taught that local ethnic groups such as the Tibetans and the other fifty-four minorities of China would disappear as their members merged into the new, classless society. Party bureaucrats in the former countries of the Soviet Union, Yugoslavia, and Czechoslovakia all taught that same theory, but instead of seeing the ethnic groups disappear, they saw their own states disappear as the ethnic groups divided the territory among themselves in mistrust and frequently in fierce and bloody violence fueled by centuries of hateful crimes remembered by each side.

Communist theoreticians did not stand alone in the mistaken assumption that ethnic divisions would disappear into the homogenity of modernism. Economic and political theories of many types assumed that the process of modernization would lead people from their underdeveloped and traditionalist forms of life into the modern production and consumer markets of the developed world. The metaphor of the melting pot in which many cultures are combined into one became a primary image of the United States; yet the cultures did not always combine so readily. Modernists assumed that along the way the ethnic groups would shed their traditionalist clothes, life-styles, languages, and religions as the world became a global village in which we all worked for interrelated corporations, ate similar diets, and laughed at the same situation comedies on television.

Neither the classless society of communism nor the global village of capitalism managed to homogenize the world during the twentieth century. Even though economic interdependence increased, and even though an international popular culture of sports and entertainment icons arose and became as known in Tibet and Timbuktu as in Toledo, the emergence of a world culture failed to obliterate local cultures. Instead, ethnic and cultural identities grew stronger, everywhere from the largest cities to the most remote jungle valleys. Rather than blending into a homogenized world culture shared by all, the various tribes, nations, religions, and ethnic groups accentuated their differences to become more varied than ever.

The global culture makes each group more self-consciously aware of its own identity and where it fits in the global society. In a world where nearly anyone can watch television or at least listen to the radio, people need more than ever a way to differentiate themselves from others. Humans have developed a global culture of communications, news, music, film, radio, and television; travel and cultural contact are far more widespread now than during any other historical era. At the same time, local, ethnic, and even tribal issues have flared into renewed fighting and the dismemberment of some nations. As world culture has become broader and more easily identified, ethnic groups have struggled to make themselves into important actors on the world stage and to define themselves to a rapidly expanding audience around the world.

Even after I left Tibet, I could not leave behind the powerful images and troubling questions that unique place had thrust into my mind. Although I did not yet realize it, my experiences in Tibet had launched me on yet another, longer journey, on a quest to explore the new cultural conflict that has burst forth in the modern world.

That world seems much less modern now than it did a few years ago. Daily news offers accounts of high-technology missiles being fired by tribal peoples whose names have rarely been seen outside a history book in the last five centuries. Ancient religions have reared their heads to put women back in veils, to condemn men to death as heretics for praying the wrong way, to attack anything modern, and to lead their followers on raids and holy wars against their neighbors. Old and new plagues have decimated tribes, cities, and nations with a ferocity more appropriate to the angry wrath of the Old Testament than to the age of modern vaccines and nuclear medicine.

Each of us today faces the task of understanding these changes, interpreting their meaning, and integrating that information into our lives as we decide how to live. We are made to feel as though we have failed in our job as global citizens when we do not understand the complex cultural struggles reported on the nightly news. Despite all the information supposedly at our fingertips as a part of the communications revolution, not only do the answers seem more illusory than ever, but we are no longer even sure of the right questions to ask.

In the struggles among cultural groups in world history, the victors usually seized the title of "civilized," and the defeated bore the stigma of being savages, barbarians, heathens, or pagans. In recent years, scholars and journalists have softened the terminology by using words such as *ethnic groups, folk tradition*, or *national minorities*, but we never quite found the right term for these *other* people who have traditionally been outside the mainstream of world civilizations.

The relationship between tribal peoples and the so-called civilized peoples of the cities changed and evolved constantly through history. In this book, I explore some of the many different facets of that relationship by looking at specific episodes and examples from around the globe and throughout human history. By examining the issues from the perspective of different places and cultures, I try to make a series of benchmarks from which to survey the changing relationship between tribal people and the constantly expanding power of civilization.

Culture contact has often proven violent, and since we are the victors our telling of the story has emphasized the violence. In some eras, the civilized people preyed upon the tribal people in order to take their land or property, as the Europeans did against the natives of the Americas. Sometimes the civilized people sought to enslave the tribal people, as the Egyptians did to the ancient Hebrew tribes or as Westerners enslaved Africans to work on plantations. Sometimes the people from the cities made genocidal war on the tribal people, as when the Spaniards slaughtered the Arawak and Carib Indians of the Caribbean or when the British persecuted the aborigines of Tasmania.

Through the centuries, tribal people also fought back against their attackers and in some eras even became the aggressors. The Germanic tribes of northern Europe eventually defeated the forces of the great Roman Empire, and the Huns temporarily seized much of the eastern empire. Sometimes the tribal people conquered the people of the cities which they then made their own. Thus, the Hebrew tribes seized the cities of Canaan, the Mongols conquered China, and the Turks took over the highly urbanized Byzantine Empire.

Despite the emphasis on violence, the relationship between tribal and civilized people also proved to be one of cooperation, sharing, and mutual assistance. Far less attention has been allotted to this cooperative aspect. People of all ethnic groups have traded, intermarried, and shared diverse parts of their culture from music and myth to religion and technology. The sparks caused by the cultures colliding produced not merely violence; they have also ignited cultural genius and innovation. The contact between different cultures has been a driving force in world history. Desert tribes such as the Hebrews and later the Arabs brought new religions to the cities of the Mediterranean. The world acquired new foods, fabrics, and medicines from the tribal people of the Americas. The horsemen of the Eurasian plains united the economic networks of Europe and Asia while the camel herders of the Sahara connected the Mediterranean world with the interior of the African continent.

In the nineteenth-century notion of human progress, the innovations that caused this progress supposedly came from Western European culture. Today, we see more accurately that the propelling force, one might even say the engine, of human progress has been the dynamic tension between different cultural groups, and the struggle between tribal and civilized populations formed a focal part of that process. Isolated populations without contact do not change; they stagnate and decline. China became a focal point for innovation when it interacted most vigorously with the tribal people surrounding it, and it stagnated when it cut itself off from outside contact. For much of history, Western Europe constituted an isolated backwater with little contact with the outside world, but Europe led the technological progress of the world over the last five hundred years during a time of intense interaction with other cultures.

After leaving Tibet, my exploration into the relationship between civilized and tribal people began in Australia, site of two centuries of struggle between the hunting and gathering natives and the full power of European settler civilization. No matter who we are or where we live today, we descend from thousands of generations of hunters and gatherers much like the aborigines. Some of us have ancestors whose cultures converted to agriculture or pastoralism thousands of years ago, and then to industrial society in the last two centuries. Others of us may have seen the same transition within our own lifetimes. For all of us, hunting and gathering constituted our ancestral way of life, and perhaps in it can be found some significant clues to understanding our own world of today, in all of its staggering cultural variety.

2

The Red Heart of the Desert

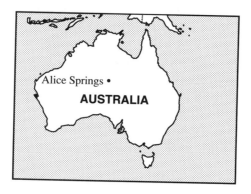

I am as free as Nature first made man,
Ere the base laws of servitude began,
When wild in woods the noble savage ran.

—JOHN DRYDEN

On a February morning in the hot summer of Alice Springs, Australia, the coolest time comes in the wonderful hour before dawn. The aborigines rise before the sun, and they sit in a large circle around a fire waiting for the water to boil for their morning tea. Sometimes they chat softly, and other times they sit silently and stare into the fire in that half-conscious state between waking from sleep and starting the day's activities.

The primary sounds at this time of day come not from people but from the thousands of energetic birds that live in the gum trees. The large, inky Torresian crows dart around among the trees and shriek with a piercing noise that rips the morning solitude. The older crows defend their territories while younger, nonbreeding males dash among the trees in small groups. They swoop down on shallow puddles of water made by the irrigation systems that water private lawns before the scorching rays of the sun strike them.

Small flocks of budgerigars, green parrots with bright yellow faces and long tails, swoop overhead in precision flying, each one taking off, turning, and landing in exact synchrony with the others. Larger and far less graceful flocks of pink and gray galahs lumber noisily through the air. The electronic-sounding call of the Australian magpie-lark bounces through the air as the male and female call back and forth to each other.

Light appears slowly from behind the Heavy Tree range of mountains, a small part of the Macdonnell Ranges. Australians call this area the Red Heart of Australia because of the persistent red coloring of the ground and rocks for a thousand miles in every direction, creating the impression of a giant rusting continent. The name "Red Heart" could apply equally to the fierce power of the sun over the desert.

Even when one is waiting for the sun to rise, it seems to pop up quite suddenly, without warning. The backlighting of the mountains changes into a fiery ball of heat as the sun springs from behind the highest peak. The sun does not gradually warm up the earth, but turns on it like a blowtorch lit and ready to weld one red rock into the next one. The white heat of the sun quickly and mercilessly desiccates and enervates everything within the striking range of its searing rays.

The largest town in the desert, Alice Springs has a population that bulges toward 25,000 in boom times, but drops back down closer to 20,000 in bust years. This excludes about three hundred and fifty nearby Americans who rotate in and out of a secluded part of the desert at Pine Gap, where they operate a secretive radar tracking and space-research station.

Alice Springs lies near the middle of Australia and in the middle of the Northern Territories, the last major area of Australia that remains a territory and has not been admitted as a state. The territories comprise 520,280 square miles, nearly 18 percent of the whole of Australia, making it very close in size to Alaska or about the size of Western Europe. Whereas the aboriginal population of Australia is now about 1 percent, the 35,000 aborigines of the Northern Territories make up 22 percent of the population, and they still own 34 percent of the territory.

By design, Alice Springs lies in the middle of Australia's Red Heart center, roughly a thousand miles south of Darwin, on the northern coast, and an equal distance north of Adelaide, on the southern coast. The community was founded as a station on the great telegraph line that stretched from London to Gibraltar, Egypt, Aden, India, Burma, Malaya, and Singapore. The line then passed beneath the ocean to connect Australia with the rest of the world. But the cities of Australia lay in the southeast, and the line entered the continent in the far north and had to pass over the entire continent before reaching the populated areas.

On such a long journey from England to its antipode in Australia, the telegraph signal weakened and had to be repeated periodically to strengthen it. For that purpose, the community that became Alice Springs was founded beside a small pool of water that was mistaken for a spring but was actually only a water hole in the usually dry Todd River, named for Alice's husband, Sir Charles Todd, the postmaster of South Australia.

To call the sandy depression in the desert a river is a bit of a euphemism except for the brief moments when it collects runoff from a sudden desert rain up in the Macdonnell Ranges. Even then the water has no outlet to the sea, but merely spills itself out into the Simpson Desert and disappears into the thirsty red earth. Far down in the sand of the river, small pools of water collect during the rains, and to the extent that the Todd is a river at all, it is an underground one. For the remainder of the year, the riverbed is a wide, meandering body of sand with scattered eucalyptus trees, called "gum trees" by the Australians. The trees survive by sending deep roots into the earth to tap into the moisture that lies trapped far below the surface of the dry river. In this arid zone, the only trees that survive do so by growing in the actual bed of the river, not along its sides.

The water that supplies the town does not come from the river on which the town was built. Instead, water is piped from a deep bore into the earth about forty miles from town. The bore cuts deep into the continent and taps an ancient supply of water. Local people say that the deep water originated many years ago as rainwater in the New Guinea highlands, sank into the ground, and percolated through the rock beneath the shallow Arafura Sea, which separates New Guinea from Australia, and then continued across the continent to collect in its remote center. That water is then pumped into Alice Springs, where it irrigates a large golf course and the manicured lawns of a small series of luxury hotels and a casino that face the dry riverbed but remain separated from it by a precise line of watered plants and stiff barbed wire.

Once a year the river becomes the focal point of community life and attention, when the local people stage their annual Henley-on-the-Todd Regatta, in which competing teams stand in their bottomless boats and run with them along the dry river. The good-humored event serves as one of the ways that the Australians poke a little fun at themselves and show their ambivalent feelings about their English heritage. The races also bring in tourist dollars and get attention for the town in the national news media.

For most of the year, the local people and visitors prefer to ignore the Todd River. The sandy riverbed is an eyesore and an embarrassment because it serves as home to hundreds of aborigines. They sit beneath its gum trees during the heat of the day, cook their meals over campfires made with dried tree limbs and assorted trash, pass bottles of beer and liquor around their camp circles, and share cigarettes. At night they sleep in the sand. A few of them have blankets, but most sleep in the same ragged clothes they wear during the day. The river is their home, their refuge in the middle of town.

Early in the morning the aborigines cluster under the trees and warm themselves around the fire. The women parade back and forth, bringing water for tea. Long accustomed to living in a dry desert with little water, the aborigines brush themselves off, but rarely make an effort to wash themselves or their clothes with water. Generations of missionaries and government officials have compelled the wearing of clothes, but prior to the arrival of the white man, the aborigines had no need of clothes. Now they wear the clothes until they rot and fall off their bodies in shreds. The slowly rotting clothes and the trash burning in the fire combine to produce a wretched smell. The aborigines living in the Todd River probably smell today much the way the first heavily clothed Englishmen must have smelled when they stepped off the boat at Botany Bay in 1788, after a long voyage without bathing.

Visitors who want to see how the aborigines live are not usually taken to the riverbed, or even to the many small compounds of government housing around the city; instead they are taken to camps at some distance from the city. There they can have meals with the aborigines on almost any day of the year. Tours take outsiders to the bush to see how the aborigines lived in the past and how they live today.

On one occasion we shared a breakfast of a large male euro, a stocky kangaroo with a ragged gray fur. The cook singed off the fur by putting the whole kangaroo into a flaming fire. She then scraped off the burnt fur with a small aluminum knife, and used a slightly larger knife to cut off the lower half of its large feet, but she cut carefully so as not to let any of the moist and valuable blood leak from the carcass. The whole kangaroo then went into a hole of heated sand, where it baked slowly for two hours. Because the kangaroo had not been gutted or had anything removed, the entrails added moisture to the otherwise dry meat.

The kangaroo had not been brought down by a traditional hunter; the aborigines had found it beside the road, where a car had hit it. As the cook explained, "We don't have to hunt no more; we just ride up the road and find everything."

The commercial atmosphere of Alice Springs emphasizes aborigines. The store signs have pictures of aborigines or the boomerang. Stores advertise aboriginal art, which forms a general motif for a basically frontier town. The pointillistic dots characteristic of aboriginal art appear in the advertising and decor of businesses throughout the community.

Despite the commercial and tourist emphasis on aborigines in Alice Springs, the line between aborigines and the whites remains clearly demarcated. The line can be seen in the signs on restaurants requiring "proper dress" or prohibiting bare feet and thongs. It can be seen in wire fences enclosing the two dozen small enclaves of aborigine houses interspersed throughout the town. It can be seen in the sharp social divisions between the aborigines living in the riverbed and the visitors living in the surrounding luxury hotels. For most of the day, the separate worlds of aborigines and whites seem to glide gracefully by and through one another, with only minimal touching. The separation comes through unconscious habits rather than through malicious thoughts or acts. It is an effortless separation that seems as natural as anything else in this unusual landscape of nature's extremes.

According to the theory of plate tectonics, two hundred million years ago, all the continents of the world were joined in a single landmass called Pangaea, which gradually split into two segments. Gondwana, the southern continent, contained the present continents of Antarctica, South America, Africa, and the Indian subcontinent, as well as Australia and its then attached lands of New Guinea, New Zealand, and Tasmania. South

America and Africa began to pull apart about 110 million years ago, and as they did so, water gradually filled the growing basin between them, creating the South Atlantic Ocean. Africa separated from Gondwana about 90 million years ago, followed by New Zealand, 10 million years later. India pulled away about 65 million years ago and headed for its collision with the Asian mainland, an impact that created the Himalayas and is still continuing today. Australia and Antarctica separated from each other a mere 45 million years ago, making them two of the newest continents on the earth's surface. Australia moved north into the Pacific, pulling with it the attached landmasses of Tasmania in the south and New Guinea in the north.

While the other continents have been drifting into one another, Australia has been cut off from the other continents for millions of years. It lacks the tigers, bears, and primates of Asia, its closest continental neighbor, but it has so many plants and animals that are unique to it that in some respects it may be considered the most different of all the continents. For a person from the northern hemisphere, Australia defies many preconceived notions about the world. It has blue frogs, black swans, and red sand. It has the platypus, an egg-laying mammal, which was thought by European scientists to be a hoax when early accounts of this weird animal reached them. Australia also had other oddities, such as the giant, flightless bird called the emu, trees that shed their bark, lizards that stand upright on two legs, and the human-size kangaroos that hop and have the largest tails and hind legs of any bipedal animal.

Australia is best known for its variety of marsupials, such as kangaroos, wallabies, and koalas, but it has a greater and even more unusual variety of lizards. Over 450 species of lizards are divided into five major families, including legless "snake lizards." The families of lizards also include the menacing-looking but quite harmless thorny lizard covered in prickly bumps, and harmless-looking but poisonous lizards. Because the sixty-five species of geckos have large, bulging eyes but no eyelids, they must constantly lick their eyes to keep them from desiccating in the dry heat of the desert, and they have adhesive pads on their feet that allow them to walk on the underside of a tree branch or upside down across a ceiling as easily as they walk on the ground.

The *Agamidae* family, usually called "dragons" in Australia, includes frill-necked lizards that grow a large, lacy collar that can be expanded like an umbrella. The monitor lizards, called goannas—a corruption of the word *iguana*—have long, forked tongues like those of snakes. The desert perentie can grow to over seven feet in length and is attracted by the garbage and refuse wherever humans camp. The skinks come in the greatest variety of all the lizards, including one with a blue tongue.

Science offers the story of the separation of Australia from Gondwana and the evolution of its unique animals, but the native people offer a different though not necessarily incompatible story of how the continent was born. According to their account, Australia came into existence when the ancestor beings, ancient humans and animals, sang the land into life. The ancestors walked along the land and sang mountains, hills, gullies, rivers, plants, and all the other natural phenomena into reality.

The aboriginal story of bringing the world into existence during Dreamtime by the use of words rather than force or magic has a close parallel in the Gospel of John in the Christian Bible. "In the beginning was the Word, and the Word was with God, and the Word was God. . . . All things were made by him; and without him was not any thing made that was made. . . . In him was life." The same idea was expressed in the *Popol Vuh*, the creation epic of the Quiche Maya of Guatemala. "And then the earth arose because of them, it was simply their word that brought it forth. For the forming of the earth they said 'Earth.' It arose suddenly, just like a cloud, like a mist, now forming, unfolding."

During the Dreamtime, when the ancestral figures moved across the unformed land, singing it into existence, they left part of their sacred life force at different sites. In singing the world into existence, they gave their life force to the mountains, rocks, trees, animals, and other things that they created. After singing the land into being, most of the ancestor beings went to sleep beneath a pool of water, in a field of boulders, or in the mountains, where they still sleep. If one knows the right way, he can commune with these beings, who are still there, but if one knows the wrong way, he can incur great danger by disturbing them in their sacred slumber.

The creation happened in the Dreamtime, but the English word *dream* is only an approximation of the aboriginal concept. When we dream, it may be an act of remembering the past, it can be an unfulfilled wish for the future, or it may be a surreal accumulation of thoughts and images during the night. Similarly, the aboriginal Dreamtime exists on another plane of reality, which includes the memory of past events as well as future events. It combines the things that have happened on the land and the potential happenings still within the land.

At the end of the creation, segments of the life force lay scattered across the continent of Australia, like scraps left from the work of creating the world. These bits and pieces of sacred power scattered across the landscape became human beings, the original people. The aborigines living in an area today are the descendants of the ancestral being who sang it into existence. These modern aborigines are the children of the lizard man, the emu, the crocodile, the sea eagle, and the kangaroo.

Even though the acts of creation occurred long before the memory of any humans alive today, the original creation repeats itself constantly through the birth of new children. When an aboriginal woman becomes impregnated, the biological act only gives her a fetus; it does not give life or a spirit to the form within her. The mother must herself travel through the land in search of the sacred spirit in order to give the fetus life, and the mother knows the moment when life enters her child. She feels it move, and she knows that this place where she is now sitting, standing, or walking gave life to her baby. The child born from a place then has the spirit of that place; it is essentially and eternally a part of that place. It matters less who the father of the baby might be than what place gave the baby life. This de-emphasis on the role of the father led many early observers to conclude that the aborigines lacked knowledge of how children were conceived. Aborigines knew that children were conceived in sexual intercourse, but they also knew that a sexual act was not sufficient to make something as sacred as life.

Creation happened in the Dreamtime, and it continues in the Dreamtime of today. The Dreamtime is the far distant past, but it is also a part of the present and the future. The Dreamtime gave life to the aboriginal people, and gives them life today, with the birth of every new baby. The Dreamtime is eternal.

The ancestor spirits that created the land also created human society. They made the laws, the customs, the kinship system, the marriage rules, the language, the code of etiquette, the tools and knowledge of how to use them, and the knowledge of how to live in the environment. The ancestor spirits created everything that humans needed to know, and there was no need to change the ancestral ways. Change did not represent progress or improvement, and it certainly did not represent good. For the aborigines, change meant deviation from the ancestral law and thus should be avoided, for in an environment as harsh as Australia, change might easily lead to death. Change destroyed the ways created by the ancestors and the way of life that the people of a particular area of land were ordained to live on that land. Those who experimented too much died out; those who upheld the past survived to pass their culture on to the next generation.

During certain ceremonies the aborigines can again commune with these ancestors of the Dreamtime or creation-time. The adventures of each ancestor being are contained in a dreaming story—the lizard dreaming, the emu dreaming, the rainbow dreaming, and other stories, one for each ancestral spirit who dreamed. Together these stories constitute the literature of aboriginal Australia, but they tell the history of the continent and its geography as well, for the stories relate how every part of it came into being. Philosophy of life, religion, the whole culture of the aborigines, comes out in their songs. Westerners have lines of longitude and latitude that crisscross their maps; the aborigines have "songlines" that crisscross theirs.

The songs give the aboriginal people their deeds of ownership to their territories, because the people who own the song and can sing the song of an area are that area's rightful owners. It would be more accurate to say that the land owns the people, and that the people who know the song describing a particular territory belong to that territory. One area may be sacred to one kinship group, while another area is sacred to a different group. Some areas are sacred to males, others to females, and still others are sacred to everyone. The people stay attached to the land by their songline, much the way a fetus is attached to its mother through the umbilical cord. Knowing the song means that one is responsible for that piece of land, because the people who know that land's song know how to care for it and how to live within it.

Much of the aboriginal history of Australia has been deliberately ignored. Aboriginal writer Sally Morgan grasped this in *My Place*, her personal search for the history of her people, in which one of the characters says, "A lot of our history has been lost, people have been too frightened to say anything. There's a lot of our history we can't even get at."

According to modern scientists, aborigines arrived in Australia about forty thousand, or possibly even fifty thousand, years ago. According to this reckoning, the Dreamtime began about two thousand generations ago, when the ancestors of the aborigines probably arrived from southern Asia. At that time, much of the world's moisture remained locked in the great ice caps of the Arctic and Antarctic, and the oceans were much lower than they are today, allowing the emergence of land bridges connecting many of the major landmasses of the world. North America joined Asia in the far north, across what is now the Bering Sea. Australia was united with New Guinea and Tasmania, and many of Indonesia's islands remained attached to the Asian mainland. With the distance between landmasses reduced, the ancestors of the aborigines came over by boat or aboard some floating object. The Dreamtime stories begin in the far north of Australia and wander toward the south, and scientists also think that this was the general route followed by the first aborigines.

By the time humans reached Australia, they were biologically modern; they were *Homo sapiens sapiens*, like humans today. They certainly arrived with well-developed human culture. Humans began making tools about two million years ago, and by 500,000 years ago, humans had learned to make fire and build hearths for warmth and cooking. The ancestors of the aborigines entered Australia with all of this cultural knowledge and skill.

The first aborigines arrived armed with the basic tools of the hunter and gatherer—the digging stick and carrying container, the spear and spear-thrower, and the throwing stick, or boomerang. These implements served as the standard tools of all foraging people throughout the world, but while the tool kit of the rest of the world continued to change, those of the aborigines remained comparatively constant over millennia.

The boomerang ranked behind the spear and the digging stick in importance for the aborigines, and it probably never accounted for even one percent of the food eaten by the typical band of aborigines. The throwing stick used in most areas of Australia did not return. The hunter threw it to hit the legs of a kangaroo or prey and cause it to fall. The returning boomerang had a very special function and was used primarily along coastal areas, near bodies of water. The hunter hurled the boomerang out over water to flush birds into flying away from the boomerang and thus toward the waiting hunters hidden along the shore. Even though the modern word *boomerang* comes from the native Australian language, the instrument was not unique to Australia; rather it was used throughout the world prior to the development of the much more efficient bow and arrow, which replaced it.

As the glaciers of the Ice Age slowly melted, the waters of the world's oceans crept higher and once again cut off Australia from New Guinea, about six to eight thousand years ago. The rising waters made it ever more distant from southern Asia and the islands of Indonesia. Innovations in tools, such as the invention of the bow and arrow, never reached Australia.

Almost all aborigines led a nomadic life of nearly constant movement, but they did not wander at whim. The wanderings followed very precise and traditional patterns within a certain territory. If they lived near the coast, they harvested fish and seafood, but they moved inland when the winter rains brought new sources of food. They gathered a large variety of roots, tubers, leaves, nuts, fruits, and seeds.

The countryside offered such a rich bounty of foods that Australian historian Geoffrey Blainey (1975, 155) called it the "harvest of the unploughed plains." Within any given day, the aborigines probably ate foods as varied as what we might eat in a day, but they would have eaten the plants and animals found on that particular day. Within any given year they probably ate a far greater variety of plants and animals than people do today, because the food varied tremendously from season to season and even from week to week. In the Cape York Peninsula of the north, the aboriginal people ate 141 species of plants (Blainey 1975, 157). These included eleven varieties of greens, nineteen different nuts and seeds, forty-six types of roots, and an amazing variety of seventy-three different fruits. They also ate a large variety of animals, birds, reptiles, fish, insects, and grubs.

In the south of Australia, around Melbourne, the modern capital of Victoria, there are few native plants that most of us would know enough about to eat. The names often betray the taste of the food, because the modern names have been given by Europeans who usually saw these plants as nuisances rather than potential food for humans. But for the aborigines the area offered a feast of bulrush roots, wild yams, tree-fern hearts, grass-tree shoots, sow thistle, nasturtium leaves, clover-sorrel, water grass, lillypilly fruits, wild raspberries, pig-face fruit, kangaroo apples, mushrooms, native truffles, native cherries, and a variety of other foods. Throughout much of the year the aborigines of the area had a good supply of fish, eels, and kangaroos, as well as smaller animals.

In the interior of the continent, around places such as Alice Springs, where even today European farmers have not been able to cultivate crops, the native people lived in relative abundance in what we call a desert. The aboriginal foragers knew which plants to harvest to supply not only food but also the scarce moisture in the dry area. In February the aborigines pick small pods called bush bananas off bushes and eat them raw; they have the refreshing taste of a small, tart cucumber. The women know to dig up the roots of the witchetty bush, in the roots of which live the fat, white grubs of the ghost moth. Living underground, inside the root, which protects it, the grubs are moist packets of protein and fat. Popped into the mouth while fresh and still alive, they retain the moisture that would be lost through cooking, and they taste slightly stronger than buttery cream. Other grubs taste more like moist coconut or shredded carrots. The aborigines searched for honey ants, which have a bloated abdomen filled with honey-nectar. The people pop the ants into their mouths, making a sweet snack of the body while spitting out the ant's head.

Over two hundred species of frogs have developed in Australia, and many of them supply both meat and moisture. In the dry season, aborigines of the desert country know the signs for water-holding frogs (*Cyclorana platycephalus*) buried deep in the mud. These frogs come out to feed and mate only during heavy rains, after which their tadpoles develop quickly in small ponds and then bury themselves in the mud to wait another year or two for the next heavy rain. While hibernating, the frogs retain water around them in their sealed holes, and they store water in a large sac on their bodies. The aborigines would dig down into the mud a few feet, pull out the frogs, and drink their moisture.

The women throughout Australia carried coolamons, bent wooden or bark trays varying in size from small ones used as dippers to ones large enough to serve as a cradle for a small child who was too tired to walk. They carried a coolamon with them almost constantly, so that they could take advantage of any possible food that they happened to see. In this way, food-gathering was incorporated into all activities of the day and consumed far less specialized time than that required by a woman who fed her family from the food she harvested in the field or from money she earned working at a job.

A somewhat typical day of foraging was recorded for October 7, 1948, in one of the last groups to live fairly traditional lives. The women began the day by trapping a bandicoot in a log, pulling it out, and smashing its head. They then added a goanna to their larder, gathered a few yams, scooped up some fish from a nearly dry pond, dug out honey ants, and pulled up several pounds of the roots of some vines growing along a creekbed. They finished gathering food before noon, but they still needed to gather a little firewood. The men took slightly longer to track and kill a kangaroo than it had taken the women to gather the other foods and firewood. In the two weeks covered by the study, this was the busiest day for the band (Blainey 1975, 165), and October represented the driest month of the year and therefore the most difficult time for finding food.

Because the earth itself contained so much food for those who knew how to find it, the aborigines did not need methods of storage and preservation. They did not need to build granaries or storage pits. They did not need pottery jars or elaborate baskets for preservation. They had no pack animals to carry large supplies, so they traveled lightly. Because the bounty of the earth shifted with each season, they did not need permanent homes. They moved across the land in an eternal cycle, and this movement severely restricted the amount of material goods that they could carry with them.

Possessing so few material objects that they could adorn or decorate, the aborigines concentrated much of their artistic talents on the surfaces of their own bodies. They frequently paint themselves with a variety of colors, made mud headdresses, and stuck feathers, down, and various leaves onto their bodies. The layers of mud, paint, and other adornments protected the wearer from insects, the fierce rays of the sun, or the morning chill, but they were always executed with a stylistic flair that made the wearer special.

The aborigines not only painted and adorned themselves but sculpted their bodies, changing them in different ways according to the custom of their group. Particularly for males, the aborigines devised a great variety of practices to alter the anatomy in accordance with the practice or commands of a Dreamtime ancestor of that group. Among the Mardudjara of the western Australian desert, the first such change came before puberty, when boys about ten years of age were grabbed and taken to the bush, where an incisor was knocked out with a stone hammer and a sharpened stick. After the boy began puberty, the elders thrust a spearpoint through his nasal septum. The boy dared show no pain, even when the point of the spear was twirled to enlarge the opening and an eaglehawk bone was inserted into the hole.

A few years later the youth underwent the most important rite of his life, circumcision. Like the ancient Egyptians, the Jews, the Muslims, and many tribal groups in Africa, the foreskin of the boy's penis was cut off either at birth or sometime before puberty. After days of preparation and exhausting nights without sleep, the aboriginal elders placed the boy on a living table made by the backs of two male relatives crouching next to each other in the dirt. As the initiate clenched his teeth on his boomerang, another man cut off the foreskin of his penis, which he held up for all to see, and then gave to the boy to swallow quickly (Tonkinson 1978, 67–79).

After another year, the young man underwent subincision, an additional genital operation, in which the underside of the penis was slit open. The slit cut deeply through the flesh to the urethra. The resulting cut and scar on the shaft of the penis supposedly made it resemble the emu penis, which has a long groove in it. The long groove in the man's penis made urination splashy and difficult to control but did not prevent ejaculation when the penis was erect. Subincision made the youth into a man, and among some aboriginal groups males underwent the rite several times as they advanced through the stages of life.

The Australian aborigines have been on earth as long as any other people; they are no closer in time to the beginnings of history than we are. But they provide us with a glimpse into human life when it depended entirely on hunting, gathering, and other foraging activities. We see in aboriginal Australia many different cultures and languages, and also a basic pattern of life that virtually everyone lived. Aboriginal Australia had no cities, towns, villages, or even permanent houses. The aborigines did not plow the ground or grow crops, and none of them worked iron, bronze, tin, copper, or any other metal. They herded no animals, nor did they use them as beasts of burden. They had no written language or wheeled vehicles.

Theirs was neither an ideal world nor a primitive paradise, but a culture that functioned and survived from generation to generation. For 99 percent of human history, our ancestors lived much more as the aborigines did than as we live today. The aborigines, with slight modifications in their life-style, could have lived in almost any time during the last 200,000 years in the temperate and tropical zones of Africa, America, Europe, or Asia, as easily as in Australia.

Foraging as a way of life is even older than humans themselves, and to some extent humans share many features of that life-style with chimpanzees, baboons, gorillas, and other primates. The ancestors of modern humans were foraging millions of years ago. Until comparatively recently in human history, all humans had the same subsistence pattern. In a certain sense, they all shared a similar, though not identical, culture. They had different words for *mother*, *laugh*, and *meat*, but they all had the same basic technology and way of life. They lived from their own energy without utilizing animals or machines; they gathered what they ate but did not cultivate it. They owned what they could carry, but nothing more. Human culture has never again been as homogeneous across the globe as it was when we were all foragers.

Humans moved slowly but persistently around the face of the earth. They moved back and forth, filling some lands as they became more productive and leaving them as they became too dry, cold, wet, or otherwise less inviting. Over thousands of years, humans roamed persistently over virtually the entire globe except for ice-covered Antarctica. As lands shifted, water levels rose and fell, and islands or land bridges appeared and disappeared as people crossed back and forth across the Bosporus from Asia into Europe, across the Strait of Gibraltar from Africa into Europe, from Siberia to North America and from North America to Siberia, from southern Asia to Australia and back again. The world formed a single, albeit large, social system that operated at a much slower pace than that to which we have become accustomed in recent centuries.

If scientists from another planet had visited the earth once every thousand years to check up on it, they would have seen a very static and slowly changing population and culture of humans living everywhere much as the Australian aborigines did for thousands of years. The alien scientists might easily have assumed that humans of all continents appeared to be culturally very homogeneous and probably incapable of major change. Aside from the humans' fondness for playing with rocks and sticks, they may not have seemed much different from their primate relatives such as the gorillas, orangutans, baboons, and chimpanzees.

The aborigines of Alice Springs are slightly less removed in time from their foraging past than most of us are, but the distinction of a few hundred years versus a few thousand years makes little difference in the total history of humans on earth. Foraging has been the most generalized and enduring subsistence pattern developed by humans. It is the only strategy proven viable over tens of thousands of years. All of us emerged only recently from this same foraging past, and none of us has quite adjusted to the sudden change in the human way of life. The aborigines, sitting ragged and dirty with the smell of alcohol on them, show the sudden transition and dislocation more clearly than we do, but our own "modern" society suffers from it just as much as theirs, if not more.

Compared with people on other continents, the Australian aborigines have stayed much the same over the last ten thousand years. Even though the Ice Age cut them off from the rest of the world, it did not produce the great social and cultural changes in aboriginal life that we see in the lives of the people of the far north.

In the last Ice Age, humans suddenly began to show great and rapid variation in their cultures. Humans in the far north of the globe faced a critical fork in the road of human history. Those who could not change died, and those who experimented with and varied their culture survived.

3

The Ice Age Revolution

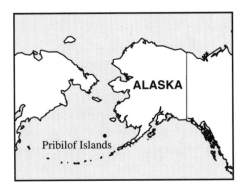

The huntsmen are up in America,
and they are already past their first sleep in Persia.
                    —SIR THOMAS BROWNE

You can smell the fur seals of St. Paul Island long before you can see them. With hundreds of thousands of them piled up on the shore—in some years as many as a million—they emit a terrific odor, a marine mammal odor common to walruses, seals, and even beached whales—the smell of rotting fish and seaweed, excrement and urine-coated rocks, placenta and trampled seal pups decaying in the nearly perpetual though misty light of the foggy summer in the cold waters of the Bering Sea. Even when it is not raining, a mottled mist rises from the seal rookeries because of the warm breath of the seals hitting the constantly cool air blowing in from the Bering Sea.

   The smell of the animals is matched by the nearly painful noise of half a million fur-seal males searching for mates and barking incessantly to frighten away other males, while another half-million females search for their pups who cry constantly for attention and food. Ancient Aleut legends claim that the barking of the fur seals was so loud that the noise first led Igadik, an Aleut from Unimak Island in the Aleutians, through the dense fog to discover the Pribilof Islands, which they called Amig. Much later, in 1787, the same loud noises attracted the Russian explorer Gerasim Pribylov, who searched through the ocean of mist for the mysterious seal islands described by the Aleuts.

Whether approaching the beaches of the fur-seal rookeries today by water or by land, one first hears the noise of the dominant males guarding their harems or patrolling far afield in search of females. Wandering up to a mile inland, unattached males search for females and defend their territory from other males. They bark at one another and erupt with long series of deep, blaring burps that sound like lawn-mower engines puttering across the beach.

The male fur seals show little fear of anything. For them, all living creatures seem to fall into one of two categories: potential mate or potential rival. Any creature larger than a fox that arrives on the shore is the subject of immediate attention from the unattached males, who want either to mate with the newcomer or frighten it away. The beachmasters, senior bulls that weigh up to six hundred pounds, bark constantly as they patrol their territory for months. Without stopping to eat even once during that time, and catching only an occasional few minutes of rest, they slowly wither from physical exhaustion and lose up to half their body weight in a summer's struggle to reproduce.

A harem of females surrounds each bull. Within the first day of arrival ashore, each mature female gives birth to the pup with which she was impregnated the previous year. Immediately after she gives birth, the bull on whose territory she has landed mates with her again and impregnates her for the following year. Considering that a female fur seal matures at age three and can survive to be as old as fifteen years, she spends 80 percent of her mature life pregnant. During most of the time that she is pregnant, she is also nursing her most recent pup.

The black pups pile up on the shore as thousands and then hundreds of thousands of females come ashore to give birth. The mother quickly abandons her pup for up to nine days as she swims to sea to feed. The mother needs great amounts of protein to sustain herself, her pup, and her fetus. Sometimes she must travel out into the ocean as far as two hundred miles to find enough fish to produce the rich milk that she then brings back to her pup. With the invasion of commercial fishing fleets into the area and their overfishing in recent decades, the trips often take even longer until the female fur seal finds sufficient fish. She may have to make a dozen such feeding trips in the course of one summer, and each trip results in a growing spurt for her pup when she returns. The number of times the pup is fed becomes permanently marked by growing rings in its teeth, similar to the growth rings in trees. During the summer, the beach is filled with pups left yelping for their mothers and trying to nurse from other females, who instinctively reject any pup but their own.

St. Paul Island, sometimes called Seal Island, stretches to a mere eight miles at its widest point and fourteen miles long, but it is the largest of the five Pribilof Islands. The tiny archipelago rises from the Bering Sea as a series of volcanic peaks between the shores of Alaska and Siberia, but three hundred miles from the closest mainland and far to the north of the Aleutian Islands. Located so far north of the Aleutians, yet south of St. Lawrence Island, the Pribilofs are some of the remotest islands in the Bering Sea.

The islands have no trees and no bushes. In the summer a uniform layer of green tundra grasses cover the ground, including beach rye and wild celery that rarely reach even knee level. Each island becomes a single large meadow dotted with splotches of color from the wildflowers—yellow arctic poppies, dandelions, and ragworts, as well as white daisies, delicate Bering chickweed, blue lupine, and purple lousewort. The only parts of the island not covered with the grasses and flowers are the gravel roads made with reddish scoria, a volcanic gravel mined on the island. The steep cliffs provide breeding areas for birds, and the rich Arctic waters attract about two hundred varieties of birds at different seasons of the year—black cormorants, thick-billed murres, horned and tufted puffins, red-legged kittiwakes, and rosy finches dart around one another on the busy island.

The pelagic seals spend most of their year at sea, but during the summer they share the islands with three other mammals. Small herds of reindeer live inland and have little interaction with the fur seals, but the seals have more intimate relations with both foxes and humans. The fur seals share their breeding ground with arctic foxes that patrol the beach and scavenge the remains of dead pups, adult seals, and fish that happen to wash up on shore. The foxes and seals seem accustomed by millennia of interaction to ignore one another even when living their lives in such intimate interdependence.

The arctic fox's lack of fear of other animals extends even to humans, who probably appear to the foxes as nothing more than skinny stray seals. When anyone walks along the beach, a fox follows and circles only a few feet away. The fox waits for the large mammal to drop a small fish, open a shell, turn over a rock, or stir up some kind of food. The inquisitiveness of the foxes almost drove the shipwrecked crew of Vitus Bering insane when they were marooned for the winter on the Komandorskiye (Commander) Islands in the Bering Sea, just east of the Kamchatka Peninsula. The foxes constantly pestered the sailors and even sniffed them and climbed over them and tried to dig under them during their sleep. No matter how many foxes the Russians managed to kill in a day, new ones arrived at night to replace the dead ones. The nosy, pesky foxes exacerbated nerves already worn thin by the extreme hardships of the environment, and several of the crew went crazy.

Because the Russians were stranded there during the winter, they did not see the great herds of fur seals that bred on the island during the summer just as they do on St. Paul, but they soon surmised that they were on another of the seal islands. Bering died on that island, which was subsequently named for him, and the Russians, who followed him to these remote outcroppings of rock, killed off virtually all the fur seals before the Russian Revolution.

The relationship between the fur seals and humans has proven quite complex. The five hundred Aleuts who live on St. Paul have always depended in some way on the seal for their livelihood. They have not only eaten its flesh but have used every part of its body. The fat provided oil for their lamps, and even the intestines found use in tailoring rainproof clothes. They preserved the flippers to make a special delicacy still loved by the locals. The Aleuts removed the seal's throat, which the women softened and then sewed into small, delicate pouches. They found use even for the penis bone, which can grow up to two feet in length, with the shape and density of a baseball bat. The men carved the bone, called *oosik*, in much the same way that they carved ivory, or they sold the *oosik* to merchants for use in Chinese medicines and as novelties for passing sailors and tourists.

The English language uses only one word, *seal*, for a range of sea mammals that have little more in common than a dog and a lion. The cute little animals that swim around zoos, jump through hoops, and balance balls on their noses are usually harbor seals, occasionally called sea dogs. The seals of the Pribilofs grow many times larger and are called fur seals, but their German name, translated as "sea bear," seems much more accurate and descriptive of them.

As the name indicates, the most valuable part of the fur seal was its fur, until modern governments curtailed the commercial hunting of the fur seal and the sale of its fur. With up to 300,000 fine hairs per square inch, the fur seal made one of the warmest pelts of any animal in the world. The Aleuts made the fur into boots and other outer garments, or sold the pelts to Russian and, later, American traders.

The Aleuts no longer trade in the fur, but they still harvest between fifteen hundred and two thousand seals a year on St. Paul for their personal consumption. The Tanadgusiz Corporation, the governing economic body owned and operated by the natives of St. Paul, oversees the entire process and the distribution of meat to its members.

The men come down to the rookeries on assigned days in the summer and, using long poles, round up some of the unattached males living on the edge of the group. They separate these bachelor males and herd them to a killing field far enough away from the rookery so as not to disturb the pups, the lactating females, and the breeding beachmasters. The hunters divide the seals into small pods of the right size and cull out males who are too small or too large, allowing them to escape back into the sea.

The hunters also single out seals of any size and either sex if they have become ensnared in large pieces of plastic bands or netting from the ocean. In the past the hunters tried to free such seals from the debris, but the process proved too dangerous to both the humans and the seals. Now the injured seals are killed by the hunters rather than leaving them to the slow, painful death ensured by the plastic that ensnared them.

Each of the hunters has an assigned duty, and together they quickly kill and skin the seal. The "pod cutter" hits the seal on the head with a long pole, rendering it unconscious, and a "sticker" quickly pierces the heart with a knife, killing the seal instantly. The "ripper" moves in to make precision cuts around the flippers and down the middle of the body. A "barman" pins the seal to the ground, and three "pullers" remove the pelt from the carcass with clamps called "nippers," which are attached to short ropes. The whole process operates with the efficiency of an industrialized disassembly line or meat-packing plant.

Some of the older men on St. Paul claim that they can skin an entire seal in less than a minute. The stripped yet warm carcass of red flesh and white fat steams in the cold, wet St. Paul air. Young boys remove the *oosik* and testes, and cut out the entrails, which they leave in special areas for the foxes. The sealers hoist the carcasses onto the back of a truck and deliver them to the doorstep of the women who have requested them.

Compared with what it was only a few decades ago, the seal hunt of today is a modest affair. It still forms an important cultural part of the life of St. Paul, and it provides an important traditional food for the people, but it occupies far less time than do the other commercial activities of the island. The native corporation of the island operates a cannery under subcontract to the Japanese, who process a variety of cold-water fish. By subleasing the cannery to the Japanese, the Aleuts thought that the good management skills of the Japanese would give them all jobs, but instead the Japanese businessmen brought in Filipino workers who had higher skills, lived in inexpensive barracks, and worked long, hard hours for lower wages. The native corporation runs the school and other public services. It even operates the island's only hotel, which offers a dozen bedrooms and two bathrooms.

In harvesting the small number of large male fur seals each year, in gathering the eggs of the seabirds, and in collecting other sea life and even the wild celery plants, the Aleuts sustain an ancient tradition, a way of hunting and gathering that once included the ancestors of everyone now living on the planet. The gathering of the Aleuts differs in climate and circumstance, but not much in skill, from the foraging of the Australian aborigines.

St. Paul is the largest and northernmost of the surviving Aleut community; due north of it lies St. Lawrence Island, home to one of the largest surviving communities of Eskimo. They hunt an even larger prey than the fur seal and walrus. The natives of St. Lawrence, like others along the Arctic shore, hunt whales such as the giant bowheads, which reach sixty feet in length and generally weigh about a ton a foot. The head makes up one-third of the whale's length and is filled with the prized baleen, averaging about fifteen hundred pounds per whale, and about one hundred barrels of the oil that made it the favorite quarry of the commercial whaling industry. The Eskimo hunt the whale for food, oil, and nonedible products such as baleen and bone; they do not hunt it for commercial sale.

The Aleuts and the Eskimo differ from the aborigines, in that the Arctic hunters belong to a special type of forager that specializes in the hunting of megafauna, the large mammals. Scattered across St. Paul are large pits dug into the ground, with the ribs of whales arching over them. On this treeless island without timber to offer building materials, the Aleuts made their *barabas*, or pit houses, into serviceable and warm homes by using the whale bones as the rafters.

Small bands of Arctic hunters survive today as remnants of thousands of such groups from the time of the Ice Age. Across Europe, Asia, and North America they stalked the giant mammoths and mastodons of their time. Using a small set of stone tools, they brought down the largest animals in the world. The hunters then used the ribs and tusks of the giant animals as supports for their large pit houses covered with earth and the woolly hides of their prey.

Just as it required a cooperating band of hunters to kill a mastodon, the size of the whale requires that it be hunted by groups of hunters and not by individuals. Hauling the giant carcass onto shore and butchering it requires far more workers than does the actual hunting of the animal. Just as the Aleuts require teamwork and specialization to harvest the fur seals, the Eskimo require the same kind of communal effort to bring in a whale. Today the Eskimo use outboard motors, two-way radios, metal harpoon guns, and any other modern technology that makes their hunt easier, but they combine this with their traditional technology when it is more appropriate. They still use their flexible, skin-covered boats because they function much better than wooden, metal, or fiberglass boats in the icy waters, and they use their paddles or sometimes even sails since the noise and movement of the outboard motors scare the game away. After the hunt, when silence no longer matters and they are anxious to reach home with their catch, they use the motors.

The Arctic was the last major ecological zone on the planet that humans colonized. For hundreds of thousands of years, while bands of people roamed the rest of the earth, foraging and killing smaller animals, the huge animal resources of the Arctic developed in relative tranquillity and isolation. Extensive herds of reindeer, musk-oxen, and caribou roamed the land, while large populations of seals, walruses, and other sea mammals lived along the shores. These large animals had few predators to worry about other than the occasional shark in the water or the wolf and polar bear on land. For hundreds of thousands of years, no humans hunted in the Arctic because they could not survive the long, harsh winter.

The safety of the large animals of the Arctic changed, not so much because the humans moved into the Arctic and found a way to conquer it as that the Arctic moved to where the humans lived. The Ice Age began nearly 75,000 years ago, when the Arctic zone extended south into what had been temperate areas. The glacial age came gradually and in waves, with intermittent millennia of warming and cooling. The people living in the formerly temperate area had to flee, gradually adjust themselves to living in the new climate, or die. In varying degrees in different areas, they probably did all three. Because the winters grew longer and colder very gradually, humans had time to adapt, to acquire new skills, tools, and coping mechanisms for the changing environment.

Foraging is insufficient in the Arctic as it must have been during the long centuries of the Ice Age. To survive in very cold areas, humans must hunt. The summer season that produces berries, roots, and other plant foods lasts only a short time, and the harvest it produces is rather trifling compared with the prodigious output of tropical and even temperate zones. The meager supply of plant food in the Arctic disappears for most of the year. The smaller animals also disappear into burrows, and a sheet of ice makes fishing difficult. Humans need vast quantities of calories, which their bodies convert to energy. Thus they had to consume large amounts of fatty meat, since fat provides more calories per measure than any other food source. The most efficient way to get such quantities of meat is to consolidate hunting expertise and energy to pursue a few large animals, rather than dissipating effort on pursuing many small animals.

By the time the Ice Age ended, humans had adapted to the Arctic. As the Arctic zone withdrew back toward the North Pole, and as the large animals moved north with it, people followed them, no longer daunted by the long, bitter winter. People who had the culture and technology to survive the Ice Age could now survive a nine-month winter each year. Even though humans have still not developed the ability to live in the Arctic in the numbers that live in the tropic zone, a variety of peoples have made it their home, including the Aleuts and Inuit of North America, the Sami or Lapps of Scandinavia, and a variety of northern Siberian peoples such as the Koryak, Yakut, Evenk, Nenet, and Chukchi.

Development of the skills to hunt large animals marked a major change in human subsistence patterns. It began the transition away from mere foraging into the more complex patterns of modern society, but before humans could make this tremendous technological, social, and intellectual revolution, they needed to develop a new tool kit that contained some large tools and also some of the smallest tools humans had ever crafted.

Hunting is an activity that humans share with many other animals. In this regard, the ancestors of humans became hunters long before they became humans. The early forms of hunting might be more accurately described as scavenging, because humans fought with vultures and hyenas for the scraps of food and bone left from the kills of lions, wolves, and other, more efficient and deadly predators. As a generalized mammal, the human came equipped to do many things, but not to do any of them very well. The human could run, but not nearly as fast as a dog, a cat, a horse, a rabbit, or virtually any other animal save the sloth. The human had a strong jaw and teeth but not nearly as strong and powerful as those of the tiger, wolf, bear, and lion. Humans had grasping hands with opposable thumbs that proved excellent for picking berries but not very good in combat, when compared to the powerful claws of a bear.

The human appears to be poorly adapted for a life of hunting, and probably would have been better off just scrounging plant foods and stealing an occasional scrap from a dog. Yet, despite the shortcomings, or perhaps because of them, humans slowly developed an amazing set of tools that allowed them to hunt and kill the largest animals on earth.

Although the arms of humans lacked the strength of a bear's arms or even the power of an elephant's trunk, humans learned to compound their strength by using rocks or sticks that could be hurled through the air. They learned that tough meat could be made edible by cooking over fire. Sticks could be made sharper and harder by lightly burning the point. Fire also kept people warm and thus allowed them to hunt and even to live in ever colder areas for ever longer spans.

Two million years ago, ancestors of humans were already using crude stone choppers in Africa, but the evolution of the tool kit that allowed humans to hunt the megafauna took millions of years to perfect. Early choppers were no more than rocks modified slightly to make them better at smashing open nuts or shellfish or crushing bones to gain access to the sweet marrow inside them. This was a long way from the thin, finely chiseled blades that could be attached to the end of a shaft and used to kill an elephant.

The early human ancestor's use of rocks, sticks, and other naturally occurring items did not significantly separate the humans from other animals. Otters use rocks to break open shells, chimpanzees strip leaves from twigs and use them to extract termites from their holes, and they have even been known to throw sticks at predators such as leopards. For early humans, toolmaking was simply a matter of stripping leaves or bark from wood or chipping stone. The toolmaker was always taking something away from the material, not adding to it.

The uniqueness of humans in the animal kingdom appeared in their amazing, almost delicate, hand-eye coordination. The same eye-hand coordination that permitted a human to reach out and gently grasp the one red berry amid a cluster of green ones, or to break off one small, tender shoot from a plant with a thorny stem, also allowed the human to pick up a single flint chip from a pile of rocks and fashion it into an even more delicate point. A large and clumsy animal in general, the human nevertheless possessed some very specific and graceful movements of the fingers and hands.

The revolution in the human use of tools came when humans started putting two tools, such as a sharpened rock and a straightened stick, together to create a spear, an invention vastly greater than the mere sum of its parts. An explosion of such inventions took place. Humans were soon using detachable blades on their spears in such a way that a damaged shaft or blade could easily be replaced by another. The new tools included items made of wood, stone, antler, ivory, and bone wrapped with sinew, strips of leather, vines, or bark, depending on the local environment.

By about 35,000 years ago, a time known as the Late Ice Age or the Upper Paleolithic, humans had assembled the tool kit of delicate yet sturdy stone points needed for such hunting. The set of tools and techniques spread with previously unknown speed from continent to continent. Within a few thousand years, hunters from Siberia to Australia and from southern Africa to Newfoundland were using a set of similar tools and skills to perform very similar hunting enterprises.

About thirty thousand years ago, humans further refined the spear by developing a small spear-thrower, now commonly known by its Aztec name, *atlatl*. The atlatl was made of antler or wood and was about the length of a man's forearm, with a small crook at the end. The hunter fitted the spear into the crook and used it to propel the spear faster, farther, and more accurately than he could do with his arm alone. Similar spear-throwers have been found from Australia to Europe and from Africa to America.

The atlatl marks the first recorded effort of humans to make a tool that only functioned to operate another tool. In a sense it was the first mechanical tool, and as such it is a direct ancestor to the machine. The atlatl threw the spear; it did not crack nuts, cut open fish, or dig up roots. Humans were thinking in new ways and making tools to operate other tools, or tools that functioned only to create other tools. All of this required extremely long sequences of thought and planning, as well as more complex series of activities. Crafting an atlatl was not the same as prying open an oyster with a stick found nearby.

This new way of thinking and planning shows most clearly in one of the smallest yet one of the most important of human inventions. In order to hunt the megafauna, humans needed more than good spears, atlatls, and finely crafted points. The kit also included a new tool without which humans could not venture into the cold areas of the northern hemisphere during the Ice Age. This vital tool was the needle, invented over twenty thousand years ago (Fagan 1990, 159). Usually carved from ivory, the needle allowed clothes to be custom-made to fit the human body. Odd-sized pelts and animal skins might have sufficed in warmer zones, where one needed only to drape them over the body to block an occasional cool breeze, but for humans to survive the severe winters of the Ice Age with its bitter winds that tore across the earth's frozen surface, clothing had to fit snugly and cover the entire body except for the eyes.

With a needle, a woman could sew together pelts and skins to make large coverings that could be draped over wood or bone and create a tent, a revolutionary and easily portable new form of habitation for humans. Chasing mammoths across the open plains or the wide tundra, humans could no longer depend on finding natural shelters such as caves, nor could they always stop and dig the large pits necessary for a subterranean shelter.

The needle allowed the sewing of small pouches that became the literal tool bags within which hunters carried the myriad blades they needed. With such pouches, which later became pockets, the travelers carried a variety of small rocks, including flint or obsidian points, over thousands of miles.

Eventually the needle lead to production of one of the most important of new inventions, the birchbark or skin canoe. Women sewed together light materials around a frame that made a kayak or canoe capable of moving faster and more easily in the hunt for the whales, walruses, and seals of the sea and for the animals that came to the edges of the rivers and lakes to drink.

The hunters followed big game or, more likely, waited for annual migrations of animals past particular points where passes or watering holes tended to concentrate them. The hunters used spears, but they had neither blowguns nor bows and arrows. They were skilled in the use of fire, and probably even used it to startle animals as well as to cook meat and process skins and leather.

The bow and arrow became another major set of complicated tools needed by hunters. The oldest preserved bow yet discovered dates from 6000 B.C., and the oldest arrows we have date from the end of the last ice age, about 9000 B.C. The use of the bow and arrow in at least some parts of the world seems much earlier, and some older stone points look like arrowheads and suggest that the use of bows and arrows came before 25,000 B.C. (McEwen et al., 1991).

The bow and arrow spread around the world, largely replacing the older tools—spear and spear-thrower, boomerang or throwing stick, and blowgun—except in Australia and a few other remote places. The newly developed set of tools allowed humans to exploit and live in new environments that had previously been too hostile for human habitation. Humans adapted the tool kit for deserts, boreal forests, tropical jungles, high plateaus, swamps, mountain valleys, and coastal plains. The basic technology spread around the world and created the first global culture.

During the Upper Paleolithic, humans hunted many of the animals that we know today, including bison, horses, musk-oxen, camels, and reindeer. In addition, the northern hemisphere had many large herbivores such as the mammoth and its slightly smaller and less woolly relative, the mastodon, as well as the woolly rhinoceros, a giant bison with horns six feet wide and fur over two feet thick, a three-hundred-pound beaver, the giant sloth, and the tapir. The environment included carnivores such as the American lion, the saber-toothed cat, the dire wolf, and the short-faced bear, which was one-third larger than the black bear. Giant sloths prowled South America and giant, flat-nosed kangaroos hopped across Australia.

The new global culture even inspired new fashions in world art. In the caves of the south of France and in the Spanish Pyrenees, we see drawings of the humans' prey—the mammoths, horses, and bison. Similar pictures can be found across Eurasia, from Spain to the Pacific coast of Siberia. Archaeologists have found pieces of stone, antler, and bone fashioned into the forms of the same animals. Similar pictures can be found carved or painted on rocks in the Sahara and in southern Africa, as well as in Australia and America. The pictures sometimes include sketches of the human hunters, or sometimes only their handprints.

The art sometimes shows fish or birds but concentrates on large animals. The artists show little interest in flowers, fruits, or plants in general. They strive to depict animals in motion rather than in static poses. The carvings of the Inuit or Eskimo today, as well as the art of the tribal people of northern Australia, still retain much of the elegant yet simple realism of Ice Age art.

The Ice Age culture varied from one region to the next, depending on the natural resources of the area and the types of animals it supported, but similar traits in subsistence, technology, and art make this a revolutionary cultural development. The Ice Age moved human technology and social organization to a new scale and thereby produced a great flowering of new and diverse human cultures.

Even though big-game hunting began disappearing in some parts of the world about ten thousand years ago, it has not quite vanished completely. Big-game hunters in a few remote places still practice it. The big game has been largely eradicated from the temperate zones of the world, such as the plains of Europe, North America, Australia, and Asia. In the tropical zones of Africa and India a few large animals, such as elephants, still roam, but there are usually too few of them to make a significant part of anyone's diet. The mammoths and other exceptionally large animals have disappeared from the Arctic, leaving only the ocean mammals, such as the whales, as survivors of the era of giant mammals.

The Aleut hunters of the Bering Sea, the whale-hunting Eskimo of the Arctic, the elephant-hunting pygmies of Zaire, and the giraffe-hunting Bushmen of southwest Namibia and Botswana are some of the few hunting and gathering people left on earth. Even for these people, however, the hunt has become a rare and exceptional activity rather than the central activity of their lives. For most humans, the end of the Stone Age occurred several thousand years ago, and now, with the heavy infiltration of trade goods, jet tourism, all-terrain vehicles, and international strife, the last vestiges of the Stone Age way of life are ending even in the remotest pockets of the earth.

Had the climate, flora, and fauna of the earth remained consistent over the past twenty thousand years, we might all still be big-game hunters today. However, the environment changed dramatically, and the skills and technology for hunting big game became increasingly less relevant as the earth warmed. The tradition helped humans to survive a difficult time of transition that wiped out many other animal species, but for humans in general, big-game hunting proved to be a temporary solution to the temporary problems of the Ice Age. The specialized subsistence pattern of hunting big game was not as versatile as foraging, nor was it easily adapted into another system that might prove appropriate for the new conditions after the Ice Age.

With the end of the Ice Age, humans faced new problems of survival in rapidly changing environments. Some groups returned to the old standby of foraging and hunting small game, but still others followed a route that eventually crossed the great technological threshold into agriculture.

4

Crops, Animals, and Diseases: The Burden of Domestic Life

When tillage begins, other arts follow.
The farmers therefore are the founders of human civilization.
—DANIEL WEBSTER

A long and decayed road connects the town of Pocona, Bolivia, with the closest provincial city of Cochabamba, in the middle of the country. The road's pavement has been chipped and eroded by years of heavy use, rains, and neglect. A driver must pick his way slowly and carefully through the potholes, gullies, slabs of broken pavement, and washboard ruts. Despite the glossy maps and the claims of the government highway office in La Paz, drivers on the road have abandoned any pretense of having two lanes of traffic going in opposite directions. Drivers follow the route of least resistance, searching for the segment with the most pavement and the shallowest holes. If two cars meet, one usually must stop to allow the other to pass, and even at the best speeds, cars and trucks barely exceed twenty miles an hour. The trip from Cochabamba proceeds only slightly faster than a burro with a medium load.

After crossing two high, cold mountain passes, the road enters the valley of Pocona. The village of Pocona lies another fifteen miles up the valley, but the road does not go in that direction.

The road creeps on toward the city of Santa Cruz, another two hundred miles away. Only trucks can tackle the road on to Pocona. To reach the village of Pocona, one must leave the partially paved road and drive on an unpaved one that consists of perpetual mud during the rainy season and cement-hard ruts and billowing dust in the dry season. This trail twists along the edge of the valley, crisscrossing the river as it proceeds up the valley. In the dry season the river is wide but very shallow and easily crossed by large trucks that find adequate traction on the bed of rock and pebbles that line the river bottom. During the rainy season the passengers sitting on top of a truck climb down to help push the truck up the slippery banks of the river. Each time it rains during this season, the river is usually so swollen for several days that no one crosses the river. Sometimes the whole valley remains cut off from outside contact for a week or more.

When the road is open, a truck will make this journey once or twice a week. The truck serves as the link with the outside world. It hauls the locally grown potatoes and corn to the market in Cochabamba, and it brings back sugar, kerosene, propane gas, and other goods that the people of Pocona need from the outside. Passengers ride on top of the produce, making the truck the local bus, and anyone who needs to send a letter sends it by the truck. The trucks that ply the road from Pocona to Cochabamba are the only link this town has with the outside world.

Life in Pocona today probably differs only slightly from the time when it was one of the most distant outposts of Inca civilization. The village once marked the edge of the Inca empire, separating the fortified Tawantinsuyu, as the Incas called their mountain kingdom, from the tribes of the lowland jungle and plains. The fortress, once manned by Inca soldiers, and the large warehouses of food that dominated the skyline now lie in ruin. Today the Catholic church is the most prominent structure in the village. The road that the Incas built directly across the mountains now serves mostly girls herding their sheep and llamas, and an occasional boy hauling firewood or straw on a donkey.

The peasants today grow substantially the same crops that they grew a thousand years ago. The mountainous fields produce a colorful array of potatoes and other tubers that come in assorted shapes, sizes, and colors. They grow corn and some beans. Since the coming of the Spanish in the mid-1500s, the peasants have added a few European crops, such as wheat, fava beans, and peaches. The greatest European impact, however, shows in the animals of the village. At eight thousand feet the village lies somewhat too low for large herds of llamas or alpacas, but there are several cows and donkeys in the pastures around the village, and pigs and chickens freely roam the streets of the town.

By Bolivian standards, Pocona ranks among neither the poorest nor the richest of agricultural communities. It even has running water, in the sense that a stream runs down the middle of the main road. The stream serves as the source of water for cooking as well as for bathing humans and a place for the animals to drink. Such a well-placed stream means that village women do not have to carry jugs of water for long distances, as they must do in many other villages.

Pocona has several ovens in different homes, and on almost any day of the week one can find at least one housewife who has baked and is willing to sell rounded loaves of light bread that look and taste like large biscuits, except that for leavening the bakers use *chicha*, the homemade corn beer. The chicha gives the bread a slightly sour but distinctive taste of Bolivian rural life.

Any family that has a freshly fermented pot of chicha ready for drinking hangs out an eye-of-God cross or a simple white flag above the doorway, and for a few days the home is transformed into a public chicha hut, welcoming anyone who can pay a few cents for a glass of the brew. The chicha sits in clay pots about three feet high and only slightly less wide. The mashed corn and water inside bubbles constantly, like a slowly boiling cauldron of thin gruel. The particles of corn float to the top, where newly formed bubbles push up the older bubbles, making a layer of bubbles several inches thick. To keep the brew from climbing out of the pot, heavy wooden planks hold down the top. When the owner lifts the top, a strong odor of silage assaults the nose. To serve the drink, the owner dips deeply into the pot to get below the thin bubbles and brings up an opaque liquid that is only slightly translucent, like a thin skim milk with a yellowish hue.

At night, drinking chicha is one of the few diversions offered by Pocona. Men and women gather to drink until they can barely walk. They then stumble through the stream back to their own huts, where they collapse onto a pile of blankets or straw on the hard mud floor.

Virtually the whole village uses straw and wood for cooking, but all sources of fuel have become increasingly scarce in recent years as the valley has been virtually stripped of wood. A development project planted the riverbanks with eucalyptus to replace the original trees. Eucalyptus trees have proven good at holding the erosion of the river, and they grow fast, but they leach nutrients from the already damaged soil. Villagers say that the area around the trees will not grow crops and serves only for grazing, and since the trees cannot be chopped down, they do not offer firewood other than that provided by an occasional fallen branch.

The village has a small school where the children are supposed to be taught the rudiments of math and reading and writing the Spanish language. The school now operates only sporadically. In the 1986 school year it was open less than fifty days. The teachers no longer received their salary of fifteen dollars a month from the government, and no money came for books, food, or classroom supplies.

In many ways Pocona seems typical of village life across South America as well as throughout India, China, and sub-Saharan Africa. Hundreds of millions of people lead village lives similar to that in Pocona. For the most part, such places strike urban visitors as backward and representative of a quickly disappearing way of life. But the settled village is a recent innovation in human history. It developed a mere seven thousand years ago, and it has been expanding around the world ever since.

Compared with the thousands of years human spent as foragers, the construction of villages represented another revolutionary change in culture, subsistence, technology, social organization, and history. In many respects, humans still have not successfully completed this major transition.

Life in villages such as Pocona continues to be hard. After a long day in the fields, working without draft animals, the exhausted villagers return to their dark, crowded homes for a monotonous meal of potatoes and corn with a little fat for seasoning. Diseases move easily through the community via the water supply and the air, from animal to animal, or from one poorly constructed and ventilated house to another.

Why did humans, from China to South America, give up their life of hunting and gathering to live in villages such as Pocona?

What events could compel them to stop wandering freely from one food supply to another in order to settle in one place and eat the same food every day?

Today, settled life seems obviously superior to the wandering life of hunters and gatherers; yet it must not have been at all obvious to our ancestors who made the transition. Disease and malnutrition climbed greatly when humans settled down. The amount of work they had to do merely to survive increased many times, and despite all that, life expectancy plummeted. Painful tooth decay resulted from the high-carbohydrate diet of agricultural life, and successive generations grew smaller than their foraging forebears as they became dependent on a small number of crops. With such drastic consequences, why did humans ever settle down?

Humans began the long transition from foraging to agricultural life about ten thousand years ago. The transformation happened in several places seemingly independently, yet within a few thousand years of one another. Farming began in Mesopotamia between the Tigris and Euphrates rivers, in Egypt along the Nile, along the Indus of modern Pakistan and India, and along the Yellow River of China. Farming began soon afterwards in the highlands of Mexico in North America, and in the Andean highlands of South America.

In Africa and Asia, the early farming civilizations arose in the temperate zones north of the Tropic of Cancer but south of the fortieth parallel. This meant that no farming originated in Europe, sub-Saharan Africa, or the South Pacific. Agriculture diffused into those areas hundreds or even thousands of years later.

Agriculture developed around distinctive sets of plants in different parts of the world. In the Middle East, grains such as wheat and barley occupied the primary position. In East Asia rice dominated, while in southern Asia that grain was supplemented by bananas, yams, and other root crops. African farmers relied heavily on sorghum, millet, and dates. In North America agriculture concentrated on the triad of maize, beans, and squash, while in South America corn, potatoes, and other tubers became the staple crops.

Did humans start to prefer grains, porridge, and a diet generally higher in plant food than in meat? Judging by the human preference for meat today, there is no reason to think that our ancestors preferred plant food. All evidence indicates that humans have usually preferred meat to plants. For humans to change their diet from meat to plants, something must have interfered with their old food supply, and the evidence for this is overwhelming in the archaeological record.

Around the world, humans seem to have switched from foraging to farming because of the whole set of changes produced by global warming. As the ice melted, the coastal and lower zones flooded, pushing back and isolating some human groups while opening up new ecological zones of larger lakes and more bountiful rivers. As the ice cap receded, new lands opened up for new species, and the annual growing season expanded greatly in the temperate zones. In the increasingly warmer era, some plants and animals thrived and colonized new areas while many others became extinct.

Particularly large numbers of the big-game animals died out. The mammoth, mastodon, ground sloth, wooly rhinoceros, giant elk, and steppe bison became extinct throughout the world. Other large animals disappeared in the temperate zones but continued to exist in smaller tropical or Arctic pockets. Medium-sized animals including the European wild ass and species of goats and antelope became extinct while other medium-sized animals, such as camels and horses, became extinct in America and seem to have retreated to less accessible places in Eurasia.

The great extinction of the megafauna in the temperate zone offers one of nature's greatest puzzles. Why did they die? The earliest explanations focused on climatic change, particularly the fluctuations of the Ice Age. This theory gained popularity in part because of the discovery of frozen mammoths in Siberia, where it appeared that they may have been trapped by a suddenly descending Ice Age. Subsequent and more sophisticated research showed that the climatic transition came much more slowly, and in any event, animals such as mammoths were ideally suited for the glacial cold. Perhaps it was global warming that killed them off and allowed smaller mammals to proliferate. Under warmer, wetter conditions, large plains became forested across the temperate world. The forest proved ideal for smaller mammals but terribly onerous for larger ones, accustomed to roaming the plains in large herds.

Throughout the twentieth century, as anthropologists and other scientists have pondered the disappearance of the large mammals, an even more sinister and tragic theory has developed for the fate of the big animals. Perhaps humans hunted these animals to extinction. According to this somewhat radical theory, the great tool revolutions of thirty thousand years ago made humans into such efficient hunters that the numbers of humans grew rapidly and their skills increased, and within twenty thousand years they managed to kill off most of the large animals of the world, leaving only a few of the large mammals, such as the whales in the oceans and the elephants on the African plains.

No matter what the cause of extinction of the megafauna may have been, it forced hunters to turn to smaller animals. They improved their trapping techniques and fishing equipment, and learned to scale down their weapons to make small points for killing birds and small, scampering mammals in the bush. Birds, rabbits, fish, deer, and other small animals did not suffice to feed an enlarged human populations accustomed to mammoth steaks and mastodon ribs. The heavy hunting of the smaller animals caused even those creatures to decline in numbers.

If the big-game hunters operated with the same division of labor that we see in foraging groups today, the males probably did most of the hunting, while the females did most of the processing of the meat and skins and gathering of berries, roots, stems, bugs, worms, eggs, and small animals. As the game died off, the gathering of plant foods by the women once again became increasingly important, and the women's knowledge of plants led the way into the radically new mode of life.

Agriculture did not have to be discovered or invented; it was probably known all along. Gatherers today, such as the Australian aborigines, show an extensive and profound knowledge of the plants they harvest. They know that if they clear the ground this year, certain plants will thrive next year. They know that they must spill some of the berries, fruits, nuts, and seeds, or else they will have nothing to harvest next year when they return to the same spot.

As meat became scarcer, the women did more to ensure that next year's seeds and plants would be as plentiful as possible. As plant foods became more important and humans became more active in their production, agriculture gradually emerged as a new subsistence pattern; it became the fall-back position for a people without animals to hunt.

Early farming arose in only a few well-watered and unique

places that usually offered good growing conditions as well as a moderate seasonal supply of birds, animals, or fish. Hence humans invented agriculture along the banks of the Tigris, Euphrates, Nile, Indus, and Yellow rivers, as well as around the highland lakes of Mexico and the small but numerous little rivers running from the Andes to the Pacific.

The actual areas brought under cultivation were often quite small. Along the Nile, farmers concentrated on only a few hundred miles of shore. The entire Nile Delta, even though rich in nutrients, annually endured extensive flooding and the incessant shifting of river channels; this area was not brought into effective cultivation until extensive water-control projects were built during the early nineteenth century. Other parts of the river proved too swampy, too sandy, or too variable from one year to another to promote agriculture.

The change from hunting and gathering to agriculture involved more than a mere change in the subsistence pattern; it represented a complete change in the social and cultural fabric of life. As farmers, humans lose their freedom to roam; they must settle down and invest tremendous amounts of labor in one very small place. Farming forced humans to become sedentary for at least the growing season, and this meant they had to build longer-term residences. Thus the village was born.

Humans also needed to store food, which required the building of granaries and storage bins. To store it, the farmers had to process it, which meant that all sorts of new tools for drying, cutting, grinding, sorting, winnowing, and storing the produce were needed. The farmers had to develop new tools and behavioral patterns to protect the fields and the stored produce from birds, insects, rodents, and larger marauding animals, including other humans.

In farming, many more calories can be extracted per acre of land than in hunting and gathering. Whereas a foraging family probably required an average of several square miles, the same family, as farmers, could live from a few acres, especially if they supplemented their crops with hunting and fishing. The larger numbers of people permitted—even demanded—further specialization of labor. Some farmed while others processed the harvest into food, and yet others smelted ore to make tools. Others would weave cloth and mats, while still others carved wood and bone. No longer could one person perform all the steps of production; the process had become more complicated and demanded greater skill.

The transition from forager to farmer required so many changes in human life that the adjustment is usually called the Agricultural Revolution or the Neolithic Revolution, since it occurred during the Late Stone (or Neolithic) Age. Until this point in human history, everyone lived by a relatively similar subsistence pattern—hunting and gathering. With the rise of agriculture, humans were divided into two major groups. Some people continued to forage while others lived settled lives, tending their farms.

The division of the world between farmers and foragers created a permanent tension between two types of subsistence with very different needs. The farmer needed to close off land, kill or drive away virtually all animals living on it, chop down or burn almost all plants growing on it, and keep other humans off it. The foragers needed free access to large tracts of land filled with many kinds of plants and animals, all of which had free and easy access to bodies of water such as rivers, ponds, and lakes.

The rival foragers and farmers shared little in common. The farmer might sometimes trade with the forager for wild products such as salt, meat, honey, and furs, but farmers usually learned to produce such items for themselves by domesticating bees and keeping animals for food, leather, and fur.

From the beginning of the division between farmer and forager, the relationship was never equal or just. The farmer had little use for the forager other than as a source of forest products such as wild game. The forager, however, frequently felt lured by the rich produce of the farmland. The crops, fruits, vegetables, and animals of the farmer offered easy and tempting food for a passing band of foragers.

The newly emerging civilizations around the globe faced common problems of how to produce crops on a large scale, how to ensure adequate but not too much water, how to harvest the crops and then process them for storage, and, of equally great importance, how to protect the crops and produce from other animals and humans. The solving of these fundamental problems represents the essential challenges to sedentary life, and therein lay the beginnings of what became known as civilization. The ways in which different societies responded to these challenges represent the varying cultural nuances that distinguish Chinese civilization from that of the Aztecs, or Egyptian civilization from that of India. Each of these problems produced unique responses and further differentiated one culture from another.

The development of farming represented only half of the Neolithic Revolution. As humans domesticated crops, they also domesticated animals. Goats and sheep dominated in the Middle East; pigs and chickens in southern Asia; cattle in Central Asia and Europe; turkeys in Mesoamerica; llamas, alpacas, and guinea pigs in South America. In addition to meat, the domesticated animals also provided eggs and milk, a versatile product that could be made into butter, cream, yogurt, and many varieties of cheese. The collection of birds and animals also provided increasingly large amounts of raw materials including hides, leather, wool, feathers, antler, and bone, which could be used to produce new forms of clothing and new tools.

Had the domestication of animals merely yielded more food and raw materials, it would have caused a major change in human culture, but not nearly as great as what happened in a few areas. Following the domestication of plants and animals, the most important innovation was the harnessing of animals to plow the fields, transport the harvest, and relieve humans of many forms of strenuous labor. Rather than breaking the ground with a hand-held stick, farmers figured out how to harness animals and let them pull the stick. In different regions, farmers used horses, donkeys, burros, cows, camels, and water buffalo, or any other strong animal they could hitch to the newly evolving plow. This innovation allowed the literal harnessing of a new type of energy beyond their own muscles. Animals could pull plows, transport crops, turn grinding wheels and water wheels, and pull wagons. The new source of energy released by the muscles of animals greatly amplified the productive capacity of humans, since the animals often had strength and carrying power several times that of the strongest man.

The Neolithic Revolution involved first a revolution in food production from foraging to farming, and then the harnessing of animal energy to supplement and, whenever possible, to replace the energy of humans. The energy revolution occurred much more slowly than the food revolution.

The harnessing of animal power marked the greatest technological innovation in human history until the massive harnessing of inanimate energy such as wind and water power and finally steam, many centuries later. This revolution did not occur in all parts of the world with equal results. In America, where dogs, llamas, alpacas, guinea pigs, chinchillas, bees, turkeys, and ducks were domesticated, there was no domesticated animal strong enough to pull a plow. Compared with a cow or a horse, the Andean llama is a delicate animal with thin bones, well adapted to living in rocky mountains and high plateaus with reduced oxygen, but not suitable for pulling a plow or a wagon. The llama serves as a fine pack animal, but its limited muscle energy could not be used in any more important way by the Andean pastoralists.

The same physical restrictions that hindered the exploitation of the llama in South America limited the usefulness of deer in North America. Bison, moose, caribou, and other animals that may have been better candidates for domestication and for heavy-duty work lived beyond the domain of agriculture. They lived in the northern woodlands in cold areas with too short a growing season for agriculture, or on the plains, where the tough sod prevented agriculture prior to the introduction of steel plows in the nineteenth century.

Aside from dogs, turkeys, and an occasional wild animal adopted as a pet, the natives of North America domesticated virtually no animals. Only the dog and the turkey lived in large numbers with humans, and it has been suggested that these two animals were not, in fact, domesticated in the usual sense of the word. Wild dogs and wild turkeys have been known to congregate around human settlements, living off gardens and waste materials, including even human feces. Turkeys lived around the cornfields, and the dogs trailed along on the hunt. Through millennia of such close proximity to humans, these animals may have domesticated themselves.

The domestication of animals came at a great price to human beings, and at critical junctures in human history it has seemed that the long-term effects of domesticated animals might prove considerably more harmful than beneficial. Animals gave humans their energy for labor and their flesh to eat, but they also gave humans epidemic diseases on a scale never before known in human history.

The humans of the Old World domesticated animals that lived

in mostly large herds, such as cows, camels, horses, donkeys, sheep, goats, Asian elephants, and pigs, or they domesticated birds that normally lived in large flocks, such as chickens, geese, pigeons, and ducks. Animals in herds provided a fertile host for all sorts of parasites and microbes. Such herd animals rub against one another and nuzzle, fight, and play together, as well as licking one another's faces, eyes, fur, genitals, and rectal areas. The animals passed among themselves a constant stream of fleas, mites, ticks, lice, worms, scales, fungi, bacteria, viruses, and a large variety of both harmful and benign parasites. With the animals packed tightly together in pens, corrals, and barns, the parasites spread quickly and have ample opportunities to evolve and develop an array of forms.

In domesticating animal herds, humans also came into close contact with the animals. During the summer, when the animals wandered farther away in search of green pastures, the shepherds lived with the animals, sleeping among them, protecting them, grooming them, and helping them give birth. Such intimate contact enabled the parasites on the animals to adapt to human hosts. Soon the humans shared the same bugs, worms, and germs as their animals did.

Usually the germs and bugs caused no damage and only a little irritation to the animal or human host, but some of them erupted into grave diseases that then traveled from human to human in much the same way that they traveled from animal to animal. Over the several millennia since humans domesticated animals, a constant stream of animal-related diseases has swept through the human population.

Cowpox in cattle is closely related to smallpox among humans and distantly related to myxomatosis among rabbits. A wide assortment of animals can contract and then infect humans with rabies. Measles may be closely related to both distemper among dogs and rinderpest among cattle. Humans and pigs frequently pass various forms of influenza back and forth. Humans and chickens exchange a variety of viruses (McNeill 1976, 44).

Every infectious or epidemic disease known among humans has a close animal counterpart. Humans share fifty diseases with cattle, forty-six with sheep and goats, forty-two with pigs, thirty-five with horses, and twenty-six with poultry (McNeill 1976, 45). In addition to these diseases shared by humans and their domesticated animals, animals act as hosts and sources of infections.

From eating pig flesh, humans can become infected with the trichina worm, a parasitic nematode whose larvae move through the circulatory system and burrow into muscle, and humans can get salmonellosis from eating poultry. Typhus passed back and forth from the fleas, ticks, and lice on domesticated animals to humans, and humans contracted a variety of ailments from contamination of water, meat, or milk by animal fecal matter.

Pastoral people who lived in large, open areas showed less susceptibility to animal diseases than did the farmers and peasants who lived in tightly cramped quarters with their animals. Part of the eternal enmity between pastoralists and farmers arose from the fact that the herders often brought diseases with them. Of all the plagues that Moses brought against the Egyptians, the worst, the one that finally convinced the Pharaoh to let them go, was the disease that killed the Egyptian children but passed over the Hebrew children. A pastoral people, the Hebrews may well have already developed some resistance to one of their animal-borne diseases, to which the agricultural Egyptians had no immunity. Many of the subsequent laws of Moses are devoted to rules of cleanliness and of relations between humans and animals. The ancient scriptures of the Hindus, written by cattle-herding pastoralists speaking an Indo-European language, also show a great concern with cleanliness or pollution, and relations among humans as well as between humans and animals.

Bubonic plague spread from the fleas living on the rats that infested urban areas and often lived on stored grain. The plague originated among the horsemen of the Asian plains, who brought it on their fleas to Europe. In 1347, during the siege of a Crimean trading post by an assortment of Mongols and Hungarian Kipchaks, a few of the horsemen died of plague. The quick-thinking Kipchak commander put their corpses on a catapult and hurled them into the fort, in one of the first documented cases of biological warfare. The disease spread among the townspeople, and when a boatload of refugees managed to escape the blockade, they took the disease with them to Sicily, from which, beginning in 1347, it spread all over Europe. The plague reached Scandinavia by 1350. Within a hundred years the plague killed between one-third and one-half of the population of Europe.

Some of the infectious diseases thrived particularly well in human hosts and evolved the ability to pass directly from human to human without any other intermediary host. Tuberculosis, measles, whooping cough, mumps, smallpox, and chicken pox developed this ability to live solely among humans. Because such germs took up permanent residence in humans, they became slow-acting diseases that did not kill their hosts, since they had no other host to which they could move. Such diseases either became childhood diseases, such as measles, that moved from child to child without killing them, or diseases such as tuberculosis, which coexisted with their hosts for decades, during which time they spread to new hosts.

The domestication of animals developed primarily in the civilizations of Europe, Africa, and Asia, but as the Europeans colonized new parts of the world and took their animals with them, they also brought their diseases. The Polynesians and Native Americans had farming but few domesticated animals, and lacked virtually all of the epidemic diseases. Australia, which had neither farming nor beasts of burden, did not have the diseases. The arrival of Europeans and their animals between 1500 and 1800 brought repeated waves of smallpox, measles, yellow fever, whooping cough, and other diseases to the Americas and the South Pacific. The diseases struck each new group of people with surprisingly similar results. Within a century the epidemic reduced the native population by 90 percent, whether it was in Mexico or Tahiti, Patagonia or Australia. For every ten people who had lived in the area before the arrival of the Europeans, only one native lived there a century later.

Every great change in human history has come at a high price, and the greater the change, usually the higher the price. During the New Stone Age, the development of tools such as bows and arrows and sewing needles allowed humans to hunt larger animals everywhere in the world, but these tools eventually led to the destruction of those animals. Farming supported much larger populations than foraging did, but it did so at the cost of a lower life expectancy, smaller stature, increased disease, deteriorated nutrition, and periodic famines. These problems further disrupted human life by increasing rivalry, conflict, and even full-scale war.

The change to new forms of energy came at even higher price than the other changes. Today we can easily recognize the costs associated with energy sources such as coal, oil, electricity, and atomic power. Pollution and environmental malfunctions have been part of the cost for tapping inanimate energy sources in the

Industrial Revolution, but the transition to animal energy carried an even higher price in the creation and spread of new diseases among humans. And just as we have not yet solved the problems created by the Industrial Revolution, neither have we solved those problems created by the domestication of plants and animals initiated nearly ten thousand years ago.

Agriculture laid the basis for a new form of world culture, but that civilization needed thousands of additional years to develop and to knit together a system that spanned the globe and brought virtually everyone on earth into it. Over the last few thousand years, most human groups have switched to agriculture for subsistence, but still today some groups continue the older patterns of foraging, big-game hunting.

Even though we now have many forms of inanimate power and industrialized production at our disposal, at its core our culture still focuses on agriculture. We may be more efficient than the ancient farmers of Pocona or Mesopotamia, but aside from the frills of modernity, we are just as dependent on crops grown in the soil for our food supply as they were.

5

Nomads Across the Heartland

In Xanadu did Kubla Khan
A stately pleasure dome decree:
Where Alph, the sacred river, ran
Through caverns measureless to man
   Down to a sunless sea.
   —SAMUEL TAYLOR COLERIDGE, *Kubla Khan*

The most spectacular lake in the world must be Siberia's Lake Baikal; over a thousand miles inland from the Pacific Ocean and more than twice that distance from the Atlantic, it is the world's largest body of fresh water. Although North America's Lake Superior has the largest surface area of any lake in the world, Lake Baikal has the greatest volume of water, and it is the deepest and oldest lake in the world. It holds 20 percent of the world's fresh water, more than all the North American Great Lakes combined. Formed in a continental rift similar to that which created the Red Sea between Africa and Arabia, Lake Baikal marks the intersection of three tectonic plates, and its deepest recesses plunge a mile into the earth.

More than three hundred rivers drain into Lake Baikal; of these, the greatest tributary of the lake is the 620-mile-long Selenga River, which drains much of northern Mongolia. Even though so many rivers flow into it, only the Angara drains out of it, making its exit from the southern end of the lake and then flowing northward into the Yenisei and on to the Arctic Ocean. Lake Baikal is home to the nerpa, the only freshwater seal in the world, as well as 250 species of shrimp and fifty-two species of fish, including the endemic omul, a tasty arctic whitefish that is the lake's most important commercial product. Despite the abundant wildlife and fish and the human communities built around the lake, the waters of Lake Baikal retain a chilling purity that allows one to see far down into it.

Even though, at 25 million years old, Lake Baikal is one of the oldest bodies of water on the earth, it is still one of the clearest because of the freshwater shrimp *Epischura baicalensis*, which consumes algae and bacteria. In the winter, when air temperature averages zero degrees Fahrenheit or minus twenty degrees Celsius, the clear water freezes to an amazing clarity that allows one to see fish swimming several feet below the ice, but the ice is so thick that, during World War I, the Russian army ran a railway over it to supply their eastern front.

Most of the lake lies within Russia's Buryat autonomous region, which forms the homeland of the Buryat Mongols, and is only three hundred miles from the Mongolian capital of Ulan Bator. The lake and the forested land around it have always been sacred to the people who live there. In Ulan Ude, the capital of the Buryat region, one hundred miles west of Lake Baikal on the Selenga, the Mongols built a large Tibetan Buddhist monastery. This monastery represents the most northerly of the lamaist monasteries, and was visited by the Dalai Lama for the first time in 1991.

Near where the Angara flows out of Lake Baikal, there flourished a sacred grove where the animist Mongols came to pray long before they became Buddhists. Generations of visitors have tied small ribbons onto the bushes and trees of the grove, and have broken thousands of bottles of white and green glass, whose shards now lie scattered among the trees. Mongols still come to the spot to pray, but so do tourists, and also vendors seeking to sell military hats, insignias, badges, epaulets, and flags from the Afghanistan campaigns of the Soviet army.

No great rivers flow from east to west across Eurasia. Along its edges, all the great rivers, such as the Yellow, Yangtze, Ganges, Tigris, Euphrates, and Rhine, flow out to the oceans. But in the middle of the landmass, many of the rivers flow into inland seas, simply dry up as they struggle to cross the immense continent, or, like the Angara from Lake Baikal, flow north into the Arctic and are frozen for much of the year. The rivers have made travel easy along the edges of Eurasia but problematic deep in the interior.

For thousands of years this great central heartland of Eurasia presented an immense barrier that separated the early civilizations of the Mediterranean from those of Asia. Thousands of miles of deserts, steppes, and grasslands intervened between the great agricultural civilizations, which developed independently of one another but often along parallel paths.

According to ancient Mongol traditions, a blue-gray wolf and a doe mated in the forests along the shores of Lake Baikal, and from this union arose the Mongol people. The *Secret History of the Mongols*, written in about 1240, claims that the progeny of this union was the greatest of Mongol leaders, Genghis Kahn himself.

Despite the importance of the wolf in their mythology, an even more appropriate totem for the Asian nomads would have been the horse. The Mongols rode into history on the horse, and with it the Mongols and their predecessors in central Asia knitted together the communication links and trade routes that eventually connected China with Europe and the Middle East. They carried technology, religion, and knowledge back and forth, and during some centuries they exercised political power that brought ever larger areas under the organization of a single nation. At various times they conquered large parts of the Byzantine Empire, Persia, northern India, Russia, and China.

The environment in the interior of Eurasia has always been hard. Without large oceans to moderate the temperature of the air and land, the area froze during winter and baked in the summer. In some years the rains never came, and in other years they brought floods. These extremes of nature prevented the spread of extensive agriculture onto the steppes, and thus kept the rice-civilization of China clearly separate from the wheat-civilizations of the Mediterranean and the Middle East.

Farmers could not grow crops on this soil, which lay far from rivers, but a number of grazing animals lived in great herds that found nourishment in the grasses that covered the area in times of adequate rain. Different parts of the steppes and plateaus appealed to different animals, but these included horses, asses, camels, goats, cattle, and sheep, as well as yaks on the Tibetan plateau and reindeer in the northern taiga and tundra. The hunters of these animals gradually became their keepers as they domesticated them. Humans could not live on the plants of the steppes and plains, but they could live on the animals who ate those plants and thus concentrated the energy of the plains into meat.

An ocean of grass separated Europe from Asia, on opposite ends of the same continent. But an ocean is a barrier only as long as a people has no boats to cross it; for a people with the right technology, the ocean becomes a link, a line of communication and commerce. With the domestication of the horse and the gradual development of equestrian technology, humans found a way to sail through the sea of grass. Over thousands of years the nomads of the area gradually developed reins, bits, bridles, riding blankets, saddles, and the other equipment necessary to control the horse and maximize its power. No human could run as fast or as long as a horse, or carry or pull as much as a horse. The humans who tapped and controlled this tremendous energy source for their own ends acquired a great advantage over rivals.

The steppe grasslands of Asia stretch like a giant crescent from Manchuria in northeastern China to Hungary in central Europe, a distance of some 4,500 miles. With the development of a horse culture, the massive steppes of Eurasia, formerly a barrier to human movement and communication, were transformed into a great highway. The grasslands have major arteries that branch southward into Iran and India, between the Caspian and Black seas onto the Anatolian Plateau of Turkey, and northward to virtually every part of European Russia and the Ukraine, and on into Poland.

Even though the horse did not evolve on the Eurasian plains, it found a natural home there. The horse, like the camel, evolved in North America. The early ancestor of the horse, *Eohippus* ("dawn horse") lived in North America during the Eocene, from 58 to 48 million years ago. By the Pleistocene, from 7 to 2 million years ago, the horse had fully evolved and crossed over the Bering land bridge into Asia, and from there on into Europe and Africa. It quickly became a favored prey of hunters on all those continents. By 6000 B.C., the horse had become extinct in its homelands of North America but was thriving in Asia, Africa, and Europe, particularly on the great Eurasian plains, which were destined to be the stage on which the horse would play its most dramatic role in human history.

The earliest evidence of wear found on the teeth of horses from the plains of the Ukraine suggests that they wore bits. Antler cheekpieces further indicate that horseback riding began as early as 4000 B.C. in that area (Anthony et al.). For centuries the use of the horse as a domesticated animal seemed confined to central Eurasia. They did not enter the Middle East, where asses were already in use as draft animals, until about 2000 B.C. Initially the horse was used simply as an animal of burden, a stronger and improved ass. Gradually it found new uses, such as for pulling chariots and, eventually, being ridden (Anthony et al.).

The horse nomads of the plains entered the Indian subcontinent between 1800 and 1500 B.C., and quickly overcame the Indus civilization (McNeill 1982, 12). In their initial forays they came in horse-drawn wagons and chariots rather than on horseback. The settled agricultural nations of the Mediterranean quickly adopted the innovation of the chariot and overcame or absorbed the invaders. Over the next three thousand years, until the climax of Mongol civilization, the nomads returned again and again with one innovation after another.

The pulling of wagons, even when the wagons had been streamlined into chariots, was cumbersome and slow. The first record of attack by warriors actually riding on the horse itself came with the pillaging of the Assyrian capital of Nineveh in 612 B.C. By this time the Assyrians themselves also had mounted warriors. It is not clear exactly where or how the transition from charioteers to cavalry occurred; it may not have been the nomadic steppe people who invented horseback riding, but they were the ones who proved most adept at it and spread it around Eurasia and into Africa.

The mounted warrior introduced a new era into Eurasian history. Following the gradual refinement of the bridle, bit, and saddle, the chariot gave way to mounted cavalry. Given the tools to control the horse with only one hand, the rider had a free hand to wield a sword, throw a spear, or even use both hands to shoot an arrow from a bow while still galloping. Because the saddle increased the rider's security, he could twist and turn in his seat to shoot in any direction; he could turn to the rear of the horse and shoot behind as effectively as to the side or front.

The invention of stirrups allowed a rider more strength to put into his lance, and even permitted him to stand rather than sit while fighting. Stirrups first appeared in about the year 500, and added one of the final great innovations for cavalry (McNeill 1982, 20). With stirrups, an archer had greater stability and thus greater accuracy, and a rider with a sword or a lance had greater power to thrust at his victim. The stirrups' potential to concentrate the rider's force made the lance a particularly formidable weapon, with greater power concentrated at its tip. This completed technology gradually gave rise to the European mounted knights and became the basic technological principle behind the medieval joust.

Each technological innovation produced a new round of invasion from the heartland. For three thousand years the nomads poured out of the heartland into the littoral states of Europe and Asia. They still inspire horrible images of barbarian hordes slaughtering millions of peasants and city dwellers and piling their heads in great pyramids outside the crumbling and smoldering ruins of their homes. All the agricultural states, from Europe and the Mediterranean through Persia and India and on to China, learned to fear and hate the nomadic tribes through thirty centuries of persistent though intermittent invasion and conquest.

Most of the nomads spoke one of the Turkish or Mongol languages, but they also included speakers of European languages, particularly Slavic and Finno-Ugric. The nomads, who combined all the racial groups of Eurasia, formed frequent alliances in which whole tribes would unite, and they frequently absorbed the people whom they conquered as affiliated clans. In addition, they made marriages with settled peoples, accepting European and Chinese women in marriage as well as kidnapping them.

The names for these people have varied through the centuries—Scythians, Avars, Huns, Magyars, Tatars, Bulgars, Mongols, and Turks. Many of the tribes are lumped together as Mongols because the Mongols were among the greatest of the nomadic conquerors, but they are also often called Tartars, or Tatars, after a Turkish part of the Mongol confederacy. The name *Tatar* probably comes from the Chinese word *ta-ta*, which simply meant "nomad." For Europeans, they were the fiends of

Tartarus, the ancient Greek word for hell, and thus they were often called Tartars.

The nomads would suddenly appear on the borderlands, sometimes literally traveling faster than the news of their approach. Seemingly without reason, they might turn in another direction, or they could sweep through cities and destroy crops for hundreds of miles. Then they disappeared as quickly as they came, but took with them thousands of slaves and new wives, and hundreds of wagons of bounty.

As completely capricious as the nomads may have appeared to the settled people, there emerged a decisive pattern and logic to their behavior. They constantly probed and tested the whole length of Eurasia. In decades when China grew strong, they turned toward the west and headed for Europe, or south into Iran or India. In years when these other kingdoms showed more strength, the nomads headed back toward China. They seem to have conquered tribes, cities, and even whole empires with equanimity.

The movement of any one group sent a sequence of shock waves across the heartland as one tribe was pushed onto another, dislodging smaller nomadic tribes and forcing agricultural peoples in the heartland to flee away from the grasslands and toward the coastal kingdoms. These wandering and displaced hordes themselves became menaces to the people whose lands they invaded.

For the three thousand years from 1600 B.C. to roughly A.D. 1500, the wandering of tribes and the warfare between settled, civilized people and their barbarian, nomadic enemies became the focal issue of Eurasian civilization. But as the two great traditions fought with each other, they constantly exchanged cultural traits and technology. The nomads sometimes settled among the farmers as their overlords or as their neighbors, but they also moved millions of people in forced relocations.

In order to survive, each side had to learn the ways and the culture of the other. The Mongols borrowed technology, animals, and ideas from all parts of their territories, and spread them to the other nations, from Europe to China.

These crucial years of world history formed a three-thousand-year arms race between two opposing cultural traditions. From the invention of the horse-drawn chariot to the spread of the stirrup, a series of technological changes in warfare permitted the momentary victory of a new group of nomads over a settled population. The settled people, however, quickly mastered and incorporated the innovations. The weapons of the nomads escalated from spears and swords to a variety of complex bows, and finally to firearms, which, in the end, helped the settled people, who learned to make ever larger artillery pieces.

Western Europe is a large peninsula that juts out into the Atlantic Ocean from the Eurasian continent, at the western end of the massive plains. If the plains are thought of as a river of grass, then the river always flowed from east to west, from Asia to Europe. Starting in the high plateau of Mongolia and stretching to fertile Hungary, the pastures become progressively more luxuriant the closer they come to the warm, moist air that flows in across Europe from the northern terminus of the Gulf of Mexico. As new groups moved toward Europe, the vacuum left by their departure enticed other groups south out of the Siberian taiga, and they too took up the nomadic life-style.

Through the centuries the river of movement flowed westward, and wave after wave of displaced nomads wandered into Europe. When the Huns, who were called the *Hsiung-nu* in Chinese records, invaded southern Russia in 372, they defeated the Ostrogoths and set the Visigoths into flight. The Visigoths headed westward, sacked Rome in 410, and plundered their way to Spain, which they ruled until the arrival of the Moors in 711. Meanwhile, the Ostrogoths took large parts of Italy; the Vandals, dislocated by the Huns, ended up in Morocco; and the Burgundians settled in France. German tribes replaced the Celts along the Rhine and the Main.

In the dislocation of people and the wandering of tribes, the Saxons, Jutes, and Angles began pushing out of continental Europe and across the English Channel into Britain, where they began the slow and methodical replacement of native Celtic people by their Teutonic invaders. An entry in the *Anglo-Saxon Chronicle* for 443 reads, "In this year the Britons sent across the sea to Rome and begged for help against the Picts, but they got none there, for the Romans were engaged in a campaign against Attila, king of the Huns" (Humble 1975, 8). The Romans and Visigoths together finally gave Attila his first major defeat in Gaul in 451, and even though the Huns left Gaul and their leader, Attila, died the next year, they went on to ravage Italy before disappearing from the world stage.

Shortly before the defeat of the Huns in Gaul and Attila's death, the *Anglo-Saxon Chronicle* records the arrival of the German brothers Hengest and Horsa and their followers from the mainland in 449. Year after year the chronicle tells of the arrival of more Saxons, Jutes, and Angles. In 495 the chieftain Cerdic and his son Cynric arrived with their followers on five ships. In 501 a chief named Port and his sons Bieda and Maegla came with two ships. In 514 the East Saxons arrived in three ships, and so on until finally the Teutonic tribes had defeated the native Britons.

No matter where the equestrian nomads of the heartland struck—China, Russia, India, Greece, Turkey, Persia, Hungary, or Mesopotamia, they conquered everyone, with two major exceptions: Japan and Western Europe. Their inability to conquer the islands of Japan can be explained easily by the fact that the Mongols were not a seafaring people, despite the efforts of Kubilai Khan to make them into a great naval as well as land power. When the Japanese refused to surrender to Kubilai Khan, he ordered a sea invasion with 4,400 ships in 1281, but when a typhoon struck the armada, the invasion failed miserably, as did every other attempt to conquer Japan until its defeat by the United States in the Second World War.

The inability of the Mongols or any other nation from the steppes to conquer and hold Western Europe raises somewhat more complex issues. Time and again, nomadic tribes overran large parts of Eastern Europe and threatened Western Europe, but a series of what seemed to be miracles always intervened.

The Mongols conquered Russia, the Ukraine, and Eastern Europe to the Adriatic. They seemed poised to take Vienna and then march on into Western Europe, when news arrived in the Mongol camp that the great Khan had died in December 1241. The leaders of the invasion folded their tents and raced back to the Mongol capital of Karakorum, abandoning their invasion of Western Europe.

For the European Christians, each deliverance seemed like a miracle from God. In the end, Western Europe may have been simply too far away for most of the heartland people, and it was not good horse country. It had massive forests, and the nomadic cavalry moved much more easily on open plains. Even the nomads' favored weapon, the bow and arrow, did not function well in a forest that was better suited to fighting with swords at close range.

The parts of Western Europe that were not forests were agricultural lands. The steppe ponies tired easily as they trod across the endless furrows. When the peasants plowed the land in a north-south direction, it made invasion from the east especially difficult for the horses, because each furrow became a small hill over which they had to step, slowing them considerably.

Long episodes of peace intervened during the three thousand years, and during these periods the nomads served as traders or as the protectors of merchants among the various civilizations surrounding them. They brought silk from China over 4,500 miles to Syria, from whence they traded it with the ancient Romans. In turn, they carried silver coins from Rome and the other Mediterranean states back to China. They traded for amber from northern Europe to Asia, and brought a great supply of sable and other furs from the forests of Siberia to the courts of Europe. Even though more than five thousand miles separated the capitals of the Chinese and Roman empires, they engaged in a slow yet persistent trade.

The nomads took new products, such as paper and ginger, to the west, and brought with them new foods such as peaches, apricots, persimmons, and rhubarb, which easily took root in European soil. During this time the nomads of Central Asia also spread the drinking of tea from China to all of Eurasia. In so doing, they created one of the first universal words as the Chinese *chai* was adopted into Russian, and became *shay* in Arabic, and *tea*, *tee*, or *té* in Western European languages.

The nomads and the agricultural people formed a single large cultural and social system. The nomadic herding warriors could not have existed without the agricultural people. Despite their dietary dependence on the meat, milk, and blood of their animals, the herders needed agricultural goods such as cereals, salt, tea, and sugar. They also needed chemicals for the tanning and processing of their leather and hides, as well as the more sophisticated crafts of settled urban people, such as metal-working, in order to make the equipment and weapons on which they depended.

The herding people and the agricultural people lived in a symbiotic relationship. During times of famine and agricultural failure, many people left their farms and joined the ranks of nomads wandering with their animals. The settled farmers and the nomadic herders intermarried, traded, maintained complex systems of tribute and allegiances, and fought against each other as well as together against other groups.

Because most written records about the nomads have been left to us by settled agricultural people such as the Chinese, Persians, and Europeans, most of the accounts portray the nomads as barbarians much less sophisticated than the farmers and urban people whom they attacked. The average herding warrior, like the average peasant warrior, was illiterate, but the achievements of the nomadic culture were just as great as those of the urban culture. Even though tribal nations such as the Mongols produced the most sophisticated and widespread systems of espionage and terrorism known, they also protected the trade routes between Europe and Asia, and greatly expanded communications.

In addition to forming the prototype for cavalry of all types and providing equipment and weapons for them, nomads made major changes in the life-style of Europeans. Even though the nomads often wore heavy coats, they also wore pants, which proved better suited to their riding life-style than the tunics worn by people in the Mediterranean or the caftans of the Middle East. The men and the women kept their pants up with belts that often had highly decorated buckles and that became very important items of clothing and symbolism among groups such as the Mongols. Eventually the trousers and belts of the nomads became the universal standard for male wear throughout Europe, even though women, who had fewer opportunities to ride horses, retained the older, flowing garments.

For the nomadic tribes of the heartland, communication was vital. Under the Mongols, who created the greatest of the herding empires, a system of post stations stretched across Eurasia, with over ten thousand relay stations built approximately thirty miles apart. An envoy could cross the continent at the incredible speed of three hundred miles a day. Not until the opening of the Trans-Siberian Railway did anyone surpass the old record of the Mongols for travel across the continent (Legg 1970, 311).

The Mongol system depended greatly on the use of written language, and the Mongol bureaucracy became one of the most efficient in the world. Borrowing from the Chinese, Persians, and Byzantines, they added their own characteristics to create a bureaucracy and record-keeping system that could stretch over a much larger area than any of these smaller empires ever covered.

The Mongol need for efficient, lightweight communication sustained a primary interest in paper made from tree bark. The paper, invented in China, proved cheaper and lighter than sheepskin, which the Europeans used, or linen or papyrus. The Mongols took papermakers with them wherever they went, and gradually spread the craft around Eurasia. In a similar way they spread sericulture, the art of silk-making, as well as the necessary silkworms, to the Middle East and other parts of the world conducive to the production of silkworms.

The same requirements they had for light paper also applied to money. Huge supplies of coins proved too bulky and difficult to transfer in massive quantities, but slips of paper representing thousands of coins could be transported easily. The Chinese already minted coins with a hole in the center so that the coins could be strung together in bundles of a thousand. Using paper money, several such bundles could be replaced with a simple slip of paper. The Chinese used paper money as early as 1024, but with the coming to power of the Mongols and their unprecedentedly large empire under Kubilai Khan, paper money became much more important.

The tribesmen of the steppes also carried playing cards made of paper to make them light and easily transported for the amusement of the warriors who spent so much time in camp away from home. The settled people quickly adopted the game and spread it on to others.

The nomadic tribes needed easy ways to communicate, but they lacked an alphabet. This problem confronted Genghis Khan as soon as he united his empire. In 1204 he sought to solve the problem with a captured Uighur scholar whom he ordered to teach the crown prince how to write. This was the first known attempt to write the Mongolian language in any script. The Uighurs had adapted their alphabet from the Sogdians, who spoke an Indo-European language that was related to Persian and was brought into central Asia by Nestorian Christians. Scholars believe that the Sogdians in turn had adapted their alphabet from Greek, Aramaic, or another northern Semitic language.

Kubilai Khan, the grandson of Genghis Khan, encountered

another problem with writing, because the Chinese whom he ruled used ideographic characters rather than an alphabet, and each of the heartland nations had a different alphabet. To make communication more efficient, he ordered the creation of a standard alphabet for all nations, including the Chinese. The new script was meant to enable the writing of any language that had not previously been written, and it was the earliest official attempt to change Chinese writing from characters to an alphabet.

Kubilai Khan entrusted the task to 'Phangs-pa, a Buddhist lama of the Saskya-pa sect of Tibet, who invented the new alphabet with heavy borrowing from Tibetan, and it became the official alphabet in 1269. All letters were formed in a rectangular fashion, similar to Tibetan and Sanskrit, but in contrast to most alphabets, which are written horizontally, the 'Phangs-pa script was written in straight lines from top to bottom, like the Chinese characters. The alphabet had forty-one phonetic symbols, which allowed any language to be written in it, and it did not require a lengthy period of study to master it.

In 1368, with the overthrow of the Mongols' Yuan dynasty in China, the nation immediately returned to writing with ideographic characters. The Mongols went back to their old Mongolian script, which they kept until the twentieth century, when the Russian Mongols and the Mongolian People's Republic adopted the Cyrillic alphabet from the Russians. The controversy over the written form of the language still rages, and many Mongols still prefer their traditional script.

Because so many scripts have been used in so many languages, scholars have not yet settled on the proper way to transliterate the name of the founding Mongol emperor, Genghis Khan, which can also be written as Chinggis, Chinghis, Chingis, Chingiz, Jenghiz, or Jinghis. Some even prefer to refer to him by his given name of Temujin or Temuchin.

The Mongols needed efficient means of accounting for their large domains. They needed to know the numbers of soldiers and animals, the amounts of taxes paid, and many other types of numbers. For this purpose they spread the use of a Chinese invention, the abacus. Using the abacus, clerks and accountants could quickly tally large sums. It became a necessary tool not only for accountants but also for merchants, and in many parts of Eurasia it has remained the primary computing device through the twentieth century.

The tribes of the heartland carried ideas and knowledge as well as material items. Traditionally the tribes had shamanistic religions and animistic beliefs based on the worship of spirits inhabiting living and inanimate objects. They freely adopted the religions of the people surrounding them in urban and agricultural areas. Many of them, especially the Naimans and the Kereits, became Nestorian Christians and spread that sect from the Middle East to China; Kubilai Khan's mother had been one of the Nestorian Christians. Many of the Khazar clans converted to Judaism, and the ancient Uighurs adopted the Manichaean religion. The Tatars and the Turks adopted Islam and helped spread it throughout the heartland, but the Mongols adopted Buddhism. The Magyars and the Bulgars converted to Christianity, as did almost all the Slavic tribes.

The nomads generally maintained a tolerant attitude toward religion. The Mongols, even after converting to Buddhism, maintained religious freedom. China under Genghis Khan was probably the most religiously free empire in the world at that time. The Mongol rulers not only tolerated the mix of Buddhists, Taoists, Zoroastrians, Manichaeans, Christians, Muslims, Confucianists, and animists, but encouraged them all to practice their diverse religions.

Even after converting to Islam, the Tatars who ruled over Russia continued as the protectors of the Russian Orthodox church, exempting it from taxation and lavishing rights and gifts on the monasteries and churches of Russia. Under Tatar rule, the church became a much stronger and more widespread institution than it had ever been under the nominally Christian Russian rulers, who tried to keep it subordinated to their own will.

The Tatars lived in camps called *orda*, and the large groups or camps came to be called *horda*. In another form the word became *Urdu*, used to describe the Muslim people and their language in the Indian subcontinent. In English this became *horde*, and even today the word carries the connotation of a chaotic and disorganized mass of people, something like a swarm of flies, and it usually evokes a sense of savagery and barbarism. This hides the ordered structure that lay beneath the military system of the nomadic herders. The Mongols, for example, organized their army on a simple, base-ten geometric progression. Ten men formed a unit; ten units formed a larger unit of one hundred;

ten of these formed a brigade of a thousand; ten brigades constituted a horde.

This simple military system translated easily into a form of
government for ruling newly conquered lands. Under Ghengis
Khan, the Mongols ruled over the largest empire ever known.
His domains stretched from what is now Finland to Vietnam.
No nation before or since has ever amassed so much territory
into one administrative unit.

During the Pax Mongolica, it was said that a girl could walk
with a pot of gold on her head from one end of the Mongol
territory to the other without ever being molested. Such an example, though hyperbolic, illustrates the organization and administrative thoroughness with which the Mongols ruled.

Unlike the antiquated Chinese bureaucracy or the bloated
Byzantine bureaucracy, the Mongol system was built for a
large territory in which leaders needed to act swiftly. Their
system became the basis for the unification of Russia and of
China, and under the Ottomans it became a much more efficient
replacement for the Byzantine system of the Mediterranean.
Under the slave-soldiers of the Mamelukes, the same system was
used to reorganize Egypt.

Mongol rule brought unity to the disparate northern and
southern regions of China, just as it subsequently united Russia
and finally India into nation-states. Modern China was shaped by
the Mongols, and Kubilai Khan greatly influenced the subsequent
history of China by locating his capital in what is now Beijing,
in 1260. Still, today the three largest Eurasian nations in both
area and population are these three nations created by Mongol
rule.

With the Mongol empire, the nomads of the Eurasian steppes
reached their political zenith, but the era was not yet finished.
Under Sultan Mohammed the Conqueror in 1453, the Ottoman
Turks overcame Constantinople, capital of the Byzantine Empire, and established the Ottoman Empire. In 1526 a group of
Turks under Babur began the invasion and unification of India
into the Mughal (Mongol) empire. In 1644 the Manchus overthrew the Ming dynasty.

These were the last three great conquests by the equestrian
nomads of the interior. By this time the conquering nomads were

already becoming indistinguishable from the settled urban people whom they conquered. The era of the horse had passed, and world history had moved on into the age of the ship and the machine. The horse and the nomads who rode it had united Europe and Asia into a single cultural history; the horse had provided the momentum that led to the subsequent incorporation of Africa and America into the system.

After the fall of Emperor Pu-yi of China and Sultan Mohammed VI of the Ottoman Empire in the second decade of the twentieth century, the last of the nomadic dynasties came to a symbolic end, but their real power had ended centuries earlier. For three thousand years the nomads of the heartland had played a pivotal role in shaping the history of Eurasia, but by the twentieth century the focus of world events had passed them and moved on to other places, leaving Central Asia a patchwork of feuding clans and tribes.

The nomads and the horse transformed Eurasia from a collection of isolated and independent civilizations into a single civilization of related parts, beset by rivalries and war, but nevertheless living within a single social and cultural arena. Over the past two thousand years, the Eurasian nomads stitched together the peoples of Asia and Europe into a continental system of shared commerce, disease, and politics.

Despite the connections that the nomads made, they did not standardize Eurasian civilization. Instead they heightened awareness of the differences between groups. Even while uniting into one civilization, the horsemen divided the people of Eurasia into new factions, created new cultural identities, and increased the rivalry, strife, and warfare among the different parts.

The horse conquered the heartland of Eurasia, uniting Asia and Europe. The horse could not, however, conquer the Sahara, which separated most Africans from Europeans. In order to bring all the civilizations of the three continents into contact, humans had to find a way to cross the desert. They eventually found the solution in the camel.

6

The Camel and the Quest for Contact

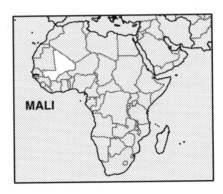

When spiderwebs unite, they can tie up a lion.
—Ethiopian Proverb

Across the southern edge of the Sahara lie many small oases and villages nestled by waterholes and lakes that appear and disappear through the years. These communities form an archipelago around the desert, and they serve as markets for salt, dates, millet, metal, camels, and a rather sparse variety of other goods. They also serve as the centers for courtship, worship, paying taxes, or hopping a ride to the next community.

One exhausting January afternoon, I sat in the dirt on the edge of a small market in the southwestern Sahara, waiting for the merchants to conclude their transactions so that I might find a ride on a small pickup truck going on to the community of Dire. The year had been a hard one in the Sahara. Rain had been more sparse than usual. Animals and even children had died in large numbers. The market offered painfully little to sell, and the men sat on their haunches in little circles, doing more talking and coffee-drinking than buying or selling.

Merchants had crossed the desert with their camel caravans laden with large slabs of salt, which they sold or traded for millet, rice, or some other staple. Special merchants also bought and sold camels in the small market, and on this afternoon there happened to be a large number of them gathered together. Most of the camel drivers hobbled their animals by tying their two front legs together just above the hooves, or by bending one leg at the knee and tying it up.

On this afternoon an irritated cow camel, apparently in heat, broke loose from her tether and raced madly around the market. A bull camel, hobbled at the ankles, followed in loud but awkward pursuit. The sellers in the small stalls jumped to gather their few baskets of produce and scattered away from the charging duo. The female charged down a narrow street of mud buildings and raced ahead at a full gallop. The tragic male loped behind her as fast as he could, running like a cartoon character. I jumped behind a parked truck when the cow suddenly turned down the alley where I was sitting. She raced down the blind alley with the bull behind her, but at the end of the alley just behind me, she could not exit. A large mud wall barred her path. She screamed and jerked her head angrily as the male raced toward her and soon caught up with her.

In one of the oddest displays of male sexual interest in the animal kingdom, the bull camel, whose penis usually points toward the rear for urination, completely reverses position and turns toward the opposite direction when sexually aroused and ready for copulation. The male pushed in beside the female and made the motions to mount her, but he could not lift his hobbled legs sufficiently high. Finally rearing back on his hind legs almost like a horse, he raised his legs high enough to put them on her back, but he could not part them because of the rope that hobbled him. He stood with his hind legs on the ground and his two front legs on the cow's back, looking like a giant praying mantis, but he was unable to complete the sexual act or to dismount from her. Both camels struggled in the awkward position until the mare knocked him free.

With increasing anger the aroused bull jumped again and again, kicking in part of the mud wall that served as their temporary jail. The camels' owners and a growing crowd of curious spectators approached the alley slowly, but no one dared approach the hopelessly frustrated and infuriated beasts. The owners had to wait until the male exhausted himself and both camels calmed down before they ventured in to separate the two animals and drag them back to the market.

The scene in the market, and the ability of the enraged camels to halt the activity of virtually the entire village for an hour, emphasized to me just how physically powerful camels are, and how different to control. I had often seen evidence of their stubbornness, but I had never seen such a display of angry vigor.

The importance of camels and the nomads who breed and sell them came comparatively late into world history, but for the history of Africa and the Middle East they had an inordinate importance. The process of domesticating the camel, developing the right technology for it and learning to breed it in captivity, proved to be a longer and more complicated process than domesticating the horse or cow. The camel may be the most difficult animal that humans have ever tried to tame, harness, and exploit, but without it, travel across the Sahara would have been nearly impossible before the invention of trucks and airplanes.

The Sahara is larger than virtually every country of the world except Russia. It is the hottest and driest large area in the world, and aside from central Antarctica and the interior of Greenland, it is the most inhospitable to life. Because of its size and severity, the Sahara forms the greatest barrier to human travel on land.

The Sahara is so large that its exact dimensions prove difficult to measure, particularly since the desert expands and contracts annually. It is like a giant, breathing creature that expands into the southern grasslands and then recedes before pushing out again in an eternal rhythmic pattern. During the 1980s the desert grew from about 3.3 million square miles to 3.6 million. Most years the desert pushed south at the rate of between 6 and 60 miles a year.

With its continental dimensions, the Sahara influences weather patterns over vast portions of the earth's surface. Its dust plays a vital role even in the Amazon, which depends on the tons of phosphates and nitrates deposited by winds from Africa to replenish the extremely poor soils of the Amazon rain forest. During the decades when the desert grows, the winds whip up even more sand and blow it across the Atlantic, helping the Amazon to thrive.

Maps can make the Sahara look deceptively tame and manageable. Mapmakers detest a void or any blank spaces because they imply a lack of knowledge. As Jonathan Swift wrote in *On Poetry, A Rhapsody* in 1733:

So geographers, in Afric maps,
With savage pictures fill their gaps,
And o'er unhabitable downs
Place elephants for want of towns.

Cartographers today use fewer elephants and pictures but more names and roads; they tend to fill in the great open space across the north of Africa with information that makes it look less formidable, less unknown, and less hostile. Small oases with only a few goatherders eking out a living have names that appear on the map as large as those of Berlin or Beijing. Even oases or salt-mining pits that have had no permanent inhabitants for decades may have a name as prominent as a department of France.

The lines connecting the oases on the map portray trails that may not have been used in generations, but the cartographers draw the trails in bold color. The lines look deceptively like roads leading to horrible mistakes made by occasional tourists driving down from Europe. For them, driving across the Sahara looks like a grand holiday adventure, like driving to Turkey or taking a family holiday in the American Southwest. They take the ferry across from Marseilles to Algeria and are delighted to find the roads almost as good as those in the poorer countries of Eastern Europe. As they drive farther south on a road, however, it gradually disappears. It is no longer a track, a trail, or a path, but merely a jumble of tire tracks headed in many different directions. Driving across the Sahara without experienced guides is like driving from Saskatchewan to the Mexican border without benefit of a highway or a road sign; one needs experience to do it.

Sahara drivers do not follow directly in the tire tracks of the driver before them, for fear of bogging down in the deepening rut. They parallel the trail and then make a wide detour where it is obvious that someone got stuck. The next vehicle makes it even wider. What looks on the map like a definite road is in reality only a belt of tracks from two to twenty miles wide. These tracks weave over and through one another, circle around, veer off toward nowhere, and disappear abruptly in the shifting sand. The family of tourists easily becomes disoriented, and finds itself circling endlessly. Suddenly they are lost and the car overheats, runs out of gas, or breaks down. One of them, or perhaps all of them, set out to search for help walking by night and hiding from the sun by day, or they all remain behind, waiting for rescue in the shadow beneath their vehicle.

We know about these people because, until their thirst forces them to suck ink from their pens, they have ample time to reflect and to write before they die. When, or if, their bodies are found, they usually have long letters or diaries in their pockets or left on the seat of the vehicle. The documents detail their torturous obsession with water, the agonizing decisions first to drink bodily fluids such as urine and blood, but they also try to slake their thirst on industrial liquids from the car such as oil, gasoline, brake fluid, coolant, and eventually even battery acid. They describe the tortured deaths of their family members and the decision to kill the children and others whose pain seems to linger too long and whose natural death seems too slow, and they sometimes rationalized drinking the blood of their dead family members.

The native people do not so much drive across the Sahara as navigate through it. Experienced drivers and guides stop constantly to make observations and calculate their location. By day they use the sun and even the seasonal wind to keep them oriented, but at night they navigate the way all other sailors do, by the stars. Like the Three Wise Men of the Bible, they know which rising stars point to particular oases and which to settlements. When they have finally crossed the Sahara from the north, they come to the Sahel, the wide belt of grassland whose name means "shore" in Arabic.

The native people of the Sahara do not travel in small groups, but prefer to go with large numbers. Truck drivers do not go alone; they wait for a crowd of people to climb up on the backs of their trucks. A truck may sit in a market all day waiting for enough people before the driver will strike out into the desert in the evening cool. The people need transportation, but the driver needs them even more, because they push and pull the truck across dunes and through sand pits. Without them he would never make it.

Every part of the trek across the desert is a guessing game. The steep dunes often defy the efforts of the driver to reach the top. The driver must back the truck up several hundred feet from the dune and then try to build up as much speed as the truck can accumulate before reaching the dune. The truck slows quickly as the angle becomes steeper and steeper. The people hold their collective breath and then give a groan of disappointment if the truck stops short of the summit and begins to roll backward yet again. If the truck makes it over the top, the passengers scream and clap and then hold on tight for the fearfully fast plunge down the other side. Often the driver must drive for miles to cut a route around a particular dune or to find a low spot where he can cross.

All trucks in the lower Sahara come equipped with two long metal tracks strapped to either side of the truck. When the truck is stuck or cannot reach the top of a particularly difficult dune, the passengers jump off and lay out the tracks in front of the truck's wheels, to get the truck to the next stretch of firm ground.

In some places there is no sand at all. The wind has blown the bedrock clean and, in the process, polished it as smooth as kitchen tiles. The trucks glide across the surface, and the passengers always enjoy the few smooth minutes, a pleasant respite from the otherwise constant lurching and lunging.

Through tens of thousands of years the history of the Sahara fluctuated between very dry eras alternating with moderately wet ones. Within these larger cycles, smaller ones make some centuries and decades much drier than others. In about 5000 B.C., the Sahara had enough grass to support herds of animals and the predators that they attracted. Transportation through the area was relatively easy for a group of people on foot.

As the centuries grew warmer and drier, humans lacked the strength to carry enough water to survive from one watering hole to the next. They needed to use horses or other pack animals, but with diminished rainfall, even the horses soon proved insufficient to make the increasingly long trips between water holes. Around 2500 B.C. the desert began another long, dry phase and became so dry that contacts across it ceased. By 1000 B.C. the Sahara had more or less reached the hot and dry climate that we still see, with only slight annual variations.

As the centuries passed and the Sahara grew wider and ever drier, ancient lakes slowly dried up and disappeared, but as they did so, they left behind thick layers of salt that eventually became the economic mainstay of the people who came there to trade.

The Romans had little contact with sub-Saharan Africa, because they lacked a means of getting to it. They did not have ships capable of sailing on the ocean down the African coast, or means of crossing the immense desert. Roman civilization, like most of those on the Mediterranean, depended heavily on the horse and on wagons for transportation. The horse could not cross such hot, dry landscapes, and the wheeled vehicles quickly became trapped in the sands. This technological liability kept the European and Mediterranean peoples from crossing the Sahara into the rest of Africa.

Even after the Eurasian steppes had been conquered and served as a corridor of contact between Europe and Asia, the Sahara cut off contact between Africa and the Mediterranean world. The connection awaited the camel and the development of technology for digging and maintaining deep wells. The camel occupies a place in the history of North Africa and Arabia similar to that of horses in central Asia and Europe, but its history followed a much different course.

The sentiment that "a camel is a horse designed by a committee" could only come from people who have never spent time in the desert. Never was an animal more perfectly adapted for human assistance than the camel in the desert. Not only can it go for long periods without food and water, but it has eyelids that keep out the blowing sand. In its own environment, it offers the combined benefits of a horse, a cow, and a sheep, because it can carry a rider and provide milk to drink and wool from which to make rope or weave a coarse cloth. Unlike the delicate hooves of the horse, which require metal shoes, the flexible pads of the camel's foot make it perfect for crossing the hot desert floor strewn with gritty sand, slippery pebbles, and sharp rocks.

The camel arrived late in the Sahara. It evolved in North America, from *Protylopus*, a dog-sized mammal that also produced the llamas, alpacas, and guanacos of South America. The modern camel evolved during the Pleistocene, and during this time it, along with the horse, wandered across the Bering Strait to Asia, where it eventually evolved into both the two-humped Bactrian camel of Mongolia and India and the one-humped dromedary or Arabian camel of the Middle East and North Africa. The camel reached Africa on its own as a still-wild animal, and fossil evidence from the Pleistocene indicates that African natives hunted it long before the domestication of animals or plants.

Domestication of the camel seems to have begun around 3000 to 2500 B.C., several millennia after the horse, and was perhaps inspired by the domestication of the horse, which had proven so successful in central Asia. The first domesticated camels in Africa seem to have been in the northeast of the continent, around 600 B.C. Nomads apparently herded them for meat, milk, and wool rather than as beasts of burden (Bulliet 1990, 116).

The camel served as an important beast of burden in Mesopotamia and Arabia, but had only a minor role to play in ancient Egypt and northern Africa. The camel's ungainly anatomy and the large hump on its back gave its first herders some unique problems to overcome in harnessing it and in riding it. From mats and cushions used as the first devices to make the camel ride more comfortable for the rider, several distinctive types of camel saddles developed quite slowly over many centuries. In 500 B.C., camel herders invented the wood-framed Arabian saddle, one of the most commonly recognized camel saddles, and after this invention, camel riding increased greatly. The camel, no longer just a provider of meat and milk, proved an excellent means of transportation for humans as well as for goods; however, it moved more slowly and awkwardly than the horse. Even today, a visit to any camel market shows that the camel has never been mastered and never responds to human commands with quite the precision and alacrity of the horse. Even the best camel riders rarely seem to develop the unity of mind and motion with their animals that skilled horse riders develop with theirs.

Despite its usefulness across the Middle East, the Europeans showed little appreciation for the camel. When Alexander the Great conquered the lands from Egypt to the Indus, he moved through lands where the camel had long been used, but he and his army showed little interest in it other than as a beast of burden. It did not rival the noble horse, which Alexander insisted on riding even on his long journey into the Sahara to consult the oracles at the oasis of Siwa. The Romans also kept their horse focus, but showed only mild interest in the camel, which was nearly as foreign and exotic to them as the elephants used by Hannibal of Carthage.

The camel belonged to people whom the Romans conquered and never fully trusted. One of the major uses to which the Romans applied the camel was pulling the plow in order to push agriculture farther south from Roman lands in Tunisia and Tripolitania. They also harnessed camels to pull carts and wagons, but in these tasks the camel never proved as tractable or as useful as the strong and docile ox.

During the time of the Roman Empire, major innovations began in North Africa with the introduction of the camel from the east and with more advanced technology for digging wells and raising water from them. In 46 B.C., we encounter one of the first Latin references to camels, in Caesar's campaign against the Numidian King Juba in what is now Algeria. In that expedition, Caesar's army captured twenty-two camels. In A.D. 363, another Roman army in northern Africa seized four thousand camels from the city of Lepcis Magna in Tripolitania (Bulliet 1990, 113).

The Romans recognized that camels transported goods more cheaply than any other animal could. In 301 the Roman emperor Diocletian, doing what many politicians in modern times have done to curry favor with the masses, ordered a price and wage freeze in order to stabilize inflation and prices. In his edict he set the prices for camel transport twenty percent below those of ox transport, a minimal ratio that probably still holds today in any place where camels compete as beasts of burden with any other animal.

Even as the Roman Empire was reaching its greatest power, the Arabs of Arabia increased their efforts at using and breeding camels. They began using camels as pack animals to carry valuable incense from southern Arabia to markets in Syria and the Mediterranean coast. The Nabateans, the first Arab kingdom, controlled this trade from their city of Petra in modern Jordan, at the head of the Gulf of Aqaba. When Rome finally conquered the Nabateans in the middle of the first century B.C., the conquerors issued a coin showing the surrender of King Aretas with a camel.

The connection of the ancient Semitic people of the Middle East with the camel endures in the etymology of the word. Most of the European languages from Greek to English use some form of the word *camel* derived from *gamal*, from the ancient Semitic language that gave rise to Phoenician, Hebrew, and Arabic. In early Teutonic documents in Old High German and Old English, variations of the word *elephant* are used interchangeably for both camels and elephants, indicating some serious confusion between the two animals. By the ninth century this distinction had become clear, and since that time neither German nor English has confused the two animals.

The Old Testament, in chapter 10 of the First Book of Kings, specifies that one of the main sources of income for King Solomon came from the Arabian spice trade, a commerce conducted via camels. The same chapter also describes the Queen of Sheba coming to visit Solomon in Jerusalem "with a very great train, with camels that bear spices, and very much gold, and precious stones. . . . [T]here came no such abundance of spices as these which the queen of Sheba gave to king Solomon."

The importance of camels and the incense trade continued into the Christian era, as evidenced in the Gospel of Matthew, in which wise men come to see the Christ child, bearing gifts of gold and the costly incenses myrrh and frankincense. According to tradition, the wise men brought their gifts by camel. Matthew 19:24 also records Jesus as saying, "It is easier for a camel to go through the eye of a needle, than for a rich man to enter into the kingdom of God."

Despite the gifts of incense brought to the baby Jesus, the Christians did not make sacrifices of incense, and they never employed as much incense in their ceremonies as the pagans and Jews had used before them. The incense trade declined steadily, but by this time the Arabs had increased in numbers and further diversified their trade goods.

The Arab city of Mecca became a center for the caravan trade because it lay halfway between southern Arabia and the Mediterranean, or between Yemen and Syria. Mecca came to prominence when Skeikh Qusayy of the north Arabian Quraish tribe took over the city at the end of the fifth century. The prophet Mohammed, who was born around 570, himself became a leader of caravans and married the widow of a merchant.

Following the death of Mohammed, his Arab followers poured out of Arabia into surrounding countries, and even though they usually fought from horses, they took their camels with them everywhere they went. The Arab conqueror 'Amr ibn al-'As entered Africa with an army of 3,500 men in 641 after defeating the Byzantine Roman army in the battle of Heliopolis the preceding year and then besieging the fortress that had been commanded by Cyril, the Byzantine patriarch and governor. The weak and preoccupied government in Constantinople had been unable to send relief to this increasingly remote part of its empire, and Cyril had finally surrendered with the provision that he could withdraw to Alexandria.

Unlike these earlier conquerors, 'Amr arrived with a new fury, slashing through Egypt and heading straight for the Atlantic coast, nearly two thousand miles to the west. Within less than a century, almost within the lifetime of 'Amr, who died at age ninety, this Arab army reached the Atlantic Ocean in northwestern Africa. Even then, the momentum of Islam could not be halted, and the stream of conquest turned north, into Spain. The Arabs crossed the Strait of Gibraltar in 711 and, in thirty years of ceaseless fighting and conquest, reached southern France. Only then, in 742, did the momentum of 'Amr's conquest finally expend itself when Charles Martel repulsed the Arab army of Tariq ibn Ziyad at the Battle of Tours.

The Arab conquest of North Africa changed many facets of life, including the means of transportation. Until this time, the northern fringe of Africa, like the rest of the Mediterranean, depended heavily on horses and wheeled vehicles for land transportation. This required a very expensive superstructure, including the building of roads and frequent watering and feeding stations along the route. Carts and other vehicles were costly to build and to maintain. The vehicles also added much extra weight to the load being pulled by the animal, but the load on the camel's back consisted almost entirely of merchandise. The heavy expense of roads and wheeled vehicles meant that land transportation proved expensive and required a reasonably large and well-financed government behind it.

The Arabs conquered the Sahara because they survived as desert nomads in Arabia, and came to North Africa with great herds of camels. Wherever the Arabs went, from Morocco to Afghanistan, the camel replaced the horse and the wheel as the primary means of transport. The camel took over commerce, and the prized Arabian horses were further specialized for show, games, and warfare.

The number of North African tribesmen using camels in the Sahara increased steadily and significantly over the centuries. As early as the fourth century, Berber tribesmen in the south of

Morocco began inching their way south from oasis to oasis, creating trade routes that would bring gold and other riches to the Mediterranean from the African interior. By the end of the eighth century, the Arab Omayyad caliphs operated a series of regular caravan routes across the Sahara, and to supply them they staffed the oases with slaves and settlers to maintain the wells and grow food for the traveling merchants and their camels.

They etched out the trails that still appear so vividly in the modern maps of the Sahara. Even though trucks now supplement camels for transportation, paved roads have not yet replaced the ancient caravan trails, except along the very edges of the deserts.

Repeatedly, throughout history, some group or another has tried to turn the camel into an animal of war. Ancient drawings depict mounted camel warriors of Mesopotamia fighting with bows and arrows, as though on horseback. Other camel riders tried fighting with swords, but for most combat purposes the camel proved completely inappropriate. Its loping stride is not smooth enough to permit use of the bow and arrow, it is too difficult to control for two mounted riders to fight each other with swords, and it stands too high for its rider to fight with someone on the ground. The best weapon for camel riders was the lance, since it was long enough to reach another animal, a mounted rider, or a warrior on the ground. In comparison to the horse, however, the camel lacked the speed and brute force necessary to give the lance a powerful blow.

In the western Sahara, the Tuaregs developed a unique saddle and way of riding the camel. Unlike the Arabs, who sit behind the hump or on it, and control the camel with a long stick or riding crop, the Tuaregs developed a shoulder saddle that allowed them to sit in front of the hump. This position has an important advantage for the camel, because it puts the rider's weight over the camel's front legs, which are significantly stronger than its hind legs. The great advantage of this for the Tuaregs was that it allowed them to guide the camel with their toes. This position proved less suited for transporting goods but was ideal for long trips carrying human riders, and the Tuareg riding style allowed the rider much more control (Bulliet 1990, 134). With their precision control, the Tuaregs became probably the most agile and proficient camel riders in the world, and they made the camel into an effective animal of war. Their effectiveness as camel warriors became evident as recently as December 1991, when, using a combination of camels and trucks, they raided the city of Timbuktu and looted it for several days in an angry dispute with merchants and the government.

Despite the episodic success of the Tuaregs in using the camel for war, the historic role of the camel has clearly been one of transportation, commerce, and peaceful activities rather than war or conquest. Yet the camel's role in world history, particularly the history of Africa and Arabia, has been just as great as the much more militaristic uses of the horse in Europe and Asia.

The Tuaregs, Berbers, and other tribal peoples of the Sahara forged the vital link between sub-Saharan Africa and the Mediterranean. The flow of precious goods, together with knowledge and culture, made sub-Saharan Africa and Europe parts of a single, growing economic system that endured until the Europeans began contact with West Africa by sea in the fifteenth century and thereby accelerated a quite different commerce.

The gradual unification of the world into a few large trading systems required a long and difficult process of domesticating animals, developing new technology, and conquering major obstacles such as deserts and mountains. That unification also came at great social cost, particularly to the tribal people living between the great centers of civilization. During the early phase of contact, these people often served as conduits and means of commerce from one civilization center to the next, but eventually, as the methods of commerce improved, the tribal people found themselves caught in a tightening vise of civilizations that persistently encroached on their world from every side.

The camel brought sub-Saharan Africa and the Mediterranean into closer contact, uniting them in trade, but also spreading the common religion of Islam, as well as literacy in the Arabic language, to many parts of Africa. Despite the spread of these cultural traits and the rise of new African empires, the contacts created new opportunities for cultural variation.

Because they had the camel for transportation, the West Africans built their great cities in the interior of the continent and not along the coast, as did the European people around the Mediterranean. The West Africans built their major cities along the Niger River, in that wide savannah that separates the Sahara from the rain forest. The plains run from the Nile in the east to the headwaters of the Niger in the west. The traditional name for the area was the Sudan, but because that name is also the name of a country in the upper reaches of the Nile, the wide plains are now more often called the savannah, the Sahel, or simply "the plains."

The key to the history of the African plains lies in its variation. In fertile spots around the lakes and rivers of the area, agriculture and fishing flourished, as did herding in the large, open expanses of grassland between these agricultural oases. Over successive millennia, the tribal people of the area developed a diversified approach to the environment. Unlike the Europeans, who had fertile and well-watered plains that were ideal for agriculture in virtually every year, on the plains the rain varied from year to year and the agricultural yield fluctuated accordingly. To maximize the productivity of the land, different groups specialized in different labors, none of which was by itself sufficient to support a people.

The central Niger River in Mali and Niger offers a vast array of peoples and ethnic groups. They speak different languages, wear distinctly different clothes, live in different kinds of homes, and have different ways of making a living. Living in such a climatically unstable part of the world, where the survival of one's family depends on the vagaries of the weather, the people have found a way to cope with it through specialization and diversity. No single way of life can be counted on to provide a living, but by having different ethnic groups, each of which specializes in a different way of life in a different environmental niche, the people have maximized the chances of survival.

The Bambara, who make up approximately one-third of Mali's population, farm dry crops, and the Hausa, who make up about half of the population of Niger, follow a comparable subsistence pattern. The Marka farm rice in the wetlands adjoining the river, while the Bobo fish the river. The Fulani graze cattle on land that is too dry for crops, while the Tuareg herd camels and goats in the even drier areas. The Songhai serve as merchants among all the groups. Smaller groups fill even more specialized niches, such as the Somono, who fish and transport goods. The specialization of labor decreases the competition for scarce resources.

Through ancient traditions that tell of common ancestry and the importance of the groups cooperating among themselves, each group has certain duties to help other groups during particularly hard times (McIntosh 1992).

This diversified approach minimized competition among groups and encouraged them to cooperate. Farmers grew millet and other grains, but their agriculture was too valuable for animal grazing, so they exchanged farm produce with nomadic tribes for milk and meat. Fishing people cultivated a few garden crops but depended on farmers for most of their grains. The fish gave added protein and variety to the diets of cattle people and farmers. This tripartite subsistence system lessened the threat of famine in such a variable ecosystem.

With the mobility provided by camels across the grasslands, the native people who lived there acted as a natural conduit between the Sahara to the north and the rain forest to the south. The people of the Sahara offered salt, which was greatly needed in the rain forest, and dates, a commodity greatly desired by the people of the rain forest, who had an even more prized commodity, gold. The people of the plains eagerly made their exchanges with the people of the forest and brought with them other items, such as leather and dried fish.

The diversity of peoples and languages sometimes makes it hard for outsiders to grasp the complexity of West African civilizations. People accustomed to the European pattern expect countries to have much more uniformity of language and culture over a large area and over a long time. Specialization of labor then occurs within classes as peasants grow crops, craftsmen or workers manufacture items, aristocrats rule, and the clergy tends to education, health, and spiritual needs. The system of the West African Sahel divides tasks not by class, which is much less important, but by ethnicity.

Joined by commerce and the sharing of religions, technology, and diseases, the Old World of Europe, Africa, and Asia formed a unified social system, even if they were not united political entities.

Contact did not promote cultural homogeneity. Instead, it produced constant variation as people learned to occupy specialized ecological or economic niches in the growing social system. The more different groups interacted, the more culturally varied they became.

Rather than promoting political union, cultural unity, or even improved understanding, the new lines of commerce stretching across the continents created one of the most nefarious trades in human history—the buying and selling of human lives as commodities. Slavery formed the basis of the first great international trade system.

7

Civilization and Slavery

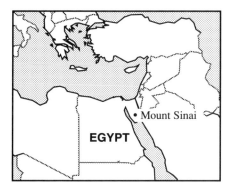

Civilization is the process of setting man free from men.
—AYN RAND, *The Fountainhead*

The Greek Orthodox Monastery of St. Catherine rises from the dusty, rocky desert of the Sinai Peninsula, where the borders of Israel, Jordan, and Egypt come close together. The monastery sits at the head of a valley roughly equidistant between the Gulf of Aqaba to the east and the Gulf of Suez to the west. Since the founding of the monastery in the fourth century, the territory around it has been claimed by the Romans, the Byzantine Empire, the Arabs, the Crusaders, the Ottoman Turks, the French, the British, the Israelis, and the Egyptians, but throughout all these centuries, only monks of Greek descent have been allowed to live inside the monastery, where Greek is the language of daily life as well as religious service.

Situated at the base of the pink granite peak of Gabal Musa, better known to the outside world as Mount Sinai, the monastery guards a site sacred to Jews, Christians, and Muslims. The Sinai is a hard and austere place, inhabited by a mere 200,000 people scattered over 23,422 square miles, an area roughly equal to that of Costa Rica or Lithuania. Most of the inhabitants of the Sinai are Bedouin herders leading lives that seem very similar to that of nomads thousands of years ago. Unlike the homelands of other desert nomads, the Sinai lacks the sweeping sands of the Sahara or the bitter cold of the Gobi. The Sinai desert is broken by mountains and numerous canyons, valleys, and crevices, resembling more the deserts of the southwestern United States and northern Mexico. The valleys of the Sinai channel the water of the scarce rains, which collect in the gullies and form small oases for the small flocks tended by the Bedouins.

Christian hermits first sought out this place, where they lived in caves, because the harsh environment shielded them from the sins and temptations of social life in the cities. According to tradition, the first building of the monastery was constructed in 337, after a visit to the area by the Empress Helena, mother of Constantine, Rome's first Christian emperor. After a series of raids on the fledgling monastery by local tribes, the Roman emperor Justinian enclosed the monastery behind protective walls in the sixth century, and he sent a force of one hundred Slavs and one hundred Egyptians to serve as permanent guards. Justinian, who was better known for building the church of Hagia Sophia in Constantinople, also built a church in St. Catherine's monastery in honor of his wife Theodora. She attained great notoriety in the ancient world as the actress-harlot turned empress and was described by the Byzantine historian Procopius of Caesarea as having made love through every orifice of her body before taking the throne as empress.

Although repaired many times during the intervening years, the monastery retains its original size and somewhat squat, nearly square shape. It has the serious, unadorned countenance of a fortress, with massive, high walls made of hard granite. Nothing about the external appearance of the place makes it look inviting or prosperous. For centuries the walls had no doorway or window other than a small, elevated opening high on the northwest wall. People and supplies had to be raised to the doorway by a basket suspended on ropes and hoisted by an ancient pulley. Today a ground-level door has been added, but it is still small and opens only for a few hours each day.

Through the centuries from its founding, the monastery has been dependent on the support of emperors, kings, popes, and czars. Pope Gregory donated furniture for the hostel; the Crusaders built the "new" dining room; and the army of Napoleon made general repairs to the walls and fortifications. British soldiers installed an electric generator before Britain pulled out of the Suez Canal in 1956.

For the first few centuries of its operation, the monastery was associated only with the Old Testament and the stories regarding Moses and the Exodus. This ancient story of Jewish history isolated the monastery somewhat from mainstream Christianity until the ninth century, when the monks conveniently discovered the bones of a Christian saint called Catherine of Alexandria; the bones had been miraculously transported to the adjacent peak now called Gabal Katrinam, or Mount Catherine, the highest peak on the Sinai Peninsula. The bones had crossed several centuries and several hundred miles to make this miraculous appearance.

Although the exact years of Saint Catherine's life were never specified, she supposedly lived during the reign of an emperor called Maxentius, who wanted the beautiful, learned, and rich Catherine for his bride. She not only refused him but denounced him as an idolater. Enraged, the vengeful emperor had her tried by fifty philosophers, whom she easily defeated in a theological debate. The emperor immediately ordered the failed philosophers burned alive as punishment for losing to her superior wit, and from this episode Catherine later became the patron saint of fire fighters.

Unable to defeat Catherine by reasoning and wit, the emperor then ordered his men to beat her and cast her into a cell, where she would starve without food or water, but a dove fed her and nursed her back to health. The emperor next sentenced her to be broken on the wheel, but the wheel shattered when it touched her, killing many pagan bystanders. Her bravery and miraculous powers converted the two hundred Roman soldiers assigned to guard her, and the emperor beheaded all of them along with Catherine. When her head was chopped off, however, milk flowed from her veins instead of blood.

To the medieval mind, this story of Catherine was certainly much more interesting than the rather dry tale of the dour Moses wandering in the desert. When Catherine's bones miraculously appeared on Mount Sinai several hundred years later, the monks of the monastery had a rich story that made them the center of a newly emerging Catherine cult. The dramatic story appealed to the romantic ethos of the Crusader era and to Western Europeans, particularly the French, who became great patrons of the monastery. The monks also made money by selling the sacred oil that supposedly came from her body centuries after she died.

The monks seemed able to flow with the times and with the vagaries of changing politics through the ages. According to another of the monks' stories, the monastery served as a refuge for the prophet Mohammed, and they gladly take credit for his subsequent tolerant attitude toward Christians as "people of the book." This story has helped protect the monastery, but after the rise of Islam, the monastery became an extremely isolated island of Christianity in a Muslim sea. The adaptable monks added a mosque next to the Church of St. Catherine in 1106, at the suggestion of the Muslim emir.

I first went to the monastery to visit its library, which is probably the greatest of any monastery in the world. It has a collection of manuscripts from throughout the Christian world, including some two thousand in Greek, seven hundred in Arabic, three hundred in Syriac, and one hundred in Georgian and Armenian, as well as many in Slavonic and Latin. The most famous of its manuscripts was the Codex Sinaticus, the oldest copy of the Gospel of Saint John ever discovered. It was written in beautiful Greek script at about the time the monastery was founded in the fourth century. In 1859 the scholar-explorer Konstantin von Tischendorf, a man of controversial reputation, acquired the manuscript by still-questioned methods and sold it to Czar Alexander II of Russia. In 1933 the Soviet government, in need of hard currency and not very interested in religious relics, sold the manuscript for 100,000 pounds to the British Museum, which has refused the entreaties of the monastery to return it to them ever since.

I arrived at the monastery with a handful of scholars and students with different interests. We had been granted access to the library in exchange for transporting a load of food and other supplies under the careful eye of a Greek monk from Ohio. As he traveled down the Red Sea road with us, he proved to be both talkative and blessed with a quite healthy appetite whenever we stopped to eat.

Like all visitors, we could not stay in the monastery after midafternoon, when the small door closed tightly against outsiders. We stayed instead in the pilgrim hostel outside the massive walls, next to the charnel house and graves. The charnel house displays the bones of the dead monks, who are usually buried first until the flesh rots from the skeleton. Then the bones are dug up, cleaned, and put on display in the ossuary, divided into precise piles of skulls stacked neatly, like grapefruits in a grocery store, next to more casually created piles of bones from the monks' limbs, hands, and feet. Occasionally one of the vacant-eyed skulls rolls off the stack and circles the feet of a startled pilgrim, but otherwise the charnel house stays rather quiet.

The piles of bones stand as a constant reminder of death for the visitors. They also signify the anonymity of the monks, the insignificance of earthly remains, and many other spiritual meanings, depending on who explains it. Only a few monks have avoided burial and consignment to the bone heap. The most notable of these was Saint Stephen, who died while sitting in a chair in 580, and has remained in that position ever since.

The simple but separate pilgrims' dormitories for males and females offered a cot and a toilet. After spending the night there, I had no desire to climb Mount Sinai, but the stirring of the pilgrims at 2:30 A.M. woke me. Knowing that the monks would not open the monastery door to let us in until around nine o'clock, I decided to go ahead and make the climb with the pilgrims.

A line of probably two hundred people snaked past the monastery and up the narrow winding path known as Sikkit Sayyidna Musa—the Path of Our Lord Moses—which has been followed by tens of thousands of pilgrims over the centuries. Each person carried a flashlight, which created a long string of evenly spaced lights climbing slowly up the side of the mountain. The pilgrims moved silently up the steep path. The only sound came from the steady wind and from the delicate tinkling of little bells strung on the camels that joined the procession. Bedouin boys led the camels, which carried some pilgrims within a few hundred feet of the top, after which it was too steep even for the camels to maneuver.

After reaching the top, at an altitude of 7,497 feet, the pilgrims waited eagerly for the first rays of the sun to break over the distant mountains and strike our peak. A group of young Italian priests began talking excitedly as they regained their breath and strength from the climb. The Muslim boys recited their early-morning prayers. A group of youthful campers, who had spent the night on the mountain, grumbled and complained loudly at the pilgrims who were now stomping on their sleeping bags and the scattered debris of their late-night party.

Shivering in the cold, dark wind after eating my breakfast supply of nuts and dried fruit, I was not in a good mood. I huddled behind some rocks that took some of the sting out of the sharp wind. Then, just as the first rays of sun darted across the mountain, a group of Chinese Christians broke into a rendition of "Swing Low, Sweet Chariot." In my irritable mood, the song seemed about the most inappropriate thing I could imagine, and I wanted the sun to hurry up so that my group could take off with a guide who had promised, for a small fee, to show us a shortcut down the mountain.

We barely made it back to the monastery in time for our nine-o'clock appointment, and when we finally gained admittance into the ancient library, I was so tired and hungry from the climb that I fell asleep in the stuffy room. I accomplished only a fraction of what I had wanted to do that day, and left with a great sense of frustration after having gained admittance to such an important collection for a few hours and not having fully utilized it.

The image of the Chinese pilgrims singing African-American spirituals on the top of Mount Sinai stayed with me long after the disappointment of the library had subsided. I was perplexed by the Chinese choice of those spirituals rather than an ancient Greek or Latin chant, which would have seemed much more appropriate to the spirit of the monastery. Suddenly the reason became clear to me. I remembered that the theme of many of those spirituals was deliverance from slavery, and Mount Sinai is the place where Moses came with the Hebrew tribes as soon as they were delivered from slavery. I realized that the spirituals and the pilgrims perhaps embodied the spirit of Moses and that place much more than did the ornate icons, the ancient walls, and even the rare manuscripts of the library, which I loved so much. Maybe the Chinese pilgrims recognized that the true meaning of the mountain lay in the spiritual realm more than in the library.

Moses came to Mount Sinai twice in search of freedom from oppression, slavery, and injustice. He fled there once for his own freedom and the second time for the freedom of the Hebrew tribes. The first time he fled to the Sinai, it was after killing an Egyptian who was beating a Hebrew slave. At the base of Mount Sinai, in a small canyon, he saw the burning bush in which God called on him to return to Goshen, an Egyptian province, to lead the Jews out of bondage.

After Moses brought down a series of ten plagues on the Pharaoh Ramses, including the killing of the firstborn in each Egyptian household, the pharaoh released the Hebrews. Every year at Passover, Jews around the world still mark the delivery from slavery, when the family sits down to dinner and the young child asks, "What makes this night different from other nights?"

Moses led the Jews out of Egypt, across the miraculously parted Red Sea, and back to Mount Sinai, feeding them manna that fell from heaven along the way. After leading the Hebrew tribes back to the canyon where he had first encountered the burning bush, Moses climbed to the top of Mount Sinai, where God gave him the long list of commandments recorded in the Book of Exodus.

The name of the monastery and the strange stories about Saint Catherine hid the older and much more important story of Moses and the first struggle against slavery. Mount Sinai and the life of Moses stand in history as the beginning of the war against slavery that has not been completely won, even today. When the African-American slaves sang about Moses, they looked back to this place and time as an inspiration for the hope that their own freedom would eventually come as well.

Even though the institution of slavery goes back several thousand years, there is no evidence to suggest that it started before the agricultural age. It apparently came into existence soon after the development of the first cities, but it is an institution virtually unknown to foraging people. Foragers could never accumulate much more than they could carry with them, and consequently they did not need the labor of slaves to produce more goods, which they could not preserve or use. Only when people had settled and could accumulate storehouses of goods did they begin to appropriate the labor of other humans to produce yet more goods.

Over the past ten thousand years, civilization has been roughly coterminous with slavery. Wherever cities arose, whether in the ancient Middle East, China, or Mexico, some form of slavery soon developed. Criminals and the very poor who could not feed themselves often became slaves, but the most common source of slaves was captives taken in war. Soon after the rise of cities, the rulers of the cities began raids and campaigns primarily to seize such captives, who were herded back to work in the fields, mines, and quarries of the captors. Sometimes these captives came from other cities, but generally it proved much easier to go out and raid tribal people who did not have large armies or massive fortifications to protect them.

Thus it was that the nomadic tribes of Hebrews tending their flocks were captured and taken into slavery by the armies of the pharaoh as well as by the Babylonians. The cuneiform tablets of the Middle East and the hieroglyphics of Egypt abound with triumphant tales of kings and princes who captured whole nations like the Hebrews, which they took into slavery. The stories of the Bible offer a unique view of this history, in that the Bible offers virtually the only account we have of that era written from the perspective of the slaves themselves and telling how they obtained their freedom, and at what cost.

The cultural division of humans into foragers and farmers came in what we may think of as a voluntary way, but slavery added a new dimension to cultural diversity in that it created a new layer of difference; it forced greater cultural change and diversity on populations by dividing them into the enslaved and the free.

The history of the ancient Jews illustrates a persistent problem from the perspective of the slaveholders: As long as a group of slaves continued to live together in its traditional kinship groups, speaking its own language, worshipping its own god, and generally following its own culture and way of life, it posed a threat to its owners. As long as the slaves maintained their culture and some remnants of their tribal social structure, they were not totally conquered or assimilated into their social position as mere slaves.

In the classical world of the Mediterranean, the social institution of slavery gradually evolved into a new form that overcame this shortcoming. Whole cities or tribes of conquered people were no longer kept together; slavery became a more viable institution and the slaves became more tractable when they were separated from other members of their families, villages, tribes, and cultures.

Centuries after the flight to freedom by the Jews, the Romans instituted this new form of slavery, which drew slaves from throughout the known world. They enslaved men and women from Britain and Gaul as well as from Nubia, Ethiopia, and the mountains of the Balkans. Stripped of their native languages, kinships, religions, and cultures, the slaves proved more easily commanded and worked rowing the Roman galleys, digging tin and gold in the mines, growing wheat and grapes on the farms, and building the many bridges, roads, aqueducts, and massive public buildings of the Roman Empire. More-educated slaves, particularly those fluent in Greek and Latin, served as tutors, messengers, and household slaves.

This more sophisticated version of slavery attained even more complex expression under the Ottoman Turks, who recruited slaves from the edges of their empire and beyond. By separating slaves from their native cultures, the Ottomans created new institutions. The Janissaries were a guard unit of soldiers born in Christian European families, but taken from them at birth. Raised as Muslims in a military setting, the slaves did not sustain the language or religion of their families. They were trained to fight solely at the command and for the interests of the sultan, without any entangling affiliations of kinship or religion.

Wherever there was slavery in the Old World, there were also eunuchs, slaves who had their testicles cut off. If the testicles were cut off after a boy reached puberty, he could still achieve erection and experience orgasm, although he could not ejaculate and thus engender offspring. To make them totally sexless, the penis was often amputated as well as the testicles.

In Moslem countries these castrated men often served in aristocratic households, protecting the virtue of the women as well as being servants. Chinese eunuchs frequently controlled the upper ranks of the imperial bureaucracy, and survived as important functionaries until the twentieth-century revolution overthrew the last emperor. In India, castrated men lived the lives of women and claimed to be a separate caste, with the right to monopolize certain occupations, such as singing and providing entertainment at family celebrations. Boys were castrated in Europe in order to preserve their youthful voices and make them into better singers. Other European men were castrated as a punishment for a crime, or sometimes they had themselves castrated as a gift to God and as a guarantor of their celibacy.

While slavery of all kinds grew in importance in the Muslim world, it lingered throughout much of Europe and Asia, but its importance declined. In the Chinese Empire, a strong emperor needed few slaves because he had the total obedience of all the people under him. In Europe, after the decline of the Roman

Empire, serfs had hereditary ties to their homes and lords, which made slavery as unnecessary in Europe as in most parts of Asia.

The importance of slaves in the work force changed dramatically with the European conquest of America. The Spaniards came in quickly and conquered Mexico and Peru, the two areas with the largest number of people. Despite the bloody toll of the conquest and the diseases brought by the Europeans, the populations of these areas remained high enough for them to supply the labor needed to work the mines, farms, and ranches of their areas. The Caribbean islands, Brazil, and what would become the United States had much smaller native populations, which were quickly decimated by the new diseases of the Europeans. Even though the Europeans made slaves of many Indians in these areas, the natives lacked the numbers necessary to operate the sugar, tobacco, indigo, rice, coffee, and cotton plantations. In contrast to the Spaniards, who outlawed slavery relatively early in their history, the Dutch, English, French, and Portuguese, who controlled the more sparsely populated parts of the Americas, had to depend heavily on slaves imported across the Atlantic Ocean from Africa.

The opening of the African slave trade across the Atlantic Ocean to America proved to be the greatest such enterprise in world history. At this point the institution of slavery reached its greatest extent, with the largest numbers involved, and with one of the greatest forced dislocations of people.

The tribal people of Africa organized their social structure around extensive kinship networks, family compounds organized into lineages or clans, but this social structure did not survive the middle passage to America, where even nuclear families found it difficult to remain together. The traditional cultures were further undermined because the plantation owners wanted predominantly male Africans. Throughout the history of the American slave trade, twice as many males as females were brought in, making it even more difficult for the slaves to form families and re-create tribal society.

According to a Kongo proverb, a person without a clan is like a grasshopper without wings (Thernstrom 1980, 8). This destruction of the tribal kinship network probably did more to cut the individual slaves off from their cultural heritage than any other aspect of the institution. Africans who came to America as

Ibo, Yoruba, Hausa, Bambara, or Malinke tribesmen became simply blacks, slaves, or Negroes. They were shorn of their native identity and issued a generic one in its place.

The slave ships hauled ten to twelve million Africans to the Americas as slaves, with about 60 percent of them arriving during the eighteenth century. The slavers took the majority of the Africans to the Caribbean or Brazil; only approximately one African out of every twenty came to North America. The slave trade into the British colonies reached its zenith between 1741 and 1760, when approximately five thousand slaves per year were imported, and by the time slavery was abolished, approximately 427,000 Africans had been imported as slaves into the United States in more than two centuries of the trade (Thernstrom 1980, 6).

The deliberate assault on African tribal culture began almost immediately in the slave trade. While the slaves were still in Africa, the traders mixed them together in large groups that combined individuals of many different languages, cultures, and societies. The new slaves found themselves in an environment where even their own language was no longer understood, much less their religion, customs, or political institutions. This cultural disorientation had an important function for the slave traders and owners, in that it minimized the likelihood that groups of slaves would conspire to escape or revolt. If the slaves could not talk adequately with one another, and if they shared little common culture, they were much less likely to assist one another in escaping. This conscientious and methodical destruction of tribal African culture persisted at every stage of the slavery system.

Aboard the ships sailing to Brazil, the Caribbean, and North Africa, individuals of many different cultures were pressed together as cargo in ships that held up to seven hundred Africans, stacked literally like sardines. On average, just a little over 80 percent of the slaves survived the trip, and once in America, they were deliberately divided before sale so that not too many of one language or tribe could be together. The slaves then marched off to their respective plantations, where they learned a creole version of Portuguese, English, Dutch, or French.

Some slaves escaped to the jungle, the swamp, or a remote island, where they created a hybrid African tribe with its own language, religion, social structure, and ceremonies. In other parts of the Americas, where there were too few escaped slaves to form a separate tribe, they merged with Indian communities. Along the Caribbean coast of Belize, escaped African slaves joined with Carib Indians and became the Garifuna, or Black Caribs. In the southeastern United States, Africans mixed heavily with many tribes, particularly the Seminoles. In Brazil, escaped slaves and their allies formed the independent kingdom of Palmares in the seventeenth century. In Suriname and French Guiana, in northern South America, slaves escaped to create their own societies in the eighteenth century. Despite repeated wars against them, about fifty thousand of these Maroons, or "bush tribes," have persisted in remote areas until the present.

In only one place, Haiti, the African slaves revolted successfully, overthrew and killed their masters, and then established their own independent government. Even though they tried to follow French and American patterns in their constitution, too few people had even minimal education in how to administer a national government. One of the richest islands in the Caribbean degenerated into a mire of poverty and corruption, and thus became one of the poorest nations in the world.

Of all the slaves transported to the Americas, the ones brought into the United States faced the greatest separation from their tribal cultures. Planters in Brazil and the Caribbean brought great numbers of slaves into their areas, and they worked many of these slaves to death. To replace the dead slaves, they had a constant flow of new slaves. Thus, African-born and tribally reared slaves were much more common in the Caribbean and Brazil than in the United States.

In the United States, living conditions were generally better for slaves, who therefore survived and reproduced at significantly higher rates than in Brazil or the Caribbean. Slaveholders in the United States depended on the natural increase of the slaves to produce new slaves, and they imported relatively few slaves directly from Africa. At the time of the American Revolution, nearly 20 percent of Americans were slaves, but only 20 percent of those slaves had been born in Africa (Thernstrom 1980, 6). By 1850, fewer than one slave in a hundred in the United States had been born in Africa (Stearns et al. 1992, 635). This meant that African influences in their lives were reduced even more for slaves in the United States than for slaves in Haiti, Jamaica, the Dominican Republic, the Netherlands Antilles, and Brazil.

During the nineteenth century, the European nations liberated their slaves over several decades. After liberation, some of the slaves, particularly those in North America, returned to their African homeland. The nation of Liberia, whose name means "land of liberty," was created in West Africa for former American slaves, who named their capital Monrovia in honor of the American president James Monroe. In neighboring Sierra Leone, British abolitionists established Freetown as a haven for emancipated slaves from British colonies.

Even when returned to Africa, however, the freed slaves could not re-create their traditional African cultures, because they had lost them. The former slaves used English as their national language, and the dollar continued as their national currency. Their religion, fashions, and social life did not follow African models; rather they imitated the culture of their former masters. The freed slaves from America had to use the only cultural pattern they knew, and they built plantations where they enslaved the tribal people living around them.

The failed efforts to make Liberia and Sierra Leone into new African societies populated by former slaves shows that, once severed from his or her tribal culture, it is very difficult for anyone to return.

After an average of four to five generations in America, they were now a different people. They adapted to their new culture much in keeping with the Lozi proverb to "go the way that many people go; if you go alone you will have reason to lament" (Thernstrom 1980, 8). Many of the former slaves continued to work on sugar and cotton plantations under conditions similar to those of slavery and without many more opportunities to be a part of the national culture and society.

Former slaves who left the plantation found increased opportunities in towns and cities, but even these had clear limits. Household slaves always had the greatest opportunities to assimilate into the language and culture of the dominant society, and they frequently established sexual liaisons that further increased the union. The mixed-blood offspring often formed a separate class, such as that of the Creoles of Haiti or Louisiana. Favored by their appearance as well as by their kinship ties to whites, these mixed-bloods often received training in a craft, or in some cases attained their freedom. They tended to live in urban areas such as Rio de Janeiro in Brazil, Port-au-Prince in Haiti, Kingston in Jamaica, or Charleston and New Orleans in the United States.

Particularly during the twentieth century, the descendants of former slaves crowded into the cities of Rio de Janeiro, São Paulo, New York, Chicago, Detroit, Philadelphia, Baltimore, and Washington. A minority of the African descendants found opportunities to be enculturated. They found employment as laborers and in some cases took over trades, such as that of porters on the American railways. Others became craftsmen or built small businesses such as tailoring shops, carpenters' workshops, grocery stores, and funeral parlors. By obtaining formal education, some of these descendants of slaves became attorneys, teachers, ministers, doctors, and other professionals. By the end of the twentieth century this minority within a minority had gained admission to political offices and positions of financial and social power in Brazil and the United States, and in the Caribbean they had taken financial and political control of most of the islands.

For the majority of African descendants, the city proved just as isolating for them as the plantations had been. They lived in large sections of town where they lacked sufficient opportunities to become socialized into the national culture. Even though radio, film, and television helped them to understand the standard languages of their nations, they continued to speak a creole or dialectic form of the national language, in their own communities where they had only limited occasions for interacting with outsiders.

Forced to be a part of the national social system but denied full access to it and its culture, the people of the ghettos, barrios, and favelas developed their own culture. This included their own forms of worship, which, in the United States, usually paralleled Christianity and in some cases Islam, but in Brazil and the Caribbean the descendants of slaves developed new and distinct forms of religion, such as voodoo and macumba, derived from traditional African religious models.

The African descendants developed new forms of music and dance that combined elements of African and European culture. African musical styles, combined with European instruments such as the piano, created ragtime, gospel, and jazz. In Brazil it led to the development of a series of dances. The rich oral traditions of Africa continued in the Americas with the development of word games and rhymes, and showed in the creation of new aesthetics.

Mount Sinai represents the end of Egyptian bondage for the Jews, but it also represents a major beginning for them as well.

On Mount Sinai, Moses received the many commandments that included the well-known prohibitions against murder, theft, adultery, lying, idolatry, and envy. The list also contained several hundred commandments regulating agriculture, property, religion, and taxation. These commandments represent the transition of the Jews from a pastoral, tribal people into the urban people they were to become. According to the scriptures, God offered the Jews a new land of milk and honey. This Promised Land represented a new way of life for them.

The experience of Mount Sinai shows great parallels between the bondage and the struggle for freedom by both the Hebrew slaves in Egypt and the African slaves in America. But Mount Sinai also illustrates a great contrast in the experience of the two groups. The Jews survived slavery with their tribal culture intact, and were gradually able to adapt this older culture to new circumstances, to transform it gradually from a tribal one to an urban one that proved viable in Europe, India, and America as much as in Israel. The African slaves who were brought to the Americas never had this opportunity. They did not survive slavery with an intact tribal culture and society; they survived it with a slave culture within which they had remnants of African words, stories, ceremonies, music, and dance. From this they had to develop their own cultural traditions and create for themselves a place in society.

The ethnic violence of recent years has produced some of the most vicious and tragic episodes of the twentieth century. In addition to being uprooted from their homes, thousands of people once again face that ancient threat of being enslaved.

After the great campaigns to end slavery in the nineteenth century, the practice seemed to make a comeback in the second half of the twentieth. In countries such as Sudan, disrupted by a long war of the Arab north against the Christian and animistic tribes of the south, slavery emerged nearly as strong as it probably had ever been.

In the markets of the smaller towns of Sudan, Dinka children could once again be bought and sold in the 1990s. Their new masters took them away primarily to work in the fields and to tend their herds, but also for the traditional tasks as household servants, water haulers, and concubines. Most of the slaves were sold through the military as they overran Dinka areas and captured the often uprooted children. In the late 1980s and 1990s, parts of the Sudanese militia conducted raids into Dinka territory primarily for the purpose of enslaving or killing the adults, whom the Muslim authorities generally regarded as rebels (Anti-Slavery Society, 1988).

Thus the enslavement of tribal people continues to be a vital part of civilization.

PART II

National Culture and the Rise of the Global Order

Every culture has its own *Civilization.*
—OSWALD SPENGLER

8

Tribe Versus City

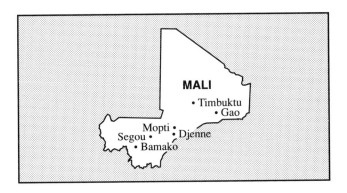

Pandemonium, city and proud seat of Lucifer.
—JOHN MILTON

Although small enough to cross in a fifteen-minute walk, Djenne, in the West African nation of Mali, is still one of the most strikingly exotic cities in the world. In the center of town the world's largest mud mosque rises up to dominate the view and the ethos of the city. Djenne lies on the Bani River, a small tributary of the Niger. During the wet season it becomes an island in the middle of a large, flooded plain. During the dry season it stands as an oasis overlooking a broad, sandy desert.

Upon entering the Grand Mosque of Djenne, worshipers take off their shoes and step inside the mosque onto a cool floor of sand. The massive mud walls of the mosque are punctuated by only a few windows that admit the minimal light needed for one to move about inside. This lack of windows leaves the expansive interior in a permanent shadowy darkness that has an other-worldly spirituality and a decisive coolness even on the hottest Saharan days.

The mosque of Djenne stands as a startling and very important cultural and technological monument. After the introduction of the camel and the building of trade routes across the Sahara, the Sahel became the logical place for the people to build cities, but the environment presented some extremely difficult obstacles.

How do people build a city in an environment with virtually no stone or trees, the most common building materials in urban areas?

The natives solved the problem through the use of the one resource they had—dirt. They added water to make mud, and caked the mud on frames made with the little wood they had. At first they built mud huts, but their structures quickly grew larger and more sophisticated. The people built mosques and schools, courtyards and palaces—all from mud. The architecture that resulted from this produced some of the most stunning and yet environmentally appropriate buildings in the world. The mud walls proved to be ideal insulation against the blasting Sahara heat, and they proved durable in the dry climate.

The people eventually learned to make the mud into bricks, with straw added for strength. Adobe architecture reached one of its highest points of expression in North Africa. The word *adobe* originated in the ancient North African Coptic language spoken in ancient Egypt during pharaonic times, long before the invasion of Alexander, the Romans, or the Arabs. Picked up by the Arab invaders into Egypt, who carried the word with them as far as Spain, the word *adobe* passed into both Arabic and Spanish and eventually into English.

The exterior of the mosque of Djenne resembles a giant fortress because its several large towers rise up from the massive walls. The mosque's windowless walls and the thin spires that cap the towers further accentuate the height and massive bulk of the building. Underneath the mud, a large timber framework supports the walls. The ends of the timberwork protrude several feet beyond the walls, giving the building a somewhat militaristic look, although the wooden spikes are used as nothing more ominous than a built-in and permanent ladder for the constant repairs needed to maintain the mud walls. Even though the mosque appears to be as ancient as the town, it dates from 1905, but it is only one in a long line of grand mosques in Djenne.

Archaeological evidence indicates that as early as 500 B.C., iron began to replace the well-established bronze industry in North Africa. Soon the inhabitants of the interior of West Africa started mining ore from the laterite crust, which had a high iron content. They mined it from pits and transported the ore to furnaces fired preferably by acacia wood, which created the extremely high temperatures necessary to smelt the ore. Modern archaeology has found it very difficult to estimate the amount of iron ore produced, but thousands of pits and furnaces have been identified. Some notion of the manufacturing capacity of the area comes from a colonial report made shortly after the French takeover of the western Sudan. Describing the metalworking center of Yatenga in what is now Burkina Faso, Captain Noire wrote that 159 native furnaces produced 539 metric tons of iron annually (Flon 1988, 316).

Craftsmen made the iron into hoes, knives, needles, spearpoints, axes, and even more specialized weapons and tools for building and farming. Iron tools permitted expansion of settlements and agriculture deeper into the jungle. These innovations in tools, coupled with the tropical Asian crops of bananas, oil palms, and yams, induced a population explosion in the rain forest and created increasing demand for iron, salt, and the other commodities manufactured in or traded through the grasslands.

The first of the great empires to arise was Ghana, which occupied the territory of modern Mali, Mauritania, and Senegal, but far removed from the modern nation that shares its name. Ancient Ghana served as a trading empire controlling the flow of gold and salt.

By the fourteenth century, power had shifted east, to the rising kingdom of Mali. Mansa Musa, the best known of Mali's ancient kings, ruled an empire as large as all of Western Europe. He earned an international reputation when he embarked on his great pilgrimage to Mecca in 1324. Tradition maintains that his caravan included one hundred camels to carry the gold alone, and their arrival in Cairo so overwhelmed the market that the value of the golden dinar fell dramatically.

Just after Mansa Musa's renowned trip to Cairo, his kingdom appeared for the first time on European maps. In 1375 the Catalan Map, made by the Jewish cartographer Abraham Creqques of the Majorca school, introduced Europeans to the new names of Mali, Gao (Geugeu), and Timbuktu (Tembuch). In the middle of the map, Mansa Musa sits regally on a golden throne drawn between the cities of Timbuktu and Gao. He wears an oversized crown and holds a golden scepter in one hand and a large golden orb in the other. A Berber merchant eagerly drives his camel toward the king with the golden orb.

The Songhai empire followed the empire of Mali, and it was

under this rule that the great cities of Djenne and Timbuktu
were ruled from the capital of Gao on the Niger River, near the
current border of Mali and Niger. They proved to be a great
temptation for the sultans of the north, and finally Sultan Ahmed
el Mansur of Morocco sent in his armies to conquer the Songhai
empire in 1591 at the battle of Tondibi, near Gao. Within a
century the Moroccans proved unable to rule an empire so far
from their homeland, and their grip slowly loosened and slipped
away. Before an extensive new native nation could arise, the impact of European exploration, trade, and colonization was being
felt, with the sequence of events that led to eventual French
colonization of this area, which they called the French Soudan.

Djenne was founded in the middle of the thirteenth century.
As a major city of the Soninke empire, it became a center of
Muslim learning after King Kunburu converted to Islam. Not
until 1828 did the first European visit the city and live to tell
about it, when the French explorer René Caillie reached it and
proved that the Niger River flowed from the west toward the
east. Even though Caillie was the first European to visit Djenne,
the city's reputation had already spread far, and had an international impact still seen on maps today. The Europeans heard
tales of the fabulous wealth of this city of Djenne (or Jenne), and
from a corruption of the name of the town, they called the West
African coast the Guinea Coast, a name still preserved in the
names of the contemporary nations of Guinea, Guinea-Bissau,
Equatorial Guinea, and even its namesake, New Guinea, in the
Pacific Ocean on the other side of the world. An alternate etymology claims that the name Guinea comes from the Berber
phrase Akal n-Iguinawen, meaning "Land of the Blacks." The
richness of the area in gold led to the use of its name for a coin,
originally worth a British pound and one shilling. Europeans also
applied the name to the guinea hen, which came from that area,
and to the guinea pig—actually a misnomer, since the animal
comes from the Andes of South America and is not a pig.

The wide assortment of people drawn into Djenne in the twentieth century reminded me greatly of the first recorded description of the city, written by a notary there in the early 1600s.
Abderrahman es-Sadi, an educated man from Timbuktu who
came to work in Djenne as a notary, wrote his history of the
city, *Tarikh as-Sudan*, around 1655. He described Djenne by
claiming that "God has drawn to this fortunate city a certain

number of learned and of pious men, strangers to this country, who have come to live here. They are of different peoples and countries" (Davidson 1959, 79).

Other than a few government employees and an occasional backpacking tourist, few people come to Djenne today, but its market still thrives as a focal point for regional commerce. Despite the difficulties I had in reaching Djenne, a wide assortment of local people flow in and out.

The mud cities of West Africa today are probably the closest extant parallels to the first cities that emerged in Mesopotamia, which had very similar environmental and climatic conditions. Like the cities of Djenne and Timbuktu, the first cities of the world were built with mud and ingenuity.

The transition from rural to urban life first occurred in Mesopotamia with the rise of Uruk, Sumer, and other cities in the area between the Tigris and Euphrates rivers, in modern Iraq. But the process of urbanization developed independently on every continent. Ancient cities all over the world, from Babylon in Iraq to Tenochtitlán in Mexico, from Xian in China to Tiwanaku in Bolivia, or from Memphis in Egypt to Angkor Wat in Cambodia, all show similar characteristics. They have large market areas for trade, where foods and some form of alcoholic beverage are available, crowded manufacturing and craft districts for production, temples with large retinues of priests for extravagant public ceremonies, and spacious palaces for their leaders, soldiers, and growing legions of bureaucrats.

The development of cities added a new form of culture and an unprecedented level of complexity to human social relations. The city became more than just a large village; it grew into something new and significantly more complicated. A village might easily get its water by hauling it from the river or perhaps a single central well, and the villagers could use the same river or a pond next to the well for bathing. The city needed canals to deliver the river water to different neighborhoods, and other canals to carry the water away. Farmers could live in a village and walk out to their fields to work each day, but city dwellers are rarely farmers. Urban people earn their livelihood as merchants, teachers, priests, soldiers, laborers, bureaucrats, builders, and craftsmen who not only live in the city but also work in it. In the village, each family produces its own food and trades for only a few items, but in the city no one produces food, and a system must operate to obtain food from the agricultural districts and distribute it among the city people. Whereas a village functions primarily as a community of residence and storage of agricultural goods, a city serves as a center of production, commerce, administration, and many varieties of secular and religious power.

Gradually, through the first few millennia after the birth of agriculture, a series of great urban centers arose, scattered throughout the temperate zones of the globe. The small urban enclaves stretched out like an archipelago of civilized islands in a sea of savagery. Gradually, almost imperceptibly, these islands began to grow toward one another. Small paths connecting them grew into roads that eventually became highways. Merchants and soldiers moved easily along the improving transportation networks. Through commerce, war, and conquest they established control over the areas between the civilization centers.

Around the world, a sequence of cities grew up as focal points for regional civilizations. Mesopotamia arose around 3500 B.C., followed by Egypt half a millennium later, in 3000 B.C., and then the Indus River Valley in what is now Pakistan, around 2300 B.C. Northern China began the transition to urban life around 2000 B.C., followed by Mesoamerica in 1500 B.C. and the Andean civilization of South America shortly thereafter. Although contact between early Mesopotamia and its two nearest civilizations on the Nile and the Indus seems possible and in some instances even likely, by and large these centers arose separately and independently of each other. Despite all the theories that purport to find Egyptian traces in Mexico and South America, there is no credible evidence that any outside civilization sparked the rise of cities in the Americas.

Over time, each of these regional civilizations depended on a cluster of cities rather than on a single one. Cities rose and fell owing to periodic changes in the weather, the exhaustion of the soil, dynastic rivalries, plagues, crop blights, foreign invasion, and any number of other variables that may have been great or seemingly rather petty. The fate of any city was always precariously delicate, and it could easily plunge from prosperity and pomp in one year to ruin and starvation in the next. As soon as one city fell, however, another arose nearby to continue its functions. Each new city borrowed heavily from the preceding one and added its own flourishes and innovations. In time, older cities might be reoccupied and new cities built atop them.

In Mesoamerica, contacts developed between the ancient centers of Teotihuacán, in the Valley of Mexico, and Monte Alban, in Oaxaca Valley in the south of modern Mexico. These in turn fostered ties with Mayan sites such as Tikal, in modern Guatemala. Local cultures began to take on a regional style as the various cities depended on a common subsistence base of maize farming, and began to borrow technology, art, gods, calendars, and myths from one another. They established networks of trade, patterns of warfare, and even alliances and exchange of family members in marriage. The civilizations retained unique aspects as Mayas, Zapotecs, and Toltecs, but increasingly they shared a common Mesoamerican culture. Even though they spoke different languages, they followed similar ways of life, interacted among themselves, and shared a similar outlook on the world.

The links from central Mexico soon spread to the Gulf of Mexico in the east and up and down the Pacific coast to the west, as far north as what is now the southwestern United States, in Arizona and New Mexico. They pushed southward to Central America, and some evidence indicates at least sporadic contacts between the civilizations of Mesoamerica and those of Colombia and the South American Andes.

The development of regional civilizations and cities produced a new set of differences among humans, for now they could be divided into several quite different groups of people: foragers, farmers, pastoralists, and city people. Until this point in history, farmers, foragers, and pastoralists all led different lives, but the city brought them together in networks of trade. Farmers and pastoralists tended to associate regularly if cautiously with each other, and both interacted with the larger cities. The foraging people tended to live on the outskirts of these regional civilizations or far beyond their influence, but the regional civilizations were growing entities that always pushed out into new areas.

The growth of villages may be seen as a transition from the life of foragers to the civilized life in cities, but the rise of cities makes the difference between rural tribal people and urban people quite clear and distinct.

The relationship between settled people and the wild people of the hinterlands formed much of the subject of the world's oldest written epic. The story of Gilgamesh, the king of Uruk on the Euphrates River, was written in cuneiform about 2000 B.C., but the story probably originated centuries earlier. In this story the people outside the city of Uruk complain repeatedly to their king about Enkidu, a wild man who lives with the beasts. In this text we have the original image of the savage. "His body was rough, he had long hair like a woman's; it waved like the hair of Nisaba, the goddess of corn. His body was covered with matted hair. . . . He was innocent of mankind; he knew nothing of the cultivated land. . . . [He] lurked with wild beasts at the water-holes; he had joy of the water with the wild game" (Sandars 1960, 63).

We see in the same text the awe and the terror that the savage inspired in urban people. The first man to see Enkidu felt fear and mistrust when he reported to his father what he had seen in the wild. "He ranges over the hills with wild beasts and eats grass; he ranges through your land and comes down to the wells. I am afraid and dare not go near him. He fills in the pits which I dig and tears up my traps set for the game."

The same words could have been used at virtually any time over the last ten thousand years for the farmer describing the hunter. The words could have been said by the Romans about the inhabitants of Britain, by a Han Chinese about the Tibetan nomads, by a nineteenth-century settler about the Indians of the Plains, by a modern rancher about the Australian aborigines, or by a farmer about the Bushmen of the Kalahari or the Pygmies of the Ituri forest in Zaire.

Gilgamesh tames Enkidu not by force but by sending him a temple prostitute who not only initiates him in the mysteries of making love but introduces him to the civilized delights of baked bread. "[T]hey put down bread in front of him, but Enkidu could only suck the milk of wild animals. He fumbled and gaped, at a loss what to do or how he should eat the bread and drink the strong wine." Finally the harlot taught him, saying, "Enkidu, eat bread, it is the staff of life; drink the wine, it is the custom of the land" (Sandars 1960, 63). This was not to be the last time that the people of the village and the city used alcohol to subdue the people of the wilderness.

The prostitute introduced Gilgamesh to herding and farming as part of the civilized way of life. His progress from a savage of the wilderness through farming and tending animals before finally arriving at the city of Uruk marked the same course that all urban people had followed in the process of creating their civilization.

Enkidu became the devoted and loving friend of Gilgamesh, and together they destroyed the forests, an act that Enkidu regretted on his deathbed. As he lay dying, Enkidu mourned having abandoned his savage life for the luxuries of the city. He bitterly cursed the woman who taught him to eat bread and drink wine, and he lamented having cut down the cedar trees and killed the animals of the forest.

In the ancient myth, Gilgamesh, who represented city life, and Enkidu, the wild man of the wilderness, managed to become friends, a relationship not always found between urban and rural people. To at least some extent, urban and tribal people in the early years of city life needed to cooperate. The city could not produce enough food for itself. The people who lived in the city depended on rural farmers for grains to make bread and beer, and they depended on pastoralists for milk, meat, and wool. The rural people also brought other commodities such as fuel, wood, honey, salt, furs, feathers, reeds, and canes. People who had no commodities to sell might sell their own labor in the city as servants, soldiers, or laborers. In extreme cases the rural people might sell themselves or their children into slavery to pay debts and taxes or to buy food.

The city housed craftsmen such as bakers, brewers, stone-masons, woodworkers, weavers, potters, basket weavers, leatherworkers, and metalsmiths, who manufactured goods of a higher quality and greater variety than rural people could make for themselves. As important as any other economic activity, the city offered markets that were just as important to the lives of farmers and nomads as to city people.

The cities controlled the major arteries of communication and travel. Roads and waterways intersected at cities, and bridges or at least ferry service provided easy passage over the rivers. Cities offered accommodation, rest, and protection for people traveling from one area to another. The city served as the place to catch a boat or join a caravan, no matter whether the purpose was long-distance trade, a pilgrimage, flight from danger, or mere curiosity and sightseeing.

In addition to the commercial needs met by the urban area, the city offered religious services of various specialties. The temples and shrines of the city housed priests who sold their services in healing the sick, divining the future, pleading for rain, making crops grow, and granting fertility for humans and their animals.

The priests offered some practical services such as writing letters, and they held out hope for some measure of orderly power over aspects of life beyond the control of the individual.

People came to the cities to pursue or settle law cases and to make appeals to the ruler over land and animal ownership, inheritance, land disputes, and hundreds of new bureaucratic issues that entered life and flourished with increasingly centralized government. People had to come to the urban areas to make, verify, appeal, or alter official records. In times of political upheaval or natural disasters, the city became the refuge for people living around it who were fleeing from famine, flood, or attack by outsiders. The armies that helped to protect people in the cities could also turn and exploit the people being protected.

The city also intensified frictions among groups of people. Potential disputes and even violence loomed over every transaction in the city. Feuds proliferated as people of different tribes and cultures came together in more intimate ways than they would as nomadic foragers or even as rural farmers. Courts and written laws arose as ways to handle but not to abolish these constant problems.

To contain the rivalries and tension in the city, and to prevent chaos, rulers made and enforced firm laws. The ability of a ruler to enforce those rules determined his level of power. A military or police group had to be created to enforce the laws, and a court or judicial system arose to interpret and apply the law. The Greek word for city, *polis*, became the root not only for English words such as *politics*, *polity*, and *polite*, but for *police* as well.

In most European languages, the concepts of city and civilization both derive from a common root, the Latin word *civitas*. The Romans first applied the word to the various tribes of the Gauls and their corresponding territory, but eventually it came to signify the main urban area of the territory. The word spread into the Romance languages, becoming the Spanish *ciudad* or the French *cité*; the latter became *city* in English. In time the word shifted to mean the primary city of each district or tribe. *Civitas* also gave us related modern words such as *civil*, *civilian*, and *citizen*. A parallel yet distinct concept can be seen in Arabic, where the word for civilization (*'umran*) comes from a root meaning to increase in numbers, to build up or to develop.

The etymology of words reveals much about the values of the

people who use and change them over time. City life, which equated with civilization, citizenship, civility, and politeness contrasted markedly with its polar opposite in rural, particularly tribal life. The Latin word *silva*, meaning "woodland" or "forest," served as the source of the English *savage*, the Spanish *salvaje*, and the French *sauvage*. The word became synonymous with crude, harsh, ignorant, violent, animallike, and devoid of the human characteristics of love, loyalty, and reason. The rise of cities created a global division of humans into city dwellers and rustics; it divided them into the civilized and the savage. This distinction allowed even the most common, uneducated, and unwashed urban dweller to feel a certain sense of superiority over rural and tribal people, no matter how noble the latter may have been.

The city offered its residents and visitors entertainment, pageantry, prostitutes, and partners for marriage or commerce. As described in one ancient Mesopotamian verse, "Every day is a holiday, the young men and the girls are wonderful to see. How sweet they smell" (Tapper 1983, 30). Compared to placid village life or the isolation of a herding camp, the city reveled in perpetual activity and overwhelming excitement of many types.

Cities quickly acquired a reputation as places of danger and sin compared to rural life. The Bible offers the best example of the perspective on the city held by rural and nomadic tribes. Unlike most ancient chronicles, which relate their stories from the heart of urban civilization and usually from within the walls of the palace itself, the Bible records the perspective of a distinctly nomadic herding people. The tribal people may have been conquered but were seldom awed by urban life, but when they did succumb to the temptations of urban pleasures, divine retribution assuredly and invariably followed quickly.

The wickedness of Sodom and Gomorrah caused God to destroy the cities, except for the virtuous Lot and his daughters. From Egypt to Babylon, the books of the Old Testament present a catalog of urban sins for which God is constantly sending angels, armies, famines, or plagues to punish one city after another. Angry prophets from the most rural areas of wilderness and desert usually deliver the requisite warnings. When the city people ignore the admonitions, God destroys them and often the entire city with them, or else He gives it to a more virtuous people, who are usually nomadic tribes.

From early in urban history, the people of the city lived in an antagonistic tension with the farmers, herders, and wandering tribes of the rural areas. The merchants and the political and religious powers of the city all wanted more of the peasant's produce. Sometimes they competed with one another for that produce, but more often they combined interests and power in order to give the outsiders as little as possible and yet to obtain from them as much as possible through trade, taxes, and tithes.

In the ancient world of Mesopotamia, Uruk acquired regional fame for its great walls. The scribes called it "Uruk of the strong walls." Around 2700 B.C., about the time of the rule of the king Gilgamesh, the people of Uruk enclosed their city of a thousand acres in a large wall built of mud bricks fired to the color of copper. From this beginning, walls became an integral part of urban life. They played a major but ineffective role in the defense of Jericho, and cities throughout Eurasia and the Mediterranean erected walls around themselves. Eventually the settled people started building larger and longer walls, giving rise to the Great Wall of China and a series of walls across the northern frontier of the Roman Empire.

The settled people built walls not only to protect themselves from attack by other cities, but even more often to forestall attack by savage barbarians. Just as when the ancient Hebrew tribes came out of the Sinai desert and invaded the agricultural and urbanized Canaan, a "land of milk and honey," agricultural land always posed a great temptation to any nomadic tribe with the strength to seize it. Despite the walls, towers, gates, ramparts, and other sophisticated fortifications, tribal warriors from the frontier frequently conquered the cities and their agricultural environs.

Cities competed with one another for the crops and goods around them. Each city had an interest in constantly expanding its zone of influence in order to increase the amount of trade, taxes, and tithes coming from the people around it. Eventually that expansion led to one city dominating neighboring cities. Cities became city-states, which grew into small empires. Either the city grew and conquered the peoples around it, or it fell prey to a mightier city and then became a subjugated city, offering perpetual tribute to its stronger overlords. Urban civilization could not stop growing without starting to decay; it had to keep growing into new areas as it exhausted older ones. Urbanization and imperialism operated as a single process.

Around the world, cultures come and go, but cities continue much the same. Each new conqueror changes the appearance and possibly the name, but the functions and activities of the city endure. Greeks from Megara founded the city of Byzantium on the Thracian Bosporus in 667 B.C., and Greeks from Sparta founded it again in 478 B.C., after the Persians destroyed it. Between A.D. 324 and 330, the Roman emperor Constantine the Great rebuilt the city, named it Constantinople in honor of himself, and made it the capital of the Roman Empire, a position it retained for a thousand years. In 1453 the Muslim Turks under Mohammed II captured the city, and in 1930 the rulers of the Turkish republic changed its name to Istanbul. Whether ruled by Greeks, Romans, Byzantines, or Turks, and whether its rulers were pagans, Christians, or Muslims, the city continued. Its growth and development seemed to have a course of its own, no matter who occupied it and no matter whether they called it a capital, as the Romans and the Ottomans did, or whether they did not, like the modern Turks.

Just as Cortez rebuilt Mexico City from Tenochtitlán and Constantine rebuilt Constantinople from Byzantium, a new civilization will deliberately remake the city and hide its humbler origins. Even a city as new as Washington, D.C., arose on top of the native community of Nacochtanke, a thriving trade settlement of the Conoy Indians when first visited by an Englishman, John Fleet, in 1623. Long before that, it had been a manufacturing site for stone tools, a fact that became evident when workmen uncovered a workshop while digging out a swimming pool for the White House during the presidency of Richard Nixon. Nacochtanke could not rank among cities such as Baghdad, Tenochtitlán, or Calcutta, but as a regional commercial center and the home of a powerful chief, it was more than a mere village.

The colonists buried Nacochtanke. The name became Latinized into Anacostia, a major section of modern Washington, but most traces of the original settlement disappeared. The new European settlers wanted to give the city the look of their own culture. They laid out the streets and circles of Washington on the model of Paris, put up a Greco-Roman Capitol, a Georgian White House, an Egyptian obelisk to honor George Washington, a Roman temple to honor Thomas Jefferson, and two Greek temples, one in honor of Abraham Lincoln and another to house the Supreme Court. The architects of Washington re-created the Baths of Diocletian in the form of Union Station, and placed a replica of the Triumphal Arch of Constantine in front of it as the grand entrance. The Catholics put up a Romanesque-Byzantine cathedral, the Protestants put up a Gothic one on the other side of town, and the Masons erected replicas of two of the Seven Wonders of the Ancient World, the tomb of King Mausolus of Halicarnassus and the lighthouse of Alexandria.

The settlers of Washington were mythologizing the landscape. Instead of singing the material world into being, they were building their myths in concrete, marble, and granite, and in doing so they combined architectural elements from many different cultures. In a sense, every city is a combination of cultures. The city was the first human institution to surpass a single culture.

The North African scholar and public official Ab-ar-Rahman Ibn Khaldun (1332–1406) wrote the first historical analysis to focus on the relationship between tribal and urban people as the key to understanding world history and human civilization. His greatest work was the seven-volume history of the world, *Kitab al-'Ibar*, in which he stated his intention to invent a science of civilization, drawing from his studies of Arabic, Greek, and Hebrew writings and from his own political service in Spain, the Maghreb, and Egypt.

Ibn Khaldun regarded *asabiyah*, loosely translated as "group solidarity" or "community," as the primary principle underlying tribal society. For Ibn Khaldun, *asabiyah* arises from kinship, mutual assistance, and affection and thereby forms the essence of tribal social life and culture. Tribal people live on the earth in a simple, natural way that satisfies basic needs, but they must maintain a strong sense of community to survive in the harsh environment they inhabit.

In Ibn Khaldun's analysis, city people needed tribal people because the tribal people reinvigorated the civilized world. Tribes brought new blood to the cities, and they brought ideas such as Islam or Judaism from the desert to the city. Most important, they brought a direct, simple, and honest way of dealing with one another and with the world around them. These strengths of tribal community account for the success of the Hebrew tribes in conquering the Canaanite cities, of the Arab Bedouins in conquering the Middle East, of the Moors in conquering Spain, and even for the success of the Turkish tribes from Asia pressing on the urbanized Arab and Persian world during Ibn Khaldun's lifetime.

The longer tribal people associated with urban people, however, the weaker the former became. When tribal people came in contact with urban civilization, *asabiyah* immediately came under attack from the luxuries that weaken kinship and community ties of the tribe and by the artificial wants for new types of cuisine, new fashions in clothing, larger homes, and other novelties of urban life.

According to Ibn Khaldun, civilization faces an eternal dilemma. Civilization needs the tribal values to survive; yet civilized urban life in most parts of the world destroys tribal people whenever contact is made.

9

Alexandria and the Gift of Knowledge

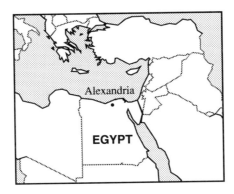

*I felt once more the strange equivocal power of the city—
its flat alluvial landscape and exhausted airs . . . Alexandria.*
—LAWRENCE DURRELL

From the wrought-iron balcony of a fourth-floor room at the aged but once grand Metropole Hotel, I look down on the city of Alexandria, Egypt. In the faint morning light and the refreshing quiet, I tried to read some of the poems of the Egyptian-Greek poet Constantine Cavafy who lived and worked in this neighborhood in the first third of the twentieth century. But the sights and smells of the city kept drawing my attention away from the lines on the page and back out onto the streets.

One side of the old hotel looks out over the modern but already dilapidated Midan Saad Zaghoul, a 1970s-style public square, and from there onto the ancient harbor and the Mediterranean. From that side of the hotel one always feels the salt in the eternal breeze that blows in from the sea, and one sees the massive Crusader-style castle of Qaytbay, built over the ancient lighthouse of Pharos, which had been one of the Seven Wonders of the World.

My room, however, does not look out over the sea. I face away from the sea and Europe and gaze instead toward Africa. My room looks over the backside of Alexandria, with its winding streets and crowded alleys. I know that only a mile to the south

lies the lake, and between me and the lake are the few classical
ruins of ancient Alexandria. There is the Odeon, where the
masses used to cheer for their favorite wrestlers and laugh at the
scatological mimes. Nearby is the misnamed Pompey's Pillar,
erected in honor of the Roman emperor Diocletian in front of
the temple to the Greek-Egyptian god Serapis, invented by the
Ptolemaic rulers to combine ancient Greek and Egyptian religions into one. Near the temple, but underground, lies the maze
of catacombs that were carved in the porous limestone and arranged with the care and financial interest of a condominium
developer.

More than two thousand years ago, Cleopatra erected obelisks
of the finest Aswan granite near this spot, as she began construction of the great Caesarium in honor of her nation's new Roman
rulers. Cleopatra had stolen the ancient obelisks from the temples
of Luxor, Karnak, and Heliopolis, where they had stood for thousands of years before she appeared in history. By the time of
Cavafy, the obelisks, or "Cleopatra's Needles" as they were misnamed, had been stolen again to grace London's Thames Em-
bankment, New York's Central Park, and the Place de la
Concorde in Paris. Distant cities have always ended up with the
treasures of Alexandria, and all the world has profited from it.

Closer to my room, I can see, on the low buildings to my
right, goats browsing on the roofs, where most people in
crowded Alexandria throw their garbage. In the building across
from me, a man slowly opens his large green shutters and takes
a deep breath of morning air. He pauses for a moment, as though
debating whether to stay at the window or go on to some more
urgent piece of business. He decides to stay at the window, leans
on the railing, and lights a cigarette. Above him a sign advertises
in English and Arabic the availability of dental surgery in his
office.

Instead of the voice of the muezzin calling the faithful to
morning prayer, I hear the captivating voice of the Lebanese
singer Fayruz vibrating over the street as she laments the tragic
history of Jerusalem, the most beautiful of flowers. The morning
breeze makes her undulating voice emanate first from one window and then from another, as it pervades the air more like the
salty haze than like musical notes.

Five well-dressed but apparently tired young men walk slowly
through the street as though on the way home from a night of

revelry. They pause, exhausted yet still playful, in front of a dozen water jugs on the streetcorner, put there by local vendors to attract and refresh potential customers. The pottery jugs sweat in the summer heat, and the evaporation cools the water. The boys pick up each jug in turn and shake it, but they find only a few drops of water left. As the boys playfully toss the jugs to one another, a policeman rounds the corner in his starched white uniform accented by a shiny black beret, belt, and boots. The boys quietly put down the jugs and continue on their way.

A fat woman in a white veil drives by and blows her horn at the boys, who seem about to step out in front of her car. The noise awakens a vendor who was sleeping all night in his stall that sells beach balls and other inflatable toys and animals for play on the beach. The vendor calls to the street sweeper to come clean up around his stall.

The view from my hotel window lacks excitement. Despite its ancient history, Alexandria always seems to be a newly deteriorated city of only a few decades ago. The buildings seem to be relics of the 1920s or, at the oldest, to have been built during the Victorian era, soon after the British seized the port in 1882. The names of the streets, squares, and buildings always represent the latest wave of invading armies or conquering revolutions, and the style of its buildings imitates the tastes of the new powers, whether they be from Rome, Macedonia, London, Paris, Constantinople, or even Cairo.

Like a painted mole on the face of Africa, Alexandria is impossible to ignore; yet it never seemed to fit the face that it adorned. The twentieth-century novelist Lawrence Durrell described Alexandria in his book *Justine* as "neither Greek, Syrian nor Egyptian, but a hybrid: a joint." In *Clea*, the fourth novel in Durrell's Alexandria Quartet, he describes the city as simply "Alexandria, the capital of memory!"

These eternally changing façades hide the history of Alexandria rather than broadcasting it. Despite this deception, every square meter of the city groans under the weight of history. My own hotel room sits just above the Trianon Café, the kind of place that causes travel writers to wax nostalgic for the beauties of an easier and more luxurious era, when only the wealthy and intellectually deserving could travel. Such books always invite summer scholars to catch up on their travel diaries while sipping cups of strong and oddly flavored coffees that they would never drink at home.

The café also caters to backpackers who write home postcards and long letters filled with newly learned phrases and the spirit of a romantic encounter with an old movie. The Trianon is one of Alexandria's spots that let visitors feel for a moment as though they have finally uncovered the "it" of the quintessential Alexandria experience. After this reflective literary moment snatched from the memories of Constantine Cavafy, Lawrence Durrell, or E. M. Forster, the traveler can return to the crowded beach and the modern exigencies of the Mediterranean tan and the perfect meal.

Just above this same café, during the time of the British occupation, the offices of the Third Circle of Irrigation groaned under the mountainous paperwork of administration. There Constantine Cavafy labored during the day in his bureaucratic job while writing Greek poems that offered a miniaturist's perspective on the great lives of Mediterranean history— Cleopatra, Alexander, Antony, and hundreds of soldiers, shop clerks, and scholars.

Alexander the Great founded and named, or renamed, a dozen cities after himself. Alexander gave his name to Alexandretta in Turkey, also called Iskenderun in Turkish, which meant "Little Alexander," so named to honor one of his many battle victories. Alexandria Troas, in Turkey, near the ancient city of Troy and in the area where Saint Paul preached the Christian doctrine to the Greeks, also bears his name. He also founded Alexandria ad Issum as a seaport that served as entry into Syria, and Alexandria in Susiana, at the mouth of the Tigris River. His name can still be heard faintly in the name Kandahar, a province of southern Afghanistan, formerly called Alexandria Arachosiorum. At what is now the city of Jhelum, in Pakistan near the border with India, Alexander even named a city Beucephala, to honor his horse Bucephalus, who died there in 326 B.C.

Many centuries after Alexander the Great died, European settlers carried his name to the Americas, where it became a name for communities or counties in six states, the most important of which was Alexandria, Virginia, which almost became the capital of the United States. Because Alexander's name was also picked up as a royal name for male and female monarchs from the Byzantine Empire and the Russian czars to the British royal house, it was also applied to a wide variety of towns, counties, and lakes around the world. In various formations, Alexander's name has become a universal one used for towns and cities from Russia to Australia.

After Alexander the Great founded the city of Alexandria in Egypt, a succession of Greek rulers, from Ptolemy I Soter to Cleopatra VII Philadelphus Philopator Philopatris, exploited the African trade from their port capital connecting the Nile with the Mediterranean. After Cleopatra's dramatic suicide and the fall of the Ptolemaic dynasty, the Romans continued to use the city to exploit the great grain-growing capacity of the Nile Valley and the large oasis at Fayum. The Christian Byzantine rulers continued this exploitation, as did the Muslim Ottomans who succeeded them. Napoleon invaded the area at the end of the eighteenth century, but was forced out by the British, who gradually took control of Egypt. In World War II, the German general Erwin Rommel tried to march on the city with his Afrika Korps and make it a base for a Nazi empire in Africa but was defeated by Montgomery in a succession of bloody battles at nearby El Alamein.

Alexandria, Egypt, contains the seeds of the modern world culture. Alexander the Great founded it in pursuit of his goal of bringing together people, knowledge, and cultures from all parts of the world as known in his era. Sitting on the edge of the African continent near where Asia and Europe meet, Alexandria arose as the first truly cosmopolitan city, a world city. If the Mediterranean world had a capital city, it had to be Alexandria. Even though the city never exercised the power of Babylon, Rome, or Constantinople, Alexandria united the cultures of many lands to produce a hybrid that became the ancestor of the modern world culture.

Alexander arrived on the Asian-African scene as a European upstart from the edges of the world. Not until the reign of Alexander I of Macedonia (circa 494–450 B.C.) did the Greek Olympic Games admit Macedonia as a part of the Greek world. Even this proved a tentative acceptance, and the Greeks continued to see Macedonia as only half Hellenic and half barbarian. Not until the second century B.C. did Macedonians fully adopt the *koine*, the common Greek speech, and the pantheon of Olympian gods.

The Greek city-states took real notice of Macedonia only when

Philip II (359–336 B.C.) conquered them in 338 B.C., effectively bringing to a close the era of the Greek city-state and starting the monarchical pattern of the coming Hellenistic era. In 336 B.C., assassins killed Philip, and his son became king as Alexander III, later known as Alexander the Great. Alexander went on to conquer the classical Mediterranean world.

What distinguished Alexander from the thousands of conquerors before him was simply that he was from one of the barbarian peoples of the northern fringes of the classical world. He was not Egyptian, Ethiopian, Libyan, Persian, Hebrew, Babylonian, Mesopotamian, Hittite, Hyksos, Sumerian, or from any of the other civilized peoples of the world. The learned priests, the old noble families, and the scribes and peasants had to prostrate themselves in the dirt before a northern monarch who appropriated unto himself both of the roles and all of the honors and powers usually accorded to the Egyptian pharaoh and to the Persian emperor.

Alexander adopted the local gods of the places he conquered into the pantheon of Greek gods, which had long been a rather open collection of deities. Even the goddess Athena had not originally been a Greek deity, but had been absorbed into the all-male pantheon of Greek gods, along with the other goddesses who were married or adopted into the hierarchy of Mount Olympus. In the Hellenistic pantheon, scholars matched up Greek gods with non-Greek gods. The Greek Zeus was the same as the Roman Jupiter, and the Egyptian judge of the underworld, Osiris, became identified with the Greek Pluto, who ruled their underworld. During the Hellenistic time, other deities were simply absorbed into an expanded pantheon. The Egyptian goddess Isis became very popular throughout the Hellenistic world, and the Greek Dionysus became particularly popular in Hellenized Egypt. When needed, new gods could be created. The Ptolemaic rulers supported the god Serapis, whom they invented as a combination of Osiris and the bull-god Apis.

Alexander worshiped at religious sites and consulted oracles in every area he conquered. In Egypt he even made the risky journey of several weeks far out into the Sahara to consult the oracles of the god Ammun at the oasis of Siwa. The oracles proclaimed Alexander to be the son of god, the son of Zeus Ammun. This represented a major change in Greek thought, because prior to this time, Greek theology and political ideology maintained a strict separation between gods and men, even if the men were rulers. From the proclamation of Alexander's godhood at Siwa, rulers such as the Ptolemys and later the Roman emperors repeatedly had themselves declared to be gods. In accepting his own apotheosis, Alexander incorporated into his Greek empire an ancient Egyptian tradition of the divine pharaohs.

Cults from Asia Minor and Egypt found wide followings among the Greeks until the beginning of the Christian era, when the Greeks abandoned their older gods for the monotheism of a small Jewish sect. Despite the traditional emphasis placed on logic and clear thinking in earlier Greek civilization, the Hellenic civilization eagerly incorporated every form of magic and astrology it encountered. This obsession with the stars and fate developed almost immediately after Alexander's conquest of Babylon, whose scholars possessed a vast knowledge of astronomy and calendars, and where astrology was widely practiced. The influence of magic, astrology, and the host of new gods effectively destroyed the older Greek religion of the classical Hellenic age, and replaced it with the amalgamated and constantly changing pastiche of the Hellenistic world.

The conquests of Alexander stretched from Greece to the edge of India and from the Black Sea to Aswan on the Nile in Africa, and it represented a new kind of conquest. Alexander united, even if for only a short time, the major cities of Egypt, the Middle East, Greece, and Persia into a single empire. Wherever the armies of Alexander marched, they left the influence of a new culture that we usually call Hellenistic, in contrast to the classical Greek culture, called Hellenic. The Hellenistic culture blended a large number of Mediterranean traits with a new, almost barbaric vitalism from Europe, which to this point had not been a major actor on the world stage.

Contrary to the wishes of the Greeks, who saw themselves as a pure and superior race that should not be diluted with foreign blood, Alexander deliberately strove to create a world civilization by mixing the blood and family ties of the Greeks with those of non-Greeks. Even though Alexander had to go against the will of his tutor and fellow Macedonian, the philosopher Aristotle, he commanded eighty of his officers to marry eighty local women in the Persian city of Susa, and he himself took as his second wife Barsine, the eldest daughter of his defeated foe, the Persian emperor Darius. Prior to this mass marriage, Alexander himself had married his first wife, Roxana, in 327 B.C. She was an Asian woman, the daughter of Oxyartes, a chief in Bactria, between the Hindu Kush and the Oxus River, near the modern borders of Iran and Afghanistan. Their Eurasian son, Alexander Aegus, born in 323 B.C. after Alexander's death, was eventually murdered along with his mother in 311 B.C., in the long struggle for control of Alexander's empire.

Hellenistic culture began as an amalgam of many cultures, and quickly became the established civilization of the Mediterranean world. The military, political, religious, and commercial elites all became a part of Hellenistic culture. Even though Alexander's empire did not survive him, the culture that he spread did survive. His empire broke up into many different states. The Ptolemys ruled in Egypt, the Antigonids in Macedonia, and the Seleucids in Syria and Babylon. Scattered among and around these major kingdoms, smaller kingdoms and chiefdoms arose that bore various degrees of allegiance to Hellenistic culture. In each of these kingdoms or miniature empires, the dynasty maintained its rule through the claim of being the legitimate heirs of Alexander and his conquest. Consequently they maintained their Hellenistic culture even when at war with one another.

Alexander helped to spread parts of Greek culture, but his long campaigns also left his homeland exhausted and depopulated of great armies, generals, bureaucrats, artisans, and the other people who set forth with him. Many of these people never returned to Greece, choosing instead to stay in Asia Minor, Egypt, Persia, Babylon, or India. Greece took many centuries to recover from this great loss; some might say it never again reached the level of civilization that it had before Alexander. After Alexander's death, Greece never resumed a position as leader in world politics or culture as important as it had during his short life.

The Hellenistic world had no single political capital, but Alexandria became its cultural and intellectual capital under the royal patronage of the Ptolemys. Not only had the city been founded by Alexander himself, but after Alexander's death, Ptolemy stole the corpse of Alexander the Great and thus started a bloody war among Alexander's generals and successors. Ptolemy brought Alexander's corpse for burial in Alexandria as a trophy that made a tangible and permanent connection between the city and the conqueror, thus legitimizing three centuries of Ptolemaic rule over Egypt. Alexandria quickly grew into the largest Greek city, with approximately half a million inhabitants at its zenith, a multicultural and international array of peoples and traditions.

When Alexander the Great founded the city in 331 B.C., on the site of an Egyptian fishing village called Rhacotis, he situated it so that it faced out over the sea toward Greece and away from Africa. He built the city away from the mouth of the Nile, putting it instead on a small spit of sand between the sea and a brackish lake, with the back of the city protected by the immense emptiness of the great Libyan desert. The Greeks never even considered Alexandria a part of Egypt. It was *Alexandros pros Aegyptos*—Alexandria toward, or on the way to, Egypt. The Romans continued this concept by calling it *Alexandria ad Aegyptium*. The Arab conquers dropped the preposition and called it *Al Iskandariyah*, Alexandria.

Situated between the traditional population and agricultural centers of Egypt and the Mediterranean, Alexandria became a great market for African, Asian, and European goods. Within the city was the world's largest grain market, as well as a market for oils pressed from sesame, safflower, gourd, colocynth, and linseed. Egypt dominated the market in all forms of oil except the common olive, since olive trees grew very poorly in Egyptian soil. A vast army of bureaucrats presided over this complex system. Ancient Egypt had been the home of a large bureaucracy since the dawn of the Pharaohs, but under the Ptolemys, Alexandria became home to the world's largest bureaucracy. One of the papyri from Hellenistic Egypt commented that "no one has the right to do what he wants to do, but everything is regulated for the best" (Grant 1982, 41). Alexandria became the first modern city.

When Alexander established his namesake city on the Nile Delta rather than on the actual river, it must have seemed an odd place for a city, so far from the center of Egyptian civilization. But the delta was the source of a new commodity that was just becoming very popular in the Mediterranean world. It was full of swampy areas where agriculture proved difficult, but where the papyrus plant thrived. It grew wild and could be harvested without the work of cultivation.

The Egyptians manufactured papyrus from a strong, reedlike sedge, *Cyperus papyrus*, that grew in swampy areas of the Nile, particularly to the south in the Sudan and in the delta around Alexandria. To make papyrus, the Egyptians removed the outer rind of the stem and sliced the pith into strips that they placed side by side and crosswise, and then pressed together and dried. Egyptians were manufacturing papyrus by the time of the Fifth Dynasty of the Old Kingdom, in the third millennium B.C. The Egyptians used this method to make papyrus clothing and baskets, and sails for ships on the Nile. Someone realized that it could also be used for writing. Simple lampblack mixed with a little vegetable gum made a permanent ink that could be applied with a reed pen.

Several centuries before Alexander, the Greeks started importing papyrus from Egypt. Papyrus supplied the Greeks with a cheap and easy way to write, and write they did. Merchants could keep better and easier records, and people could exchange letters. Everyone seemed to have a story, a poem, an idea, a song, a play, or a philosophical discussion waiting to burst forth onto papyrus and be shared with friends. The proliferation of Greek texts of all sorts in the fifth through third centuries B.C. owed much to the increasing availability of papyrus from Egypt. The Greeks received many Egyptian texts written on papyrus, but they also imported large amounts of papyrus that they used for writing new texts.

Alexander cut a dramatic and tragic figure in world history, but he was not the greatest conqueror of history. The Persians under Cyrus the Great and Darius the Great had already conquered much of the same territory that Alexander took, but we know much more about Alexander's short life than we do about virtually anyone who preceded him. So much was written about him and spread around the world, not because his name was engraved in stone like generations of kings, emperors, and pharaohs before him, but because his story was written on thousands of sheets of papyrus in an easily read alphabet.

In the ancient world, the elaborate and complicated technology of reading and writing meant that a small, specially educated class of clerks could keep a monopoly on literacy. Frequently, kings and generals could not read a word or even sign their names, an act far beneath their dignity and better handled by professional scribes. The Mesopotamians wrote with a stylus punched into a clumsy clay tablet. The Chinese invented paper, but instead of an alphabet of a few dozen letters, a scribe needed to learn a different character for each word. The ancient Egyptians who developed papyrus wrote with a complex system of hieroglyphs. Even the early Greeks had to carve their writing in stone or scratch it onto pottery.

The Hellenistic civilization focused on the Greek language, which was written with an alphabet derived from Aramaic and ultimately from the Phoenician writing system. Unlike its predecessors, the Greek alphabet had vowels as well as consonants. This made it a more efficient written language. Compared to Egyptian hieroglyphics or Mesopotamian cuneiform, the Greek alphabet proved substantially easier to learn and use, and much more flexible for adaptation to new words, names, and concepts. This alphabet and its descendants eventually became the most commonly used ones in the world.

As Alexander carried the *koine*, the common Greek language, with him, it became simplified by new speakers who learned it later in life. Speakers of the new Greek did not need as many cases, tenses, and moods as were used in the highly educated Greek of Plato and Xenophon.

Anyone could learn to read and write the increasingly simplified Greek texts. Once the student knew the basic letters and sounds, within a few years he could read almost anything that was written, even if he could not fully understand it. The Greek student could sound out strange words or easily figure out how to write a word, even if he had never before seen the written word. The Chinese student had no such luxury with Chinese characters, because the characters could not be sounded out or deciphered; each one had to be taught and learned separately. Even the Semitic languages, which already used an alphabet, did not have the flexibility of Greek, because their alphabets lacked vowels. The language was written in consonant clusters, which meant that one had to be able to speak the language fairly fluently in order to begin reading it, and learning to read required much memorization.

Hellenized Jews spoke and wrote Greek. Even their worship was done in the synagogue, a building with a Greek name meaning "meeting place." Because of the difficulty of Hebrew and other Semitic scripts, the New Testament of the Bible was written in Greek rather than in Hebrew. Anyone, even those who were not fluent in Greek, could sound out the words and read them. They could learn as they read. The Bible was written and read in such simple and often incorrect Greek that it was often referred to as "God's poor Greek."

This combination of an Asian alphabet, an African technology for making papyrus, and a European language created Hellenistic culture. The legacy of Alexander, and particularly of the city of Alexandria, was the creation of a basis for widespread literacy. Alexandria exported knowledge, information, and literacy itself.

Egypt manufactured papyrus for sale throughout the world, and this abundance of papyrus, in part, accounted for why Alexandria contained the greatest library in the world, a center of learning called the *museion*. Founded by either Ptolemy I or II, the name *museion* meant "the place of the muses," the goddesses of learning. Even though our modern word *museum* derives from this Greek word via Latin, we might more aptly call the Museion of Alexandria a research institute, since it provided a place for the best scholars to live and study all the branches of knowledge. The Ptolemys encouraged education not only because it brought them great prestige and legitimacy, but also because a better-educated public demanded more of the papyrus that they controlled, and copies of the books whose copying and sale they also controlled. The Ptolemys exercised an intellectual monopoly. Education, learning, publishing, and the equipment needed for these enterprises helped make the Ptolemys not only famous but also quite rich.

The spread of knowledge promoted by the Museion and the vital publishing industry of the Ptolemys in Alexandria caused the greatest information revolution known to that time. It also created new problems, for the government could no longer control what was being written. Socrates himself was one of the first victims of this newly emerging tension between scholars and politicians. Condemned to death for corrupting the youth of Athens, he drank hemlock and died in his prison cell, surrounded by his disciples, in 399 B.C.

When the Roman orator and writer Cicero attacked Octavian and Mark Antony for their destruction of Roman freedoms, Antony became so outraged that he had Cicero executed in 43 B.C. To emphasize exactly what Cicero's offense had been, Antony had his hands cut off and nailed up in the Roman senate, so that all might behold the hands that had penned the attack on Antony.

In laying the foundations for a literate public, Alexander the

Great unleashed a great problem for his successors through the centuries. This tension between scholars and politicians probably lay at the heart of the eventual destruction of the great library of Alexandria.

For two thousand years, intellectuals and academics have mourned the loss of the great library in Alexandria, which contained the largest collection of manuscripts and books known in the world. In addition to copies of works from across Europe, Africa, and Asia, the library housed many unique works not available outside of Egypt. It once contained nearly half a million scrolls, the majority of which were the so-called "mixed" scrolls, each of which contained more than one work. Stored in bins along the wall, each of the scrolls had a label, or *syllabus*, attached to the end, on which was written a list of contents, the name of the author, and a précis of the entire scroll.

The destruction of the library generated many myths. In one version it was burned by the conquering Arabs, who took the city from the Christians; in another the Christians burned the city when they seized it from the pagans. Neither is true. In fact, the great library died gradually over many centuries. It suffered its first great purge in 145, under the Ptolemys themselves, when the intellectuals of the library sided with Ptolemy VI Philometor in a struggle with his brother, who succeeded him as Ptolemy Euergetes II. Many of the scholars fled, taking manuscripts with them.

Through succeeding centuries manuscripts were removed, lost, or stolen, or allowed to deteriorate. Occasional riots between Christians and pagans or among the numerous warring factions of Christian theologians added to the destruction as a small annex was burned or the works of a particularly unpopular scholar or school of thought went up in the flames administered by the followers of a rival philosophy.

Today we do not even know where the great library of Alexandria stood. Guides differ over several contending spots for that honor around the city, but one place stands out as the most likely. Beneath the giant column called Pompey's Pillar lie the ruins of a temple library that may have been one of the annexes of the great library. The caverns of this library now lie empty. Deserted underground corridors repeatedly echo the voices of visitors as lifelessly as catacombs. No great papyri lie in the niches on the wall. The many great works in various Greek scripts, Egyptian hieroglyphics, Coptic script, and Latin letters are now gone, forever lost.

Because we, as educated readers, do not want to believe that scholars would neglect their own work or that they would wantonly destroy the works of their rivals, we have developed the myths of an apocalyptic destruction at the hands of the untutored infidel. We would much rather picture barbarians torching the great library than imagine generations of scholars neglecting their own charges, pilfering old manuscripts and selling them, using them for wrapping paper, papier-mâché, and toilet tissue, or even tossing them into a fire.

In world history, much more knowledge has been lost through neglect and petty fights than in the grand struggles and wars of great civilizations and conflicting empires. Knowledge dies through carelessness because the information lacks relevance to the practical concerns of the moment, or because it contradicts prevailing modes of theological, philosophical, political, racial, or economic ideology.

Even though the library of Alexandria died of neglect, the idea symbolized in the universal city continued to live through the more than 2,500 years since its founding. The culture of Alexandria took from all other cultures, and it gave back to each one more than it took.

Alexandria has represented many things to many people in different eras since Alexander the Great founded the city. Its significance has constantly changed through the centuries, and its former power is now gone. If we look closely at Alexandria, however, we can see clearly the origins of the modern, global society.

In his poem "The God Abandons Antony," composed in Alexandria in 1911, Constantine Cavafy wrote,

When at the hour of midnight
an invisible choir is suddenly heard passing
with exquisite music, with voices—
Do not lament your fortune that at last subsides,
your life's work that has failed, your schemes that have
    proved illusions.
But like a man prepared, like a brave man,
bid farewell to her, to Alexandria who is departing.

The city of Alexandria has itself departed from the center stage of world history, but its influence endures. It rose above the ranks of regional cities to become the first world city. Alexandria offered a brief glimpse into the city of the future, a glimpse of the increasingly decisive role cities would play in shaping the modern world system.

10

The Technology of Nationalism

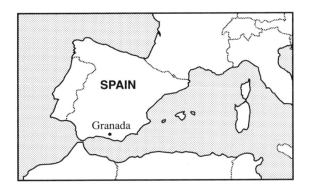

The three great elements of modern civilization,
gunpowder, printing and the Protestant church.
—THOMAS CARLYLE,
The State of German Literature (1827)

The sun always seems just a little too bright around the Alhambra palace in the Spanish city of Granada, but the layout and architecture of the place seem designed to lessen the power of the sun. The palace rooms have high, vaulted ceilings, large, shaded porches, and porticos protected from the sun by lacy grilles of wood or carved stucco. Colorful ceramic tiles of intricate geometric designs decorate floors and walls and always feel cool to the touch of a hand or a bare foot. Most of the rooms open onto large, tree-lined courtyards with sparkling water fountains and slowly moving channels of cool water, in which wives of the sultan might dip their fingers to refresh themselves on a hot summer day. The dark clay walls of the palaces and surrounding fortifications do not reflect the sun so much as absorb it, giving the walls a reddish glow from which the Moors gave the place its name, Alhambra, meaning "red fortress."

From the walls of this fortress, Mohammed XI Abu-Abdullah, the last Muslim ruler in Spain, looked out over the plains below the city in 1491 and watched the gathering armies of King Ferdinand of Aragon and Queen Isabella of Castile, who had united their kingdoms, fortunes, and armies through their marriage in 1469. The Muslim king, usually known as Boabdil, the Spanish corruption of his name, watched as the invading soldiers pitched their tents for the long siege of his beautiful city, and he watched as they defiantly built a town of brick and wood to show Boabdil and his soldiers that they had come to stay and would not budge until the surrender of the city. From the edges of the Alhambra, that permanent encampment can still be seen today as the village of Santa Fe, the namesake of Santa Fe, New Mexico, and Santa Fe de Bogotá, Colombia.

Strolling through the grounds of the Alhambra, one can hardly help but wonder how Boabdil spent those waning months of Muslim civilization in Europe as he withstood the long siege of Ferdinand and Isabella. Did he wander sleepless along the walls, staring into the dark night and wondering about the Spanish troops waiting to exile him and destroy the world crafted by his ancestors? Did he sit cross-legged in the official Court of the Lions, plotting strategy with his advisers, or did he seek guidance in the cool quiet of the mosque and the scriptures of the Qur'an? Did he forget his official woes and amuse himself with the concubines of his harem, sitting by the fountains of the Court of Myrtles, listening to the wailing ballads of the Arabic troubadours, and smelling the orange blossoms floating in the water?

Boabdil stood at the end of 780 years of Muslim presence in Spain, which began in 711, when an army of some ten thousand Arabs and North African Berbers left from the base of Gabal Musa, on the shore of Morocco, to cross the Strait of Gibraltar. Known as *moros* in Spanish or Moors in English, because they crossed into Spain from Morocco, they brought a whole new civilization under the leadership of Tariq ibn Ziyad, whose name is still recalled at the strait by Tariq's Mountain, better known by its English name, Gibraltar. The Arab army of Tariq defeated the Visigoth army of King Roderic at the Battle of Río Barbate, south of Cádiz, and raced up the peninsula to the Pyrenees and even into southern France.

The Arab armies demanded unconditional surrender; the word *Islam* itself is Arabic for "submission." Contrary to western stereotypes, however, the Arab armies demanded only submission but not conversion. The subjects of the Arabs remained free to be Christians or Jews and to speak Spanish so long as they paid their taxes and remained loyal to their Moorish overlords. Because the

Muslim rulers could collect more taxes from their Christian subjects than from Muslim ones, they did little to encourage conversion. Most of the Spaniards who converted to Islam did so through marriage or for their own personal or financial reasons.

The Moors reached as far as France in their blitzkrieg, but the French quickly repelled them from the south of their country in 732, and gradually the Christian armies of the Spaniards beat them back toward the south. *La Reconquista*, the reconquest of the Iberian peninsula by Christian armies, went slowly but persistently forward and became one of the dominant themes of the next half-millennium of Spanish history. King Alonso VI of Castile and León seized the Muslim city of Toledo in central Spain in 1085, Córdoba in 1236, and the Almohad dynasty's capital of Seville in 1248. The story of the reconquest still resounds in *The Song of El Cid*, the Spanish epic with an Arabic name derived from *al-sayyid*, meaning "lord."

Between 1248 and 1354, after the fall of the other great centers of Muslim power in Spain, the Nasirid dynasty of Granada's sultans defiantly built the great citadel and palaces of the Alhambra as a gesture of intent to remain in Spain, no matter what the Christians did. The palace was a piece of stone and stucco propaganda meant to impress all visitors. They decorated the palace with phrases from the Qur'an, particularly the family motto of the Nasirid dynasty, "There is no conqueror but Allah." Above the arches, the architects wrote in the angular, formal Kufic script, but on the walls they used the curving, flowing, graceful Maghribi script more commonly associated with Arabic. The beautiful curved script was intertwined with representations of vines, leaves, and geometric designs, but with no images of animals or humans, which would be contrary to the laws of the *Qur'an*.

Some of the finest tile and stucco work in the world can still be seen in the Alhambra, which was located so far from the Arab centers of culture that its inhabitants developed their own style. The builders of the Alhambra added more ornamentation than is usually seen in Arab architecture, particularly in the uniquely Arab decoration of the *muqarna*. Using the delicate material of stucco, the architects made the *muqarna*s by forming a sort of symmetrical stalactite that hung down and formed a series of vaults on the ceiling. Each vault had a superimposed tier of arches that looked like a honeycomb hanging from the ceiling.

Boabdil was the last of his dynasty, which ruled for 254 years in the southeastern corner of Spain, the last foothold of Muslim power on the peninsula. The great fortress of the Alhambra never fell in battle. Knowing that he had been completely defeated and that his armies could no longer hold off the Christians, Boabdil left the fortress to surrender his sword in an area of the city known as Albaicin, now a district of small restaurants opening onto open plazas where Gypsies sing and dance for diners and old men play cards in small cafés.

Legend says that Boabdil wept as he left the beautiful Alhambra. When he reached the pass through the mountains, he looked back on his beloved Granada for the last time at a place still called Suspiro del Moro, the Moor's Sigh, and in one of the most biting comments in history, his mother, Aisha, supposedly turned to him and said, "It is right that you cry like a woman for what you could not defend like a man." A broken man, Boabdil retired with his loyal followers to Fez in Morocco.

The Arabs and Berbers had entered Spain as a collection of nearly wild tribes, but they did not leave as a tribal people. They left as urban people with some of the best-trained doctors, linguists, architects, philosophers, and lawyers in the world. The Moorish craftworkers made the most prized lusterware pottery, tiles, and textiles of the era. These people would not return to a life of nomadic herders in the desert. They had evolved what was probably the highest standard of living in the Old World, and even though they faced exile, they could never return to the place where they had started.

In defeating Boabdil, Ferdinand and Isabella had welded the land into a nation, a single people, and in its cultural homogeneity they had no room for deviation. Even though the Spanish monarchs had promised Boabdil to respect the Muslim religion of their new subjects, they quickly broke that promise. The Catholic monarchs were not to be as tolerant as the Muslims; within months of their final conquest they issued a proclamation ordering all Muslims and Jews to convert to Catholicism or leave the country.

The Spanish and church authorities quickly closed every synagogue, mosque, and Koranic school in their territory, converting most of the buildings into churches, convents, and monasteries. Ferdinand and Isabella had already established the Spanish Inquisition in 1480, well before the conquest of the last Moorish stronghold, and under the guidance of the Inquisition, the authorities escalated their persecution of Jews and Muslims. Thousands fled, while other thousands converted to Catholicism in the hope that they might find peace.

Even though Isabella and Ferdinand had a backward medieval mentality in regard to religion, in another sense they were modern monarchs who realized the importance of having a homogeneous population speaking a single language, following a single religion, and leading culturally similar lives. It was not enough for them that the Jews and Muslims who stayed behind swore their loyalty to the Spanish monarchy, converted to Christianity, and worshiped in the Catholic manner. In edict after edict, the monarchs and their successors hammered away at the *conversos* or *moriscos*, as they were called. They forbade the use of the Arabic language or writing in their kingdom, and outlawed Arabic dress and any other sign of Arab cultural identity. They forbade any observance of the Jewish Sabbath or of the Muslim holy day of Friday. The people had to give their children Christian names, and the monarchs even outlawed the public baths that had been so important in Muslim and Jewish culture.

Despite the efforts of the converts to follow Spanish law, religion, and custom, the royal authorities never trusted them and never gained their loyalty. The *moriscos* withdrew into the remotest parts of the Alpujarras Mountains, seeking to be left in peace, but there was no relief from Spanish persecution. When the *moriscos* revolted in 1568, after nearly a century of steady persecution, the Spanish government defeated them thoroughly and then exiled all *moriscos* from Granada to other provinces of Spain. They opened the lands of *moriscos* to colonists from the north much the way that they opened Indian lands for such colonization in the Americas. In 1609 the Spanish monarchy finally exiled all *moriscos* from all parts of Spain. Some 300,000 citizens of the nation fled. Some made their way to America or to distant Spanish colonies, but many fled to Al Maghrib, as the Arabs called northwestern Africa, or to the protection of the Turks and their flourishing Muslim empire in the eastern Mediterranean.

The effects of the Jewish and Arab flight from Spain still reverberate through the Mediterranean and Middle East. Thousands of Jews in Turkey still speak a form of Spanish, called Ladino, as their mother tongue. In a certain sense, the Arabs never fully surrendered the glory of Muslim Spain. In recent years many

Lebanese Arabs have settled along the Mediterranean coast, which reminds them of their own homeland before it became so war-ravaged. Each summer, thousands of wealthy Arabs flee the oppressive heat of the oil-rich Persian gulf sheikdoms and move to the Mediterranean coast of Spain, where they have whole Arab resort communities, but the Arabs come to Spain very much as tourists, vacationers, and temporary residents, not as citizens.

The fall of Boabdil and Granada marked the end of an era, not just the end of Moorish civilization in Spain, but of the old-style empires and colonialism as practiced in the Mediterranean world since before the time of Alexander the Great. Ferdinand and Isabella marked the beginning of a new kind of nation and a new kind of colonial empire.

In conquering Granada, the two monarchs created their new country of Spain. While still at Granada, the monarchs also sent Christopher Columbus on his voyage of conquest across the ocean. The Spanish went from a virtually tribal people to an imperial nation within the lifetimes of Isabella and Ferdinand.

The bitterest influences of the *Reconquista* probably are those on the Spaniards themselves, for they have had to endure a terrible history of racism, persecution, and intolerance within their own society and sanctioned by their clerical and secular powers. The rulers of Spain became obsessed with stamping out all effects of the Jews and Muslims. Under a sequence of chauvinistic and bigoted leaders, the government and church imposed rigid and narrow restrictions on religion and cultural life.

Spanish families lived under a fear of finding some drop of Semitic blood in their ancestry. For them, *sangre pura*, pure blood, became a national obsession. No parents wanted their son or daughter to marry anyone with the slightest suspicion of having Jewish or Muslim ancestry. The Spanish word for "aristocrat" became *hidalgo*, derived from the simple phrase "son of someone," meaning someone with pure European blood, untainted by Semitic, African, or American Indian strains. Through the years after the eradication of Muslims and Jews from Spanish society, the focus shifted gradually from religion to blood, ancestry, or family heritage. In a society in which everyone practiced Roman Catholicism and thus at least appeared to be Christian, the mere taint of non-Christian blood was enough to ruin careers, marriages, and all prospects of advancement in society.

Ferdinand and Isabella conquered Spain by force of arms, but they made it into a new nation in a cultural war that depended in part on arms and force, but also on a new technology that allowed them to standardize their language and culture. The year 1492 witnessed not only Ferdinand and Isabella's conquest of Granada and Columbus's voyage to America, but also the publication of the first Latin-Spanish dictionary and the first book of Castilian grammar, when the Spanish humanist Elio Antonio de Nebrija published *Dictionarium Latino Hispanicum et Hispano Latinum* and *Gramatica sobre la Lengua Castellana;* the publication of these twin volumes marks the birth of the modern Spanish language, as clearly distinct from Latin. The radical new technology of the printing press gave the rulers of Spain a far mightier tool than they ever had in the armor and swords of Isabella and Ferdinand. With the conquest of Granada and the publication of these two books, the modern nation of Spain and the modern Spanish language appeared simultaneously on the world scene.

Just as the spread of writing and the use of cheap papyrus in the Hellenistic centuries helped to lay the foundations for a modern global culture, the development of printing and publishing made possible the new national consciousness and promoted the rise of modern nation-states.

Communication technology has always operated at two levels. By increasing people's knowledge of and access to other people, it also increases ethnic and national identity by making people more conscious of the differences between themselves and their neighbors. This occurred most clearly with the invention of the printing press and movable type by Johann Gutenberg around the year 1440 in Mainz, Germany.

Gutenberg did not invent any one thing so much as he brought many things together in a system that worked to produce books more quickly and cheaply than ever before. In China, printers had long used xylography, the process of carving a wooden panel in reverse, inking it, and making an impression on paper. They began using movable characters in their presses around the middle of the eleventh century, when Pi Cheng made characters from pottery and attached them to a metal form with wax. Later they tried tin and wooden type, and finally various metal alloys. It is not yet known how or even if Gutenberg or someone else in Europe learned of this, or if they reinvented the process independently of the Chinese. It is usually assumed that Gutenberg utilized the type developed by Peter Schoeffer, who used an alloy of lead, tin, and antimony.

In the West, the screw press, which was used to press grapes, had also been used to print money and textile patterns long before Gutenberg's time. The Europeans also used the screw press to press paper. The making of paper also came from China. Ts'ai Lun supposedly invented it from tree bark around A.D. 100, but papermaking probably predates that time by several centuries. By 590 the Chinese had enough paper to use it in their toilets. Papermaking gradually spread via the Mongolians, Persians, and Arabs to Spain, where the first paper mills went into operation in 1276.

The mechanization of writing required many technological and social innovations. The production of paper alone required tremendous amounts of water, but once all the technology was in place, printing reduced the cost of books greatly. When relations broke down between Egypt and Europe after the Arab conquest, the papyrus trade died, and the Europeans had to write on much more expensive substances, such as parchment. A 150-page manuscript written on parchment required the skins of a dozen sheep and weeks of labor, compared with the mere 150 sheets of paper and a few hours of labor used to make the same book by printing press.

Rarely has the world been so ready for an innovation such as the printing press. After Gutenberg, publishers opened their presses in one European city after another: Paris and Venice in 1470, Naples in 1471, Lyon and Louvain in 1473, Cracow in 1474, and Poitiers in 1479. By 1480, presses operated in 110 towns and cities in Europe, and by 1500 they were operating in 236 communities, and they had printed a combined total of some 20 million books (Braudel vol. 1, 1979, 400). By 1557 the first press was at work in Goa, Portuguese India. In 1589 the first European-style press went into operation in China at the Portuguese colony of Macao, and in 1590 the first press was imported into Japan through Nagasaki.

Gutenberg printed the Bible and other books in Latin, the language of the educated class of his time. It probably appeared to any educated person of that time that Gutenberg's invention would help spread the Latin language and increase communication and homogeneity among the people of Europe. For a brief moment this appeared to be true, as the humanists flourished and traded Latin books and treatises with one another. Thanks to publishers such as Aldus Manutius (1449–1515), who operated the Aldine Press in Venice, learning in Latin and even Greek increased dramatically. Over twenty years the Aldine Press published the complete works of Aristophanes, Aristotle, Demosthenes, Herodotus, Plato, Sophocles, and Xenophon in Greek, and Manutius and his son, Paulus Manutius (1547–1597), published editions of the writings of Cicero, Vergil, and other Latin texts. They became so successful as printers that Pope Sixtus V called Paulus to Rome in 1588 to take over the beginnings of the Vatican press.

Despite this initial spurt of classical learning, there were only so many Greek and Latin masterpieces to print, and relatively few writers actually had the ability to write new materials fluently in either of the languages. The printing press revived Latin, but it was the last gasp of a dying language. The publishing industry needed vast amounts of new materials to pay for their presses, and when they could not find enough Latin texts, they began printing in the vernacular, the language of the common people. The printing press allowed the modern languages of French, German, Spanish, Russian, and Italian to come into being in a standardized format. Later it did the same for Finnish, Danish, Hungarian, and the languages of other, smaller countries. Even the Aldine Press contributed to the rise of national literatures by publishing Dante and poets such as the Florence poet Pliziano, writing in the vernacular that became Italian.

Martin Luther laid the foundations for High German when he translated the Bible into German and published it in 1521. Luther translated the Bible, not from Latin but from the original Hebrew and Greek texts, which had recently become available in printed form. For the Greek of the New Testament, Luther relied on Erasmus's edition. For most of the Old Testament he relied on the Hebrew texts published by Jewish scholars in Soncino and Brescia, Italy, and an edition of the Psalms published in Basel by the scholar and printer Froben. Even though the Bavarians and the Swiss spoke differently from people in Hannover or Prussia, with the appearance of the Bible in a standardized German form, all of them after Martin Luther read and wrote the same form of German.

Printing not only gave each country its own language, but promoted a proliferation of different styles of printing for the various countries. Gutenberg printed his first books in the heavy

Gothic print that became standard for Luther's Bible and then everywhere that the German language was used. Not until the founding of the modern German government after World War II did the Germans switch from their nationalist print to the style of letters now commonly used throughout Western Europe and the English-speaking world.

The Aldine Press used a much more cursive and slightly slanted form of printing that resembled handwriting. This typeface became known as *Aldine*, after the publishing house, and eventually as *italic*, just like the new vernacular of Italian that they printed.

The French under Louis XIV developed a new style. They did not like the slanted and curled italic form or the thick and extremely ornate Gothic of the Germans. Abbe Jaugeon of the French Academy of Sciences lead the development of a new alphabet of letters of nearly equal size, produced on a grid composed of sixty-four tiny squares, executed by the engraver Philippe Grandjean. With modifications over the centuries, this became the model for modern print.

Europe was once home to thousands of languages or dialects, but the steady movement of civilization has consistently reduced their number. The Celtic languages that once covered large parts of the European continent have now been virtually eliminated. The standardization of languages created new linguistic minorities such as the Basques of Spain and France, the Cornish and Welsh speakers of Britain, speakers of Breton or Alsatian German in France, or Yiddish throughout Eastern Europe. People who spoke Prussian, Frankish, or Bavarian had to understand German to function in their own lands.

Almost from the beginning, the printing press began to erode the power of the Catholic Church, the most wide-reaching institution in Europe. The printing of Bibles in different languages allowed people to interpret the scriptures for themselves, so long as they could read their own language. The Council of Trent, which met from 1545 to 1564 to shore up the Catholic Church against the spreading Protestant Reformation, tried unsuccessfully to control Bible translations. The Church then introduced censorship by publishing its Index, a list of books that Catholics were forbidden to read.

In 1536 the authorities of the Holy Roman Emperor arrested and then burned at the stake the Englishman William Tyndale, for the great crime of translating the New Testament into English and for his general agreement with the newly emerging Protestant theologians on important issues of doctrine. In its quest to fight the new learning, the Church burned at the stake the printer and philologist Etienne Dolet in Paris on August 3, 1546. He had published the works of Erasmus, François Rabelais, and Clement Marot, and the Church accused him of heresy. This act effectively cut off the Catholic world as the new center for communication and knowledge, as printing of new materials now took place almost exclusively in the north, particularly in Holland.

For a scholar of that era educated in the classical manner, it must have appeared that the world was coming apart, or at least that its social institutions were collapsing with dizzying speed. Educated Europeans were abandoning the classical language of Latin and writing instead in dozens of other languages. Now, instead of talking to all educated people, writers were communicating only with people who were literate in their own languages. The Church had splintered into several factions centered around languages. The Lutherans clustered around German, the Anglicans had their own Bible in English, and the people who stayed loyal to the Roman Church were primarily those who spoke French, Italian, Spanish, and Portuguese, languages all descended from Latin. Education and literacy increased, but the power of the Church and the university over education declined as people became able to read books for themselves and see them richly illustrated with engravings of everything from classical characters and contemporary personalities to human anatomy and diagrams of the planets and stars.

The foundation for the national culture rested primarily on a uniform national language that could be written and spoken the same way in all parts of the nation. Castilian became the Spanish language that supplanted local Andalusian, Galacian, and Catalonian dialects in official circles. The French court and later republican governments imposed Parisian French on all provinces. People in all countries faced similar pressures to conform to new national standards. Europe coalesced into a few major reading audiences focused on a few standardized dialects of the many dialects spoken in each country: London's English, Castilian Spanish, Parisian French, and High German.

Along the borders between the large language areas, small buffer states arose almost as no-man's-lands. Some of these small nations have their own languages, such as Dutch or Luxembourgish; others have no language of their own but share the languages of their neighbors, as in Belgium and Switzerland.

The nation-state evolved slowly in Western Europe, as a particular kind of political entity based on a people who shared a common language, a common religion, and a common general culture. It took the English, the French, and the Spaniards centuries to develop their individual national cultures, and the national culture often came at the price of great violence and repression. The central governments in London, Paris, and Madrid had to fight hard against regionalism and minority languages and religious groups to forge the identities of their people as English, French, and Spanish. It took centuries of interaction and frequent warfare for the Celtic, Saxon, and Angle tribes to form the English, just as the Picts and Celts merged to form the Scottish, and the English and the Scots in time became part of an even greater nation, Britain. Despite all of the pressure to assimilate, minorities such as Basques, Jews, and Gypsies persisted in their apartness on through the twentieth century.

The modern names of the Western Europeans often derived from a single tribe—Franks, Angles, and Germanen—but not necessarily from the dominant tribe. England's name came from the Angles, who came over from Germany, and their common designation as Anglo-Saxon derived from two German nations. Great Britain, another name for the area, came from Brittany, a province in France. France derived its name from the Franks, a German tribe whose name is still preserved in Germany in the city of Frankfurt and in Franconia, the northern part of Bavaria. English speakers applied the name of the Germanen to the country of Germany, or sometimes they used the name *Teutons*, derived from yet another tribe of the area. The speakers of Romance languages, however, called it Allemania, after the Allemanen tribe. The Germans called themselves *Deutsch* after yet another of their tribes. For English speakers, *Deutsch* became *Dutch* and was applied to the people of the Netherlands.

In 1475, William Caxton began operation of the first press in English, and he published in the newly developed English language with titles such as *The Recuyell of the Histories of Troye* and

The Dictes or Sayinges of the Philosophers. During the early years of printing, the English language still used different words and odd spellings, but gradually it became standardized with the publication of the King James version of the Bible, the Anglican Book of Common Prayer, and the large volume of new literary work, particularly that of William Shakespeare.

Using Shakespeare's printed editions of his plays, acting troupes around the country could recite the words exactly as Shakespeare had written them and not as the actors happened to remember them. The actors no longer needed to rely on the small repertoire of plays that they could carry around in their own heads. Also, with printed editions of his work, people no longer had to wait for a performance on stage, but could read Shakespeare in the privacy and leisure of their own homes, lounging by the fire or in a library, or sitting on a park bench by the pond.

By the time of Shakespeare, there was a real flowering, not only of printing and literature, but of a new and vibrant nationalism as well. A people who read the same works share a common language and culture, even if they are sometimes divided by religion. We can see in Shakespeare's time that the audience no longer thought of themselves as merely Christians or as subjects to a particular lord; now they had a new identity. They were *English*. Even though Shakespeare wrote about people as varied as Hamlet from Denmark, Cleopatra from Egypt, and Caesar from Rome, he wrote from a newly emerging English consciousness of history. This new consciousness is most apparent in his series of plays on English history. The most famous of Shakespeare's nationalistic monologues appeared in 1595, spoken by the character John of Gaunt in *Richard II*, Act II, scene i.

This royal throne of kings, this sceptered isle,
This earth of majesty, this seat of Mars,
This other Eden, demi-Paradise,
This fortress built by nature for herself
Against infection and the land of war,
This happy breed of men, this little world,
This precious stone set in the silver sea,
Which serves it in the office of a wall
Or as a moat defensive to a house
Against the envy of less happier lands—

This blessed plot, this earth, this realm, this
England . . .

Extreme nationalist sentiments such as these seem far removed
from a century earlier, when Sir Thomas More wrote his *Utopia*
in the older learned language of Latin. In it he sketched the
romantic story of an ideal world. Even though More's writings
reflected political issues in his own country and time, the setting
for his book was not meant to be England or any other particular
place; the title itself meant *Nowhere* in Greek. More wrote for a
small yet widely dispersed audience of educated people scattered
wherever men had a higher education, but Shakespeare was
clearly writing for an English audience that did not even need
to be educated in order to appreciate his works, which they could
watch on the stage, and which they understood with great delight
and emotion.

Printing presses added more than just words to national consciousness; they gave new life to the engraver's art. Books came
accompanied by engraved pictures that could also be produced
separately as items of interest in their own right. Engravers such
as the master Albrecht Dürer of Nürnberg made pictures of the
cities, towns, villages, and countryside around them. They made
people more aware of their own country, particularly in the numerous pictures printed of the monarch. As long as pictures had
to be made by hand, only the richest aristocrats might have a
portrait of the king or queen, but with the spread of printing,
engravings became far more common, along with paintings of
nationalist symbols, such as the monarch's coat of arms.

Presses also produced maps and atlases in great quantities.
These gave people not only a better sense of the world, but
also more information about the area immediately around them,
because the cartographers surrounded their maps with pictures
of the places and people marked on the map. Most of the early
world maps, like many still made today, place the country where
the map was printed as the center of the world, fostering a sense
of increased national importance for that country.

Printed illustrations helped to make books come alive, but after
the development of the printing press, the painted and sculpted
image declined greatly in importance, particularly in Northern
Europe. The printing press made the *word* much more important.
Illiterate peasants needed simple pictures in their churches to tell

them simple stories, but a literate people could read the words themselves. When people could read what they thought was the true word of God, they did not need to see paintings of angels performing miracles. The Protestant churches stripped their buildings down to basics, without statues, crucifixes, or elaborate stained-glass windows. The new ministers and their assistants wore simple black rather than the richly embroidered vestments and ornate capes and hats that had characterized medieval Christianity. The church became a place to hear, speak, sing, and contemplate the word, but not to *see*. Nowhere did this emphasis on the spoken word become more evident than in African-American Protestantism, where simple churches with only minimal decoration produced a tremendous emphasis on gospel singing and on sermons.

Parishioners in the church could now hear new forms of music and singing, thanks to the printing of music and of hymns. Martin Luther himself wrote some of these, including "Ein' Feste Burg," which became popular in English as "A Mighty Fortress Is Our God." Printing and the development of a new musical instrument, the church organ, led to a whole new development of music, culminating in the fugues of Johann Sebastian Bach in the seventeenth century.

In their religious zeal and bigotry, Ferdinand and Isabella seem very much like medieval characters, but viewed from another perspective they seem quite modern. Unlike rulers before them, who had been willing to rule over many different nationalities speaking different languages, wearing different clothes, and practicing different cultures, Ferdinand and Isabella installed a new homogeneity that was very much a precursor of the totalitarian movements of the twentieth century. They equated nation, language, race, and religion. To be one of their subjects, one had to speak Spanish and be of European ancestry and Roman Catholic faith. Anyone who deviated from one of these requirements could not be a true Spaniard. Ferdinand and Isabella imposed on their subjects a rigid system that allowed little room for cultural deviation from the standard, orthodox culture they controlled.

The modern ideology of Ferdinand and Isabella could not have been more different from the classical ideology of someone like Alexander the Great, who founded his empire based on the principles of diversity and mixture. Whereas Alexander wanted people of many languages and religions to live and intermarry in his empire, Ferdinand and Isabella outlawed those very same things. Whereas Alexander sought to create a universalist culture with room for all the people of the world, Ferdinand and Isabella sought to create a nationalist culture with which they could impose uniformity on the large part of the world that they controlled.

The cultural uniformity of Ferdinand and Isabella set a standard for the totalitarian ideologies that followed in the coming generations, from the regime of Cromwell and the Puritans in Britain of the seventeenth century on through Italian fascism, German Nazism, and Soviet communism in the twentieth century. It is hard to imagine two governments more different in their approaches to cultural issues than the empires of Alexander and of Ferdinand and Isabella. In this regard, Ferdinand and Isabella may be seen as opening the modern nationalist era. Over the past five centuries, their nationalist ideology of cultural uniformity has reigned among the nations of the West and slowly spread to the other peoples of the world.

11

The Silver Ship Across the Pacific

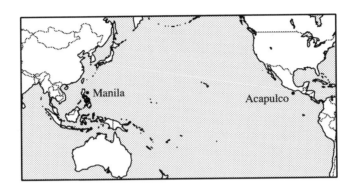

They that go down to the sea in ships,
that do business in great waters.

—PSALMS 107:23

Sailing north from Panama and up the Pacific coast of Central America, one sees few towns. The major cities stand well back from the ocean, in the higher and cooler mountains. The steamy tropical ports tend to be small, primitive, and no larger than necessary to ship supplies in and out of the small Central American republics, where most of the population lives at higher elevations in the interior. The coastal communities are small fishing villages and ports such as Costa Rica's Caldera, a name that means "boiler" and indicates why so few people live along this green coast.

Before dawn on the fourth day of sailing up this tranquil coast and across the usually choppy Bay of Tehuantepec, I saw a dim halo of lights gradually come into view just beyond the horizon. As we drifted closer, the lights became a long arc, almost like a crown of thousands of lights shimmering in the inky darkness of a moonless night. The arc of lights crowned the city of Acapulco, Mexico's greatest Pacific port.

As the sun rose and we docked at the wharf, the beauty of nocturnal Acapulco faded quickly with proximity and light. Like an aging movie star, Acapulco is best seen at night, preferably at a distance, in dim, artificial light, and not examined too closely in the full glare of the sun. An infectious tropical fungus seems to cover the varied forms of concrete used to build the city, and the cracks in the buildings leak a gray stain that discolors walls, awnings, and doorways. As the sun heats the pavement, the gutters and ditches exude a persistently rancid smell of too much decaying vegetable matter.

Vendors come out to hawk their blankets and ponchos woven from bright acrylic fibers, as well as to sell leather belts and jackets, cheap silver, alabaster chess sets, crude Mayan vases, copies of Aztec pottery figures, and a thousand types of dolls with "Acapulco, Mexico" embroidered on their clothing. Taxis and buses pull up to the docks of the tourist ships and the fronts of hotels to take on another load of passengers who will gawk in uncomfortable curiosity at the young men diving from the cliffs, at the surrounding homes of movie stars complete with their own heliports, and at the Princess Hotel, where the reclusive billionaire Howard Hughes spent his dying months.

Acapulco became a major resort in the second half of the twentieth century. After the fall of Cuba to Castro and the collapse of elegant hedonism in its casinos and beachfront hotels, Acapulco arose as a new resort for the well-heeled. In the 1950s, with the rise of air transportation, Acapulco became a favorite vacation spot for California's newly emerging wealthy class, but well before the end of the century it lost its sheen. The rich visitors kept moving their homes and hotels ever farther from the town. The hotels booked larger and larger tour groups of swinging American singles, German factory workers, and Swiss backpackers.

The story of Acapulco did not begin with tourism. Its place in the history of great cities has been eclipsed by other cities in Mexico, but it played a unique role in the development of the modern world system. As soon as he had conquered the Aztec capital of Tenochtitlán and well before he had secured the provinces of Mexico, Captain-General Hernando Cortez himself ordered the founding of Acapulco. The founding of the port took precedence over many seemingly much more important issues, but Cortez wanted the city for one primary reason, as a port for the express purpose of sending expeditions across the Pacific to Asia.

From the time Christopher Columbus first sailed away from

Spain, in August 1492, the Spanish monarchy wanted only one thing from their overseas explorers: a sea route for trade between Spain and the Orient. Columbus failed his commission to find that route to Asia. Despite the riches that were beginning to come into Spanish ports from the newly conquered lands of America, the Spanish authorities initially viewed America primarily as an impediment to reaching the lucrative markets of China, India, and the Spice Islands. Cortez arrived in America determined to be not merely the conqueror of Mexico but the one who might finally offer his monarch the passage to the Orient and the riches of that trade.

Other explorers and other nations rushed to be the first to establish a sea route westward from Europe to Asia. Before Cortez had consolidated his hold on Mexico, Ferdinand Megellan sailed around South America in 1521 and became the first European to cross the Pacific. When he arrived in what became the Philippine Islands, he found a lively trade conducted by the Muslims, who had already claimed a major foothold. Magellan died in the Philippines, but his ship sailed on toward the west and, upon returning to Europe, became the first ship to circumnavigate the world. Magellan had proved that a ship could sail to the west and cross the Pacific from America, but no one knew how to sail east across the Pacific, to make the *tornaviaje*, the return trip.

For almost half a century, sailors searched for a way to cross the Pacific from west to east. Without it, Spanish ships could not return from the Philippines without sailing through Dutch or Portuguese islands, where they were quickly captured and imprisoned. To sustain trade or even communications with its distant islands, the Spaniards needed a return route from the Philippines.

The first galleon to cross the Pacific from North America left the Mexican port of Zihuatanejo, near the current resort city of Ixtapa, on October 30, 1527, under the command of Captain Alvarado Saavedra y Seron. Before Spain had even conquered the Incas of Peru and nearly a century before the first English colonies would be established in North America, Saavedra y Seron sailed across the emptiness of nine thousand miles of ocean. The Hawaiian Islands lay near the middle of his trip, but he sailed south of them and, like the other European sailors for the next two centuries, never saw the islands.

The problem for Saavedra y Seron, like the captains who followed him, was that even though they had found the currents and winds to take them safely from Mexico to the Asian islands of the Philippines, they could not sail back across the Pacific. For another two decades, navigators searched for the eastward passage across the Pacific in vain. They went south to New Guinea and north through the Marianas and Caroline islands, but not until 1565 did the Basque sailor Miguel López de Legazpi discover that the route back to America lay in the far north, across the Pacific from Japan, following the Kuroshio Current. Legazpi found the west-east trade winds by sailing far to the north and picking up the Kuroshio Current and then the North Pacific Current, east of Japan. He laboriously sailed the North Pacific to California and then south to Acapulco, thus establishing the first permanent round-trip route across the Pacific.

The Acapulco-Manila connection, and the spur on down to Panama and then to Callao in Peru, became a mainline from which some early Spanish voyages of Pacific exploration began. At first the Spaniards explored the coast with repeated expeditions from Acapulco as far north as Oregon and south to Chile. Several of the earliest explorations of the Pacific followed a clockwise route from Peru to Asia and back to Acapulco.

In 1567, Alvaro de Mendaña de Neiro (1541–1595) left Peru to follow the route pioneered by Magellan in search of a great southern continent. Along the way he discovered the tiny islands of the modern nation Kiribati (Ellice Islands) and the Solomon Islands, whom he named for the biblical king because Mendaña thought that he had discovered the source of Solomon's fabulous mines of gold. He then sailed back to Peru via Mexico. In 1595, nearly a quarter of a century later, Mendaña set out on yet another long Pacific voyage, but on this one he took families of potential colonists including his own wife, Doña Isabel, and her three brothers.

In July 1595 the expedition came upon the beautiful Polynesian Islands, which Mendaña named Las Marquesas de Mendoza in honor of Antonio de Mendoza, who served as the first Viceroy of New Spain in 1535, and as Viceroy of Peru from 1551 to 1552. A skirmish broke out between the Spaniards and the Polynesians of the Marquesas Islands, and it resulted in the massacre of all the natives Mendaña's men could find. The Spaniards left some of the bodies on display as a warning to any other islanders. To underscore the message and to identify themselves, the Spaniards erected three wooden crosses at the site and carved the date of their bloody visit.

The voyagers fought fiercely with the natives they encountered, and they fought among themselves as hunger, disease, and the ravages of the torturous trip exacerbated tensions for everyone. The unpopular Doña Isabel hoarded food while the sailors began to die around her. Captain Mendaña died less than six months into the voyage. His wife buried him in February 1596, when the exhausted and decimated company reached Manila, where she promptly took a new husband.

The thirty-one-year-old pilot of Mendaña's ship, Pedro Fernandes de Queirós, a Spanish citizen originally from Portugal, took command and sailed the ships back across the Pacific to Mexico. Once back in Peru, Fernandes seemed to have inherited Mendaña's obsession to find the great continent in the South Pacific; so he finally got royal approval for a new voyage of exploration. He became one of the greatest and probably one of the most humane explorers to sail under the Spanish flag. He was an exact navigator, a deeply religious man who believed in fair treatment of all native peoples. His crew often resented him because of his attitude toward the natives, but just as much because of his prohibition on gambling and cardplaying on board his ships.

Fernandes set out in 1605 with three ships. After discovering a number of small Pacific islands, including the islands of modern Vanuatu (New Hebrides) in 1606. He mistook the largest of the volcanic islands for a part of the great southern continent. He named it Australia del Espíritu Santo, but today it is simply known as Espíritu Santo. He came close to the continent we know as Australia, but did not discover it. He sailed north to Guam and then across to Acapulco. Despite his pleas, the monarchy never let him explore the Pacific again, and he died in Panama in 1615.

One of Fernandes's pilots, Luis Vaez de Torres, did not return with him. Instead he sailed on to New Guinea, which he proved was an island and not part of the southern continent when he sailed south of it in 1606, through the ninety-mile strait that separates it from Australia's York Peninsula. Even though the strait still bears his name and he claimed to see "islands" to the south, it is unclear whether he actually saw the continent of Australia.

While the exploration continued in the South Pacific, the Spanish colony of Mexico used the harbor of Acapulco to colonize the Philippines, and thereby made the Philippines the colony of a colony. In 1565 the viceroy of Mexico sent Miguel López de Legazpi to be the first governor of the Philippine Islands. After subduing the army of the local Muslim sultan, the new governor established his capital at Manila Bay on Luzon, the chief island of the Philippines. The name for the new city came from the native Tagalog language and indicated the place where the *nila* flowers grew.

Spain did not publicize its newfound route across the Pacific. The world did not learn of it until more than a decade later, in 1578, when the English pirate Sir Francis Drake raided the Pacific coast of South, Central, and North America and found an abundance of Chinese and other Asian trade goods that had been brought over on the Manila galleon. From that moment, the Manila galleon became the most sought-after ship in world history.

The vitality of the port can be seen quite easily in an old copper engraving of "Aquapolque," made in 1590 (Wolf 1982). The print shows a large harbor with a handful of colonial buildings and a fortress. The buildings look more like Dutch colonial buildings of the Caribbean than Spanish buildings of the Pacific, but they still convey the idea of a trading center. In the harbor, five newly arrived galleons lie anchored. Sailors row many small boats laden with boxes of merchandise to shore. Cannons from the fortress fire a welcoming volley, which is answered by a volley from the ships. On land, merchants are arriving with their mule trains to greet the arriving ships. Acapulco played a unique trading role because it served as a linchpin uniting North and South America with Asia.

The real story can still be seen today, in the middle of the bay, just where the tourist ships dock at the foot of an immense stone fortress called San Diego. A Spanish galleon sailed from here each year for 250 years, from 1565 until 1815. The Manila galleon left Acapulco each April and headed straight across the high seas of the Pacific, maintaining a consistent latitude of thirteen degrees north. Crossing to the south of the Hawaiian islands, the galleon did not see land until Manila, on the opposite shore of the great ocean. In October the ship left Manila, moving north by northeast and skirting Japan, of which the Spaniards were apparently still ignorant. The ship continued across the ocean, far to the north of Hawaii, until the crew sighted land somewhere along the California coast, which they then followed south back to Acapulco. The nearly twenty-thousand-mile round trip was the first regularly scheduled commerce across the Pacific Ocean.

Immediately after the appointment of the first Spanish governor of the Philippines, the Spaniards set about building the fortress of Santiago within strong city walls. Only Europeans were permitted to live inside these massive walls, called simply *intramuros* in Spanish; Filipinos, Chinese, and other Asians lived outside. Manila became a great international trading bazaar, but unlike other such centers in the world, it was the first truly global port because its markets united the commercial systems of the Europeans, Asians, and South Pacific islanders, as well as North and South Americans.

The Chinese merchants came from Xiamen (Amoy) and Ningbo, and were called *Sangleys*, which came from *seng-li* and meant essentially "trader" in the Xiamen dialect. By the end of the sixteenth century so many Chinese lived in Manila that Spanish authorities created the Parian, a special market quarter for them.

Tensions among the varied cultural, racial, and economic groups operating in Manila repeatedly flared into violence. One of the bloodiest episodes occurred in 1603, when the Chinese attacked the Filipino community and lay siege to the Spaniards. In the ensuing fighting, half of the Spaniards in the fort lost their lives, and to frighten the surviving Spanish soldiers, the Chinese displayed severed Spanish heads on poles throughout Manila. The Spaniards, Japanese, and Filipinos managed to fight off the attacking Chinese and killed roughly 23,000 of them in retaliation for the uprising.

Despite such episodic eruptions of violence in Manila, the colony continued to grow and prosper. By the middle of the seventeenth century, the population of Manila climbed to 42,000, of which the Chinese constituted the largest segment.

Manila also became a major port for intra-Asian trade, as merchants traded Chinese goods for exports from India and other distant parts of Asia. Whereas the Manila galleon primarily traded American silver for Chinese porcelains, the India trade exchanged Chinese tea for Indian opium, a trade later monopolized by the British. Merchants brought cinnamon, nutmeg, and cloves from the Moluccas, which the Europeans called the Spice Islands, and which are now part of Indonesia. Japanese merchants brought amber, copper, bronze, and craftwork such as knives, swords, and intricately made furniture. Rubies, sapphires, ivory, ebony, and musk came from Siam (Thailand).

In addition to being a trading market, the Philippine Islands produced many natural products and crafts. Artisans in Manila turned out gold work and furniture that rivaled work from China and Japan. The Philippines also produced native crops such as the *abaca*, a relative of the banana tree, and from the leaf-stalk of this plant, the Filipinos made Manila hemp, which in turn was made into rope, cordage, or a thick, smooth paper, since known as manila paper.

The Manila galleon opened up new connections among the nations of the Pacific, and it became one of Japan's most important connections to Europe via America. Because the galleons had to sail north from Manila, they soon found the route to Japan, but in Japan they found themselves in vigorous competition with the Portuguese and the Dutch, who reached Japan by sailing around Africa and India. Both the Dutch and the Portuguese wanted desperately to open and monopolize the Japanese trade for themselves, as they had already done in India and the Spice Islands of Indonesia. Japan wavered between opening its borders and sealing them completely.

In 1610, Japan sent its first mission across the Pacific on the Manila galleon to Acapulco. The merchant Tanaka Shosuke sailed in hopes of opening direct Mexican-Japanese trade without the goods having to pass through Manila. His effort failed, but another mission soon followed, headed back on the Manila galleon for Acapulco. In 1613, Hasekura Tsunenaga of Sendai province left on a seven-year trip to Acapulco and on to Mexico City, Madrid, and finally Rome. By the time the envoy returned in 1620, his homeland showed no interest in his long journey because the country had once again turned its back on the outside world. Ieyasu, the founder of the Tokugawa shogunate, had outlawed Christianity and was leading Japan back into an isolationist era.

*   *   *

The tenuous thread of contact that began in 1565 with the
first round trip of the Manila galleon quickly expanded into a
network of connections knitting together the ports of all the
continents of the world and crisscrossing all the oceans, eventually including even the treacherously difficult and unpredictable
Arctic Ocean.

During the same centuries when a fervent and uniform nationalism took hold and grew in the political spheres of the European
powers, a new kind of economic internationalism repeatedly challenged and broke the bonds imposed on it. The trade network
knitted ever tighter bonds over ever larger stretches of the earth's
surface. The rise of political nationalism, occurring at the same
time as the rise of economic internationalism, created a lasting
tension between economics and politics that has continued to
plague modern society.

The trans-Pacific voyage of the Mexican galleon to Manila
each year was the longest and probably the most dangerous voyage of any ship in the world. It covered the longest distance on
the high seas without sight of land of any other route. Particularly the return voyage, which sailed far to the north in order to
catch the North Pacific Current, passed through treacherous waters plagued by typhoons, Japanese pirates, and the constant
threats of scurvy and beriberi.

The Manila galleon put the cities of Spain in direct and continued contact with the cities of China. By today's standards, the
two years that it took to make a round trip from Cádiz to
Canton seems long, but compared with the years that it took
Marco Polo to make a similar trip by land, the Manila galleon
made a new and fast connection. The sea route proved not only
much faster and more secure than the land route, but it was
considerably cheaper because the goods had to pass through
fewer hands. From the time the goods were loaded onto the ship
in Manila until they were unloaded in Spain, they were under a
single authority, that of the king of Spain, who ruled not only
Spain but Mexico, Central America, South America, and the
Philippines.

In the Spanish imperial administration, the Philippines constituted a part of New Spain (Mexico), which lay much closer to
the islands than did the mother country. The Spaniards even
called the Filipinos *indios,* or Indians, the same name they used

for the Mexicans and other Native Americans. A letter from the Spanish court left Madrid by land, sailed from Seville in the spring, and crossed the Atlantic and Caribbean by ship, landed at Veracruz on Mexico's eastern shore two months after leaving Europe, was transported by hand or horse across the mountains to Mexico City, then down the mountains to Acapulco, to wait for the Manila galleon in April.

Even though Spain and the Philippines lay on opposite sides of the same Eurasian landmass, the commercial and bureaucratic lines connecting them ran the other way around the world and across the Pacific. Madrid and Canton sat on opposite sides of Eurasia, separated by 6,500 miles of land, but connections between the two went in the opposite direction from Madrid, 5,600 miles across the Atlantic, a few hundred miles overland, and then 9,000 miles by water to Manila, and then another 775 miles to Canton, a total distance from Madrid to Canton of 16,000 miles, two-thirds of the way around the earth. Acapulco served as the key link between the two distant lands. A letter from the king took more than a year to travel to Manila via Acapulco, and the response to the letter might take even longer traveling eastward from the Philippines back to Spain. For a letter to go and return even within a decade must have seemed momentous to the people of that era because the Manila galleon made communication around the world quicker than it had ever been.

The fast new sea routes across the world meant the nomadic tribes who traded across Eurasia and the Middle East no longer played a significant role in global commerce. Once necessary, albeit slow and expensive, the cheaper, faster sea routes made them obsolete. Their crossroads of civilizations became the back roads, and often these atrophied into the niggling routes for a few local products such as metal pots, firearms, tea, and sugar, for which they sold their laboriously woven and knotted rugs and other handicrafts, and sometimes even their own children. To this day, the tribal merchants of central Asia have never recovered from this financial setback of the Manila galleon, and they have never again flourished as they did when they controlled the trade. They descended from being the conquerors and the arbiters of power to being the pawns of China, Russia, Persia, Turkey, and other invading armies.

The fleet across the much more heavily traveled Atlantic sea lanes from Spain numbered from eighty to a hundred ships each year. By contrast, the Manila galleon usually crossed the Pacific alone. The distance of nine thousand miles in each direction was far too great to risk more than one ship at a time. Accompanying ships would have required more water, food, and supplies than could be furnished, and even then they were little protection from a shipload of determined Chinese, Dutch, or Philippine pirates.

Most of the goods on the Manila galleon were not destined for Mexico or other parts of the Americas; they continued on across Mexico to Spain and other parts of Europe. Mexico was the stopping-off station for European-Asian trade, but relatively little of the goods or wealth of either continent stayed in America; instead, the American colonies had to work hard to produce inordinate amounts of gold, silver, and other precious materials for their European overlords.

In some years the Mexican merchants sent more silver across the Pacific to Asia than across the Atlantic to Spain. Scholars estimate that between one-third and one-half of the silver mined in America ended up in China (Braudel vol. 2, 1982, 198). The total amount of silver shipped over in a little more than two hundred years of commerce was approximately five thousand tons (Wolf 1982, 154). The silver added greatly to the wealth of the late Ming and the Qing dynasties, but it also made China a more visible target for colonial powers wanting to wrest that silver away from the Chinese.

The exact amount of the wealth that flowed from America to Europe and Asia will never be known. It included the accumulated wealth of virtually all the American Indian civilizations—all the gold, jade, and silver accumulated by the Aztecs, the Mayas, the Toltecs, and other now-forgotten people who preceded them. It included the great wealth of the Chibcha of Colombia as well as the Incas of Peru and Bolivia and all the pre-Incan civilizations that flourished there. Later it included the rich furs of North America, the pitch tar and lumber of the greatest forests of the world, American Indian cotton and dyes, and the world's widest assortment of plants, ranging from corn, potatoes, and beans to pumpkins, squash, and chocolate.

The transoceanic commerce enriched the Europeans above all others and the Asians secondarily. It cost native America and

Africa a bitter price in property and lives, in return for which they received only a few crumbs from the lucrative trade that sucked out the interiors of their homes and their cultures.

So much Mexican silver crossed the Pacific in the galleons that the American coins minted in Mexico, Bolivia, and Peru became the standard currency throughout coastal China and the offshore islands. These coins, which had already become the general currency of North America and the Caribbean, quickly became that of the Pacific as well. "Dollars" of various weights and values eventually became the unit of currency for Pacific countries including Australia, Hong Kong, Fiji, Singapore, the Solomon Islands, and New Zealand, as well as for the North Pacific nations of the United States and Canada.

While the Spanish trade empire stretched across America and the Pacific to Asia, the Portuguese extended the long tentacles of their commerce around the African coast and north to India, Indonesia, and China. Even before Columbus crossed the Atlantic in a Spanish expedition bound for Asia, the Portuguese had set out to reach it by sailing south and around Africa. Bartolomeu Dias rounded the Cape of Good Hope in 1488, and ten years later Vasco da Gama rounded the cape and reached India in 1498. The Portuguese established a series of trading centers and forts along both African coasts and across India and Indonesia, terminating in the Portuguese colony of Macao, China, established in 1557 at the mouth of the Canton River. The Lisbon-Macao route served much the same place in Portuguese commerce that the Madrid-Manila route served for Spain.

The slender thread of trade created by the Manila galleon and by the Portuguese and then Dutch ships became the first completely global trade network. These were the last and longest parts of a journey around the world from east to west and from west to east. With the annual run of the Manila galleon, humans had spanned the widest ocean on earth, and with the ships around Africa, humans had created ties running in both directions around the world. Since the inauguration of these routes, we have intensified these ties, added more ships, built more highways, and added railway and finally airplane links, but basically the world has merely been elaborating on this accomplishment.

The unification of the world into a single economic system, a truly world economy of global dimensions, took roughly eight thousand years from the settlement of the first agricultural villages until the completion of the first trans-Pacific route from Acapulco to Manila. The process required three major sets of technological and social breakthroughs: the unification of Asia and Europe via the horse, the connection of sub-Saharan Africa with the Mediterranean by means of the camel, and the voyages connecting Europe and Asia with America across the high seas of the Atlantic and the Pacific. Each of these three breakthroughs required a host of secondary technological innovations, such as the invention of stirrups, bridles, and saddles to maximize the energy of the horse; the digging of wells to provide water while crossing the Sahara; the use of paper to maintain contact over thousands of miles across Eurasia; and the mastery of celestial and compass navigation to cross the oceans.

The Manila galleon's annual crossing of the Pacific marked a major triumph in human technology and organization. With the inauguration of this route, humans had finally conquered the high seas and thereby moved from mere exploration to sustained commerce and communication. In the truest sense, the modern age began with those voyages. From the year of the Manila galleon's first round-trip crossing of the Pacific, the world had become a much smaller place; the commercial ties, stretched so thinly across the two great oceans, grew into religious, cultural, and political ties in the coming centuries. The modern global order had begun, and only a matter of time and effort remained to bring every country, island, nation, village, tribe, and band into that unified system.

Today, Acapulco is still Mexico's major Pacific port. Ships registered in Panama and Liberia bring in multimillion-dollar cargoes of Japanese cars and machines, Korean textiles and televisions, and Chinese toys and crafts. The modern ships, however, are bringing goods for Mexico and not for shipment on to Europe. That cargo now heads south, through the Panama Canal, and on across the Atlantic by an all-water route, without the need to pass near Mexico.

Acapulco has evolved from its former status as a major link in creating the modern world economic system to that of a bit player in world tourism. The ships that sail in and out of Acapulco harbor today are as likely to be cruise ships running the Mexican Riviera route as they are to be cargo ships from Asia. The young Filipino men and women who wear starched white uniforms and serve drinks on the promenade deck or by the pool serve as a faint reminder of the role that the Philippines and Mexico once played in world trade. The children and old women hawking tawdry souvenirs along the beach of Acapulco represent an ever-fainter version of the merchants who traveled down each year from Mexico City to trade with the merchants from the Philippines, Peru, and Japan for some of the most exotic and costly merchandise in the world. The tawdry trinkets made of silver and sold in modern Acapulco do not hint at the billions of dollars in silver bars and coins that once sailed out of this harbor to change forever the economy of Asia.

The merchants and their families still come down from Mexico City each weekend and holiday season, but they come to escape work and commerce, not to expand it. They come to stay in the luxury hotels scattered among the palms, and to board the luxury boats that pay their courtesy calls on the aged city. Like many of the visitors, the city of Acapulco has retired from its active role as a major player on the international stage of commerce and has settled into an easier routine of fun in the sun, golf, swimming, boating, touring, fishing, drinking, shopping, dining, and even some occasional snorkeling.

12

Civilization and Its Environment

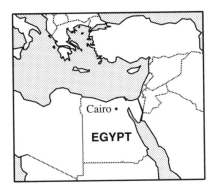

What man calls civilization always results in deserts.
—MARQUIS, "What the ants are saying"

Adel Hussein tramples a small mound of clay beneath the shade of a thatched roof over a shed cleverly but pathetically rigged from discarded gasoline cans and sewer pipes stuffed with mud. Adel is a scrawny, unshaven man in his early twenties, but with the yellow teeth and bent shoulders of a much older man. He wears a sleeveless undershirt and large, blowsy pants caked with mud and marred with dozens of rips and holes. Even though he is short, he must bend to avoid hitting his head on the roof of the shed as he rhythmically plunges one bare foot and then the other into a pile of oozing clay.

Adel lives and works in a place called Fustat, at the ancient heart of Cairo. Crowded together with him in the work shed, Adel's younger brother works a slab of clay with his hands on a board dusted with sand. Except for the dirt surrounding him, he might be a baker's apprentice kneading dough. The middle brother, Magda, sits in an open pit in the middle of the hut, where he turns a creaking wooden potter's wheel with his right foot. He works a symmetrical mound of clay that rises up from the wheel like an ancient Mesopotamian ziggurat, and with a deft motion of his hand he lifts off a small piece that resembles a two-inch candle holder or perhaps an egg cup. But this pottery is much too crude for such refined objects as eggs or candles.

Magda sculpts an object called a *kursi*, which is Arabic for "chair." The *kursi* is a small clay bowl that sits atop the large glass water pipes that men use to smoke strong Turkish tobacco in the cafés of Cairo. In every café, waiters scurry around in this alcohol-free environment with strong cups of overly sweet coffee and with a small *kursi* filled with tobacco and topped with three or four bits of live charcoal to keep the tobacco burning.

Working with his nimble fingers, Magda can produce seven *kursi*s in a minute. The pieces make no pretense of being finely crafted, but they are sturdy, cheap, and disposable. In addition to *kursi*s, he produces water jugs and flowerpots by the hundreds. He covers a slab of wood with rows of his mass-produced creations, and his brothers work together to load thousands of these items into a kiln about fifteen feet high and fired with sawdust and the crushed residue of sugarcane from which every drop of sweet juice has been squeezed.

The burning kiln belches forth a thick black smoke that hangs eternally in the air around the workshop. Next to the kiln, a man stands in a large brick pit filled with a thick, viscous brown mud. As the man's son lifts buckets of water and pours them into the pit, the father stands naked in the muddy water and laboriously slogs through it to make the clay necessary for the low-grade pottery of Adel and his two brothers.

The hut, kiln, and clay pits of Adel and his neighbors are surrounded by more huts, kilns, and clay pits exactly like them. In every direction one sees men marching in pits, kilns spewing out black smoke, and mud people darting back and forth from the pits to workshops, carrying the dripping clay.

No women enter this zone where the men work, but filthy children of both sexes dart around among the workers. The youngest boys wear dresses as a precaution against the evil eye, on the assumption that no one will look jealously at a small girl the way they might at a small boy. I can tell the girls from the boys only because some of the scrawny children have dirty, ragged pieces of string through their pierced ears—an optimistic practice arising from the hope that the girl will survive to adulthood and may one day be prosperous enough to wear earrings. The children help with the work, and their small bodies are quickly covered with mud. Some of them have deliberately dabbed the mud on their bodies and heads to reduce the itching from scabies and lice.

Goats wander among the children eating garbage, and small donkeys strain to pull carts that seem to be nearly buried beneath mounds of sawdust, pressed sugarcane stalks, pots, and garbage. Several of the huts have a large eye drawn on them and, underneath this ancient hieroglyph, the Arabic letter *ayn*, which begins the word for "eye." For untold thousands of years this eye has served to keep evil away from the household. The same symbol peers from the top of the pyramid on the reverse side of the Great Seal of the United States, which appears on every U.S. one-dollar bill.

Yet, even in this place, one hears the ritual and elegant exchange of beautiful Arabic greetings. As each person tries to outdo the greeting of the other, they escalate through a series of ornate compliments.

—Good morning.

—May your day be filled with light.

—May your day be filled with jasmine.

—May your day be filled with cream.

Such phrases seem out of place here, where nothing grows, where the smoke obscures the light of the sun, and few people could ever afford a bowl of cream.

Fustat is one of Cairo's many garbage dumps and salvage areas for recycling. Between the pottery huts, the garbage pickers return each day from their patrols through the streets of the city. Each part of the dump has its own specialty. The huts in one area seem nearly buried in mountains of rusted scrap metal and old cans. Another section contains shredded paper, newspapers, and mounds of packing material and torn cardboard boxes. Another rests atop a mound of broken glass, and yet another appears devoted to plastic. The garbage pickers and potters live amid this refuse, just behind the cemetery, where their richer neighbors have built huts among the marble and brick tombs of many generations of dead Cairenes.

As I wander among the bizarre mounds of trash and smoky kilns, I am constantly climbing up and down and out of pits and over embankments, and I have to watch each step carefully because what appears to be nothing more than a small pothole in the ground may turn out to be a vent into an underground living chamber, a storage room, or another empty pit. In this trash dump of a thousand years, there is no longer a ground level or any top. At one moment I am pushing my way through a narrow ditch, but at the next moment I realize I am walking across the weak roof of a mud hovel. The place has become a maze of aboveground and underground passages and chambers, with little differentiation of inside and outside. At times I can hardly tell whether I am walking through an alley or through a corridor into one of the workshops or huts. It hardly matters, for the space may fill both functions equally well.

Fustat was not always a dump. One thousand three hundred years ago, the conqueror 'Amr chose this spot just outside the walls of a Byzantine Roman fortress on the Nile as the place where he built the first Muslim city in Africa. For two centuries Fustat supplied the needs of 'Amr's fortress, and it acquired a reputation as the source of excellent glass and pottery. While it thrived, Fustat was one of the most modern cities in the world. 'Amr laid out the city with military precision on a grid. Fustat utilized an elaborate underground sewer and water system. In 1168, Fustat was destroyed in the war with the European crusaders. Fustat's ruler, Shawer, burned the city rather than allow it to fall into the hands of Amalric, the Christian king of Jerusalem, who had besieged Fustat. The next generation of rulers built the capital farther north along the Nile and named the new city Al Qahira, Arabic for "The Triumphant One," but better known to us as Cairo.

Adel, Magda, and their younger brother now live and work in the ruins of this once-powerful settlement. Fustat had been best known for its workshops, where craftsmen produced fine glassware, ceramics, and metal utensils that were traded throughout the Mediterranean. Ironically, Adel and Magda now continue the production of ceramics, but their products are only the cheapest of wares for the poorest of Cairo's people. Not only has the quality of their product declined, but they do not have the running water or the underground sewage system that their forebears had on the same spot a thousand years ago. Instead they now make their homes and workshops amid the steadily deteriorating ruins of this former civilization.

The choking air and the smoldering piles of rubble of Fustat contain the garbage of a thousand years of civilization. Garbage piled up here long before Egypt became a republic, before the British colonized it, before Muhammad Ali tried to modernize it, before Napoleon conquered it, before the Mamelukes arrived, and even before the Turks founded the Ottoman Empire and conquered Egypt. Almost like the hole in a doughnut, Fustat forms the hollow center of a sprawling metropolis. After Fustat declined, new cities rose around it, including the medieval city of Cairo's Muslim merchants, the massive Citadel and mosques of the Turkish Ottomans, the nineteenth-century city of Parisian boulevards, and the twentieth-century city of high-rise buildings and dense suburbs. Still vibrant and healthy, the new sections surrounded the old decayed center.

Thousands of people in Cairo, Nairobi, Calcutta, Lima, and similar cities around the world literally live on, from, and in garbage. They wear it, burn it, eat it, and use it to build their homes. Across the world, from Lagos to Manila, from Calcutta to Managua, garbage collecting became one of the fastest-growing occupations of the twentieth century. In the larger cities, such as Mexico City or Lima, whole communities of thousands of people not only spend their lives working the garbage, but they live in the garbage dumps in order to be close enough to grab the best of the refuse as soon as it arrives. The dumps for Mexico City have grown so large that in some areas they reach nearly two hundred feet in depth, as deep as a twenty-story building is tall.

Humans compete with dogs and vultures for the food. I learned from years of travel in poor countries that one could easily judge the prosperity of a town by the vultures at the garbage dumps; only prosperous communities had the luxury of throwing away enough food to sustain such scavengers. In the poorer communities, the garbage pickers killed the birds. The twentieth century may be known to future archaeologists as the Age of Garbage.

To fulfill their role as markets, manufacturers, administrators, builders, and conquerors, the urbanized centers of the world produce a tremendous amount of garbage, and they strip the resources from the surrounding area. People of the cities channel and redirect rivers to quench the urban thirst; they rip up large pieces of land to extract stone to make their homes, and metal to make their tools and machines. They chop down giant forests to make buildings, bridges, walls, and ships. They require ever more fuel to feed the fires for cooking, for heat, to smelt ore and execute other crafts. After only a few generations, this activ-

ity destroys the forests and denudes the land within several days'
journey in every direction from the city.

Cities always encourage intensive agriculture as close to them
as possible, in order to feed the large population. The exhausted
land exposes the tilled soil to rain and wind, which blow away
the fertile topsoil. The dust in the air even alters weather patterns, creating more unpredictability for the farmers. In ancient
Mexico City, farmers gradually filled in much of Lake Texcoco
by making *chinampas*, the so-called floating gardens. These highly
productive gardens had a constant source of rich soil and water
from the lake, and thus permitted constant harvests throughout
the year. When the Spaniards arrived, they completed the filling
in of most of the lake, and built the expanding Mexico City over
it. The building of the city over the gelatinous mud, without
bedrock for support, created a structurally vulnerable city that
shook violently and caused extensive damage in even a relatively
small earthquake.

In ancient Mesopotamia the urban appetite for agricultural
goods fostered extensive systems of irrigation, which steadily increased the salinity of the soil produced by inadequate drainage.
The more irrigation the farmers used, the more quickly the soil
became saline and the faster crop productivity declined. Just as
urban life exacted a heavy toll from the agricultural lands around
it, the need for animals encouraged overgrazing on the land already too poor for agriculture.

In ancient Egypt, irrigation and soil depletion posed less of a
problem than they did in Mesopotamia, because of the Nile's
annual flood. The flood flushed out the land and annually deposited tons of fertile soil washed down from the highlands of Ethiopia. The problems of Egyptian farming, however, may yet
duplicate those of Mesopotamia. The Aswan High Dam, built
by Soviet engineers between 1960 and 1971, stopped the annual
flooding. Without the annual flushing of the canals, ponds, and
streams around the Nile, malaria-bearing mosquitoes thrive, as
do the snails that carry bilharzia, which causes widespread blind-
ness among rural people.

The Egyptian farmers had to extend their irrigation systems
and add large amounts of artificial fertilizers to replace the rich
sediment that now deposits itself uselessly behind the Aswan dam
in Lake Nasser or washes out into the Mediterranean. Almost
immediately after the inauguration of the dam and the termina-

tion of the annual flood, salinization began. The salts not only accumulated in the fields but began wicking their way up the porous limestone monuments, such as the Sphinx, on the Giza plateau, and like some subterranean cancer, the creeping salts cause the stone edifices that have stood for millennia, through thousands of floods, to erode and crumble at the base. Within a decade, a thin line of deposited salts could be seen forming around the edge of Lake Aswan itself.

The effects of the Aswan dam are best seen underground, at the base of ancient monuments such as the fortress built by the Romans and confusingly called Babylon, even though it was a thousand miles from the ancient city of the same name. Today the massive south gate of Babylon fortress lies ten feet below ground level, and the Nile River, which used to flow past its ramparts, has retreated toward the west, leaving the fortress to the slowly accumulating sands that have gradually climbed up and covered the walls over the past millennium. To get to the former entry passage of the gate, I had to climb down beneath the Coptic church of the Virgin that was built atop the ruins of the Roman gate in the seventh century and thus acquired the Arabic name of al-Muallaqah, the suspended or hanging church. The small complex of buildings built around the old gate includes the spot where Mary and Joseph supposedly took refuge with the infant Jesus during the time of Herod's persecution and slaughter of the innocents in Israel. Just behind that spot is an ancient synagogue that is claimed, like dozens of other spots in Egypt, to be the place where the infant Moses was found by Pharaoh's daughter as he floated in the bulrushes.

I crossed a small yellow-brick courtyard of African palms and Mexican cacti surrounding the original Roman well and interspersed with diminutive Greco-Roman columns. On this particularly hot afternoon in the summer, the only activity in the courtyard came from a stately procession of Japanese ladies in flowered summer dresses and carrying brightly colored parasols for protection from the piercing sun.

From the courtyard I descended a narrow staircase that burrows down into the ancient entryway of the gate. The massive fortifications meant to stand sternly out on the plains now seem oddly out of place underground and beneath a church. The ruins look more like catacombs than the entry to an old fort. The distinctly Roman construction of alternating layers of red brick and white limestone appears clearly, even in the dim light of this netherworld. As my eyes become accustomed to the darkness, I slowly discern the finer craftsmanship of a series of columns that seem too ornate for such a military structure.

The shrill screeching of bats cuts through the dim light as I enter their private world, in a large, vaulted chamber that was once the main arch of the gate. Water has seeped up into the foundations and now varies from a few inches to several feet deep. Even though the Aswan dam now stops the summer flood of the Nile over its banks, the dam is powerless against the underground flood that still pushes upward in July and August, as it has done for thousands of years. The flood pushes up sewage along with the water.

Wherever light trickles into this chamber, a thick, green scum thrives on the sewage that floats atop the water, making it almost appear to be a lush green carpet. Only the floating drums and plastic bottles show that real water underlies this living carpet. Where the light fails, minute worms propel themselves through the water with a quick lashing motion of their bodies.

I traverse the ruins on a makeshift series of planks forming a bridge that sways and creaks with each step. Even though the arches rise more than fifteen feet above the water in some places, in other spots I have to crawl along the planks and squeeze between the stone foundation and the pool of sewage below.

On one side of the south gate are the ruins of an open court that still houses the water-soaked remains of a wooden mill that would have been turned by an ox, a donkey, or slaves. A brick oven over four feet in height fills another corner of the yard, and an olive or wine press occupies the opposite corner. The other side of the gateway is flanked by a much less domestic set of artifacts. In the base of a former tower I can still see the evidence that this was used as a dungeon. According to tradition, the Romans imprisoned Christians here during the most vigorous part of the persecutions under Diocletian.

'Amr and his descendants initiated a new type of conquest— total subjugation that included the complete destruction of the old culture and substitution by a new one. For the Muslims, everything that proceeded the Prophet Mohammed was the time of the *jahiliyya*—the era of sin and ignorance. Nothing from this era had value. The only valid knowledge was explained to them in the Qur'an. Their book told them the way to live in the world; it prescribed the path, or *sharia*.

The Arab invaders hacked the faces from statues and wall paintings and generally banned the arts of painting and sculpture. When they found the great statue of Ramses II in the Ramessium of Thebes, they could not hack it to pieces, since it was the largest statue in history. Instead they built great fires around it to heat the rock, then threw cold water on the statue, causing it to crack and break into gigantic chunks of broken granite. In utter contempt for Egypt's great monuments, they used them for building materials to make their new palaces and mosques in a completely new architectural style. The columns of the old churches and temples were used to make arcades and mihrabs for mosques, and can still be seen today, scattered throughout Cairo. The Arabs substituted more oriental styles for the Egyptian style as they introduced tall minarets and soaring *liwan*s or vaults from Samarra.

Even when they could not use the old monuments to make new buildings, the conquerors tried to destroy them simply because they were from the *jahiliyya*, the time of ignorance. In 832, Khalif Mamun excavated a tunnel deep into the pyramid of Khufu, searching for treasure. After using the granite and limestone blocks that faced the pyramids, the Muslims tried to destroy the monuments by disassembling them. Only those monuments that had been buried by nature or man in the drifting desert sand survived the destruction of the new conquering culture.

Even the bodies of the dead were not safe from the new civilization. The medieval Arab doctors claimed that they had found medicinal value in the mummies scattered throughout the desert cemeteries of Egypt: the ground-up bodies could be used as a medicine that helped to restore health and prolong life. The doctors and pharmacists began a lively trade in mummies, which people ate in the form of a powder. The Crusaders took the practice back with them to Europe, and thus began a long tradition of eating the dead of Egypt in the courts and cities of the Europeans.

Cities destroy. They consume the area around themselves, and if they cannot find new materials, they die. Historically, the destruction from urban areas has followed a pattern of destroying

or severely disrupting first the animals and plants of the surrounding area, then inevitably, the soil, the water, and finally
the air.

The whole discipline of archaeology arose from the study of
dead cities, large stone and adobe carcasses strewn across the
landscape of the world. Cities and centers of civilization such as
Babylon, Nineveh, Ur, Uruk, and Persepolis were long ago left in
ruins, and until nineteenth-century archaeologists and explorers
relocated them, they were often lost to human awareness. We
see in Mesopotamia, the oldest urbanized area of the world, the
greatest ruins. The oldest cities perished first. Babylon, which
was once one of the Seven Wonders of the Ancient World because of its luxurious Hanging Gardens, became a pile of dry
rubble.

Today Iraq, the modern successor to the states of Mesopotamia where Babylon once flourished, lives mostly from oil. Gone
are the great trees, the luxuriant fields, the large numbers of wild
animals, and the Hanging Gardens described in ancient documents. It is hard to imagine that this land could once have been
thought of as a virtual paradise.

After devastating the land of its origin, urban civilization
spread out from Mesopotamia to other parts of the world, but
wherever it went, it carried the extravagant habits of consumption
and destruction. The needs of the newly emerging civilizations
quickly destroyed the great cedars of Lebanon and denuded the
hills of Greece and Anatolia as well as the once-forested Valley
of Mexico. The civilized way of life consumed everything around
it—water, stone, metal, trees, plants, animals, and even the land
itself—leaving behind a decimated landscape. It took civilization
thousand of years to consume and destroy Mesopotamia before
moving into the Mediterranean and Europe.

In Europe the cultural pattern has continued much the same.
The great forests of Europe disappeared, along with the animals
who once lived there. Generations of humans have mined,
plowed, and stripped the land. The only salvation for European
society came in finding new resources in other places. The European discovery of America and the move into sub-Saharan Africa
gave the Europeans the opportunity to acquire new forests, new
minerals, and new lands to feed their large populations.

When European settlers arrived on the Atlantic coast of North
America, trees covered the entire coastal plain from Canada to

Florida. The Indians lived in small villages that they cleared out of the forest for their homes and crops. Within three hundred years the settlers had cleared the land first for farms and then for urban and suburban development. The strip of land around Montreal in the north, and running from Boston to Washington along the coast, became a virtually endless urban sprawl. The coastal plain became one of the most urbanized parts of North America, and the forest was reduced to a series of small parks regulated for recreational uses of the middle and upper classes.

Potosí, Bolivia, was one of the first cities built by the Europeans in America, and for several decades it was the largest city in America. It is now a decaying and decrepit place. The great silver mines have been closed, and the miners eke out a living from traces of tin left in the great Cerro Rico, which was once the world's greatest silver mine. The people today mine the tailings and residue of previous centuries, searching for traces of silver left behind from the earlier mining. The people of Potosí live from their past. They are remining what their grandparents and great-grandparents first mined over the last four centuries.

Potosí limps along today as a tragic example of what has happened to South America as a whole. One great boom after another has ripped through some part of the continent. After Pizarro seized the ransom of Atahualpa and looted the Inca empire, the conquistadors turned to the silver. When that ran out, there was a cattle boom in Argentina, a guano boom in Peru, the tin boom in Bolivia, a copper boom in Chile, the rubber boom of Brazil, the oil boom of Venezuela, the coffee boom of Colombia, and, more recently, the new cocaine boom throughout the Andes. Each boom left the population more devastated than had the preceding one. No one seemed to care about the future. No one planned for the orderly exploitation of South America's treasures so that future generations might find a way to live from them.

By the start of the twentieth century, civilization had run out of new lands to conquer and untapped continents to exploit. Only a few marginal swamps, jungles, polar ice caps, and deserts remained untouched, and the cost of massive exploitation of these areas seems higher than the potential rewards until new and cheaper forms of technology might be developed.

Rural and tribal people always paid a much higher price for the degradation of the environment than did city dwellers. So long as the city obtained its supplies, it mattered little to the urbanites from where they came. The process of environmental destruction had its first and most immediate impact on the hunting grounds, fishing waters, and grazing and agricultural lands of the people living outside the cities, but as communities such as Fustat show, the cities eventually pay a deadly price.

The threat of modern, civilized society became quite graphic for me one afternoon when I set out from Bandiagara, in Mali, on the way to Mopti with a pickup truck filled with twenty-seven passengers. Our legs were jammed into one another and went to sleep from excessive pressure. Babies cried and crawled over one person to another, occasionally causing an outcry, and one of them released a stream of urine or runny diarrhea. Even though the trip only took two and a half hours, it proved to be one of the most uncomfortable journey of my travels in Mali.

Less than a third the way from Bandiagara, we had to pull off the side of the road. I suspected that the truck had broken down, and I looked forward to the opportunity to escape from the stinking pressure of the small truck. But as I unfolded myself and stepped out from under the truck's canvas cover and into the late-evening light, I saw that the truck had not broken down but had been forced from the road by a swarm of motorcycles kicking up dust so thick that we all tried to wrap our faces in anything we could grab. These motorcycles were not the mopeds that often serve as taxis in the smaller towns; they were huge, monstrous machines that roared like some living animal on a rampage. The riders seemed as aggressive as their machines were loud. Although some of them had removed their shirts, all of them wore oversized helmets and goggles that matched the color of their machines, making them look like some inhuman combination of animation and mechanical horror.

Although I did not count them, well over a hundred of the large machines must have flown past us in the half hour that we waited for this dusty plague to pass. A few of the passengers laughed and waved to the menacing riders, but they ignored us. Our group gradually fell silent, and we watched impassively from slits in our face coverings, or curled up and simply waited.

What we had witnessed was an Italian motorcycle race through Africa. It proved to be only a small part of the fun industry across the Sahara. When I arrived in Mopti I saw gigantic trucks perched on top of what seemed to be an army of oversized tires. These support vehicles crossed the desert with the racers, carrying whole repair stations, bedrooms, kitchens, and all the supplies that might be needed in this distant, lonely place.

All of this was only a small offshoot of the larger convoy that made up the fabled annual Paris-to-Dakar race, in which six hundred racing vehicles leave Paris on New Year's Day to race across France and then be ferried to Algeria, where the real race begins. The monster caravans of support and supplies are already in place all along the eight-thousand-mile route through Algeria, Niger, Mali, Mauritania, and Senegal. The race ends, three weeks after it started, in Senegal's Dakar, the Paris of West Africa. It is a grueling trip. According to racing aficionados, it is the most difficult race in the world, and it averages two to three deaths a year in accidents. Of course, that does not include the occasional African child run down or the market woman who is forced off the road to lose her whole week's produce or even her life. In the 1988 rally, the screaming horde killed at least two children and one woman, according to official reports.

This annual expedition costs approximately $100 million, which is half of the total annual exports of the entire nation of Mali. If divided among the seven million people of Mali, that money would represent an increase of over fourteen dollars to their annual per capita income of less than two hundred dollars.

Even when they do not need the resources of the areas around them, people from the cities still find novel ways to destroy the world around them for the sake of recreation and entertainment. Living in the very unnatural environment of a city so far removed from the living conditions of their ancient ancestors, civilized people lost their understanding of nature, and humans rarely value what they do not understand.

13

The Lonely Tasmanian

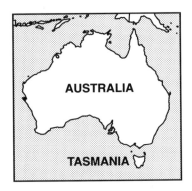

*The societies of primitive man are virtually extin-
guished when they come in contact with civilizations.*
—WALTER A. FAIRSERVIS, JR.,
The Threshold of Civilization

Even on a summer day in February, Port Arthur, an inlet in
southern Tasmania, can be quite cold. Facing south, nothing but
open ocean lies between the small peninsula and the frozen ice
continent of Antarctica. The cold wind blows unimpeded across
the South Indian Ocean from the South Pole, picking up moisture as it comes. The air, some of the purest in all the world,
carries a crisp feel and a clean smell. When the wind from Antarctica strikes the island of Tasmania, it creates a moist, cool
environment rich and nourishing for the giant plants that grow
there and for the sea life that swirls around the jagged peaks and
rocky promontories along the shore. Collapsed caves near the
coast have created some dramatic but dangerous blowholes,
and columns of dolerite rise up out of the water to punctuate
the coastline.

Port Arthur lies at the southern tip of the island's Tasman
Peninsula, making it one of the southernmost communities in
the world. On this peninsula, in 1642, the Dutch explorer Abel
Janszoon Tasman became the first known European to visit this
land. He landed his ships *Heemskerck* and *Zeehan* in Tasmania

while on a voyage from Mauritius in the Indian Ocean to Tahiti in the Pacific. Since Captain Tasman sailed under the sponsorship of the Dutch East India Company, and Anthony Van Dieman was the governor of the Dutch East Indies, Tasman named the island Van Dieman's Land in the governor's honor, but the peninsula where he landed became known as the Tasman Peninsula.

The moist air nourishes the Tasman Peninsula, providing it with a lush, green appearance throughout the year, similar to that of the islands along the Pacific coast of British Columbia and Washington State. That green color contrasts with the luxuriously creamy yellow limestone used to build the nineteenth-century structures on the tip of the peninsula. The ruins of the large buildings give the place a very European, almost classical, atmosphere. The Gothic chapel on the hill overlooking the bay provides a religious feeling reinforced by the rows of uniform windows on the large ruins that could easily be an ancient monastery in Ireland or an old boarding school in the English countryside.

But these buildings never served as a monastery or a university, or any other purpose quite so noble; instead, they housed one of the world's largest prisons. The British colony of Australia was founded as a penal colony in 1788, after the British crown could no longer dump its prisoners in Georgia and its other North American colonies. The British built the first penal colony in Australia at Sydney, but within a few decades the people of the newly founded community of Sydney decided that they needed an even more remote site for the prisoners who could not adapt properly to the colony. In its growing sophistication, the citizens of Sydney wanted to rid themselves of the most difficult and dangerous criminals. They selected isolated Van Diemen's Land, the name by which the island of Tasmania was known to them, as one of the most remote places on earth. Thus Tasmania began its modern life as the penal colony of a penal colony, the place of exiles from among exiles. Between 1830 and the closing of the penal colony in 1877, approximately thirty thousand male convicts passed through this dreaded place, and many of them never left the island again.

Even though the colonial authorities built Port Arthur's penal colony for recalcitrant and unruly prisoners, most of the men and women shipped to Australia had been convicted for relatively

minor offenses—petty theft, delinquency, prostitution, lewd behavior, unnatural vices, and, very commonly, political dissension.
Under British law, two hundred offenses were punishable with
"transportation," as it was called, but people convicted of the
most serious crimes were hanged, not exiled. Many Irish, Scottish, and Canadian political prisoners faced deportation, and in
general the legal establishment of Britain, in the scientific environment of the Victorian era, advocated deportation as the ideal
way to rid the streets of their cities of so many derelict, unemployed, and uneducated people. Authorities cleared many of the
children from the streets and emptied the crowded orphanages
by exiling the children on almost any pretext.

The penal colony at Port Arthur began operation in 1830 as
a sawing station to harvest Tasmania's large trees in a hard-labor
camp. The early generation of convicts lived in bark-covered huts
and worked themselves to death in their primitive, exposed way
of life, with few rations or other supplies from the outside. As
new generations of prisoners arrived from Britain, they erected
stone buildings, and the population grew to 1,200 convicts and
nearly as many free people working as guards and custodians.

The colony soon boasted industrious activities of many sorts.
In addition to timbering and farming, the men cut stone, manufactured brick, built ships, made furniture, cast iron, raised sheep,
wove cloth, and manufactured clothes and domestic items. The
colony was truly a model institution, in which anything could be
done with human labor. Farming was an easy activity, despite
the lack of strong oxen to pull the stumps and break the virgin
soil. Convicts were hitched to the plows and forced to pull them.
They were sometimes chained in great numbers, like yokes of
oxen, to pull large carts.

The convicts of Port Arthur built Australia's first railway to
transport goods and officials across the peninsula. What they
lacked in technological equipment and knowledge, they easily
compensated for in the labor of the large and dispensable work
force. Men served as the locomotion for the train carriages by
running behind them, pushing them up and down the hills. The
railway covered five miles from Norfolk Bay to Long Bay.

Other men were harnessed to a treadmill that looked like the
paddlewheel of a ship, and it turned continuously but performed
no function other than forcing the men on it to suffer. As the
prisoner stepped down on one blade of the wheel, it descended

and the next one came down, making him constantly go through the motions of walking up a flight of stairs. If the prisoner slowed for even a moment, the turning wheel quickly slammed into his shins, causing bloody pain.

Port Arthur housed only males, but English judges condemned boys as young as eight years old to exile there. Rather than keep the young boys in the main facility, the authorities sent most of them out to a separate prison on the island of Point Puer. The boys had their own quarters and a chapel, and they learned the trade of woodworking. Women were also exiled to Van Diemen's Land, but they were far fewer in number than the males, and were not sent out to Port Arthur or anywhere on the Tasman Peninsula. Other sections of the island offered numerous small jails and prisons, but most of the women were given in consignment to work as domestic laborers or craftspeople.

As early as 1825, the Van Diemen's Land Company was chartered in London to entice free settlers to emigrate to Van Diemen's Land on the promise that they would have free land and a limitless supply of convict labor to do their work for them. Even under these conditions, however, the company found it difficult to persuade settlers to go voluntarily to a place that had so quickly acquired a terrible reputation based on the prison and the convicts housed there.

One of the oddest buildings at the site is the Model Prison, built in 1848 and patterned after London's Pentonville. It was an expression of the latest ideas of the penologists, bureaucrats, and politicians of the early Victorian era. Four large corridors radiated from a central hall like spokes on a wheel, making it possible for a single guard placed at the hub of the system to see all cells from one central spot. Walled exercise courts occupied the open spaces between the spokes.

The philosophical premise underlying the architecture of the prison was that no corporal punishment could be used. At this time, flogging, sometimes to the point of death, had been common in British prisons and penal colonies, as well as in the army and navy, but flogging had proven to be largely ineffective in reforming men or preventing crime. Within the prison, a certain status system had arisen whereby men gained prestige among their fellow prisoners according to their ability to accept large numbers of lashes without showing fear or pain. In 1841, seven years before flogging was abolished in Tasmania, the guards ad-

ministered 18,469 official lashes to 684 prisoners, an average of
twenty-seven lashes each. More than one-third of those lashes
went to young boys, one of whom received three days in solitary
confinement followed by thirty-six lashes for the crime of having
his hands in his pockets (Weidenhofer 1981, 71). Some men
received such severe and frequent flogging that their backs gradually scarred over into a mass of hardened flesh.

To overcome the horrors of corporal punishment, the building
for the Model Prison incorporated the most scientific social engineering of the enlightened Victorian era. It functioned under
what was termed the "silent" or "separate" system. Inmates lived
in individual cells, in anonymous silence. Each inmate had a
number but no name, and his uniformly gray clothing bore a
badge with his number but no name sewn onto it. The rules
forbade the inmates to speak to one another, to guards, or to
anyone else. To ensure silence, inmates could signal their guards
only with a flag, and the guards themselves communicated with
one another using sign language rather than their voices. The
guards even wore soft slippers inside the prison to muffle the sound
of their steps as they patrolled the long hallways. The prisoners
lived in a world as close to absolute silence as the planners
and authorities of the prison could make it. According to the
plan, the silence provided the prisoners with the opportunity
to reflect on their crimes and on the importance of leading a
moral life.

Most of the day, the prisoner stayed in his room, working at
one of the quiet trades assigned to him. Such jobs might include
weaving or sewing, but no noisy work requiring the use of ham-
mers or heavy equipment. To ensure anonymity and prevent
prisoners even from recognizing one another, a prisoner had to
wear a cloth cap and mask over his face whenever he was allowed
out of his cell, for whatever reason.

Each man left the cell daily for an hour of solitary exercise,
facing a blank wall. Five times a week they went to a religious
service, either Catholic mass or Anglican chapel, but this proved
no less communal a time than the exercise hour. In the chapel,
each man entered a separate booth that completely hid him, except for his face, which was turned in the direction of the chap-
lain's pulpit. Securely locked into his individual booth, no
prisoner could see any other person. Some prisoners found a

way to communicate with adjacent prisoners by leaving notes or through a laborious code tapped on the wooden walls of their booths. If intercepted by the guards, any such communication carried the risk of extended confinement or further punishment.

For a prisoner who violated these rules, an even harsher regimen of punishment awaited him. The guards dragged him off to the "dark and dumb" cells, which were smaller than the regular cells and lacked a light shaft. With walls approximately three feet thick, no sound or light could enter the room, where the man was left to contemplate his errors in total silence and darkness. In some of the confinement cells, prisoners received daily food rations of bread and water, but guards delivered it at random hours to prevent the prisoner from using the arrival of meals as a way to time his stay. In other confinement cells, particularly unruly prisoners wore iron leggings attached to a chain in the wall. When guards at the end of the hall pulled on the chain, it snatched the prisoner off the floor and raised him up in the air, where he hung upside down in the silent darkness for hours or until the guards released the chain, upon which, without warning, the prisoner crashed down onto the stone floor.

The Model Prison succeeded in quieting even the most unruly prisoners. Chained to this harsh regimen, the will and spirit of the men snapped. The Model Prison produced madness. Without social contact or even conversation, the isolated convicts quietly descended into insanity. The mental and emotional condition of the convicts became so acute that in 1867, less than two decades after the opening of the Model Prison, the authorities built a new building, a lunatic asylum, next door. The asylum had twenty wards and a large dining hall, but it soon housed far more than the one hundred patients for which it was designed.

Convicts passed directly from the Model Prison into the lunatic asylum next to it. The asylum provided new work demands on the men in the Model Prison, who now had to sew many more canvas jackets to use as restraining devices for the men in the asylum. A man working in the Model Prison making confinement jackets might well be the one wearing the jacket a few years later, after his assignment to the lunatic asylum.

A visitor described the lunatics as showing one of two dispositions: either they were howling mad or they cowered like frightened animals. The Tasmanian *Mercury* reported in 1877, after the lunatic asylum had been in operation for a decade, that no person ever left the asylum cured, and that most of its inmates would be better off if killed (Weidenhofer 1981, 116).

One reason that the ruins of Port Arthur today do not look like a prison is that they do not have walls surrounding them. The open feeling of the community belies its status and function to imprison and limit mobility. The authorities deemed walls around the compound completely unnecessary in that environment. Prisoners saw that their prison lay surrounded by rough, cold waters that they had been told were infested with sharks. The small neck of land that connected the Tasman Peninsula to the main part of the island was easily guarded by a line of men and a series of staked and very angry dogs trained to attack anything that approached them. At Port Arthur, walls were unnecessary because the whole society had been made into a prison.

Even when an occasional prisoner did escape, he faced a harsh and isolated island interior that was almost another prison of its own. The land was so inhospitable for the prisoners that in one successful escape by two convicts in 1837, one of the convicts ended up eating his companion.

The very name of Van Dieman's Land became such a hated one that the convicts shortened it to Demon's Land. The transportation of criminals to the island ended in 1853, and the island moved toward making itself into a normal community. One of the first requests of the people was that the hated name be changed because it was so soaked in the memory of the penal colony. The people decided to rename the island in honor of the Dutch explorer who first visited the island and made it known to the world. In 1855 the island became Tasmania, and it has remained the smallest and poorest of the Australia states.

Colonialism is as old as civilization. The ancient Phoenicians sent out colonists to start settlements in the eastern Mediterranean in places such as Carthage, founded by settlers from the kingdom of Tyre, in the eighth century B.C. In the third century B.C., according to tradition, settlers from Cathage, under Hamilcar Barca, founded a colony that became Barcelona, the capital of Catalonia in the north of Spain. The Greeks sent out their colonists to build communities along the coast of Turkey, in Cyprus, throughout Italy and Sicily, on the coast of Libya, and even in Spain. The first Greek colony in Italy was Cumae, founded about 750 B.C., and about 150 years later refugees from Cumae founded Naples on the site of ancient Parthenope. The Italian name *Napoli* came from the Greek name *Neapolis*, meaning "new city," in much the same way that American cities later bore names beginning with *new*. Greek colonists from Corinth also founded Syracuse, the largest city of Sicily, in 734 B.C.

In the middle of the ninth century, Norsemen from Scandinavia settled the coast of France and made it Normandy, derived from the words "north man." The Vikings of Norway established colonies across the North Atlantic, including Iceland in 874, Greenland within another fifty years, and the Canadian coast of Labrador by the year 1000. Danes settled in England and on many of the smaller island chains in the North Atlantic. To the east of Scandinavia, Swedes sent colonists throughout the rivers and coasts of what would become Russia.

The ancient inhabitants of India proved to be great colonists of the islands around them, such as Sumatra, Borneo, and Java, which Hindu princes began invading as early as the first century A.D., producing the Madjapahit empire, which controlled all of the Malay Archipelago at its zenith around 1380. The residue of these ancient kingdoms can still be seen in the elaborate Hindu ceremonies and cremations on the island of Bali in modern Indonesia, now a substantially Muslim nation.

The Incas were not only great imperialists but also great colonizers. They frequently moved whole villages or tribes of people to new areas in order to open up those areas for agriculture, to pacify a formerly belligerent group, or simply to serve as teachers and models for newly conquered tribes. Villagers living today in Ecuador trace their ancestry back to Bolivian tribes forced by the Incas to colonize new lands in Ecuador, more than a thousand miles from their original home.

The myths and legends of many people point toward some form of colonialism early in their history. According to Vergil's *Aeneid*, the Trojan prince Aeneas and his followers founded Rome after fleeing the sacking of Troy. Much later the residents of Paris, France, claimed a tie back to colonists from ancient Troy, a claim supported by the similarity in the name of their city to that of the legendary Paris who seduced Helen and started the great Trojan War.

By the time colonization began in Van Diemen's Land, to the south of Australia, the colonial system had reached the most distant places on the planet. The penal colony of Van Diemen's Land represented a certain pinnacle of civilization for the British. Their ability to create and maintain such an institution on very nearly the most distant point on earth from Britain illustrated how much civilization had advanced and how close the Europeans had come to controlling the globe. The voyage itself took many months, and the people of Van Dieman's Land lived for months at a stretch without contact with the outside world, yet their institutions continued to operate precisely as mandated by London. The penal colony was a true institution in that it operated in much the same fashion, no matter who came to administer it. It was an institution beyond the power of any individual in it, and it showed the great power that the new global bonds held as they encircled the earth and tightened the grip on it.

The people who planned, organized, and controlled the settlement from London gave meticulous care to the smallest details of daily life, but no one seemed to care at all about the impact of the various prisons on Van Dieman's Land, for this was no uninhabited corner of the world. It was home to a unique people.

Even though we call the native Tasmanians "aborigines," the same name used for the Australian natives, the Tasmanians differed in physical and cultural ways from the natives of Australia. The Tasmanians were shorter than the mainlanders and had woolly hair rather than the Australians' straight and sometimes curly hair. The Tasmanians' skin was a dark brown color rather than the matte black of the Australians'. They also differed in technology. The Tasmanians used digging sticks and spears, but they lacked the primary Australian tools of the boomerang and the woomera, or spear-thrower. The Tasmanians' tools were coarse; they lacked the finely crafted small points, or *pirir points*, used by the Australians, and the Tasmanians did not know how to haft or attach stone tools to wooden handles. The Tasmanians lacked domesticated dogs, so essential a part of most Australian bands.

The Tasmanians puzzled the English greatly because they seemed so remarkably different from the Australian aborigines. Scientists developed many wild hypotheses to explain how these people reached this distant land. Scholars assigned them different homelands: they were Bushmen from Africa; Ainu from Japan; Andamanese from the Andaman Islands, between India and

Burma; Melanesians from New Caledonia; and dozens of other origins.

What little we know of this people's history reveals a story even stranger than any of these creative accounts. At the end of the last Ice Age, about ten to twelve thousand years ago, the rising sea cut them off from the Australian mainland, and virtually sealed them up on remote Tasmania. The Tasmanians probably lived in nearly total isolation from the rest of the world until the rather recent arrival of Abel Tasman in 1642. Their twelve thousand years of separation from outside human contact constituted the longest isolation of any known group of people in world history.

Throughout the year, including the damp, cool winter, Tasmanians usually went naked, but both men and women had extensive decorative scars over their bodies. They wore necklaces of kangaroo sinew, kangaroo teeth, and strings of shells, and they decorated themselves with flowers and feathers. For protection against the humid cold, they coated their bodies with fat and charcoal. Early sketches show the men standing on one leg, leaning against their spears and clutching their genitals. The natives sometimes wore small cloaks of kangaroo skin that also served as the means to carry children and food gathered during a day's search.

For some unknown reason, the Tasmanians would not eat fish, even though the waters around their island teemed with them. Archaeological evidence shows that ancient Tasmanians did eat fish, but more than four thousand years ago they stopped doing so, even though they continued to eat other seafood such as oysters, mussels, and abalone. Early chroniclers reported that the Tasmanian women gathered the seafood by diving naked into the chilly waters, a feat that seemed too difficult for the males to accomplish. They also ate wallabies, wombats, possums, seals, and muttonbirds, and harvested a variety of plants, although generally they ate much more meat than plant foods.

Their technology remained so simple that they probably lacked the knowledge or tools to make fire. Even though they used fire and kept it burning at all times, no visitor ever mentioned seeing them make fire, and no firemaking tools have ever been discovered on Tasmania. Perhaps they captured fire from lightning strikes and kept it burning. The inability to make fire is also characteristic of some other jungle peoples, including some of the Amazonian natives of Bolivia. The reason for this seems as much environmental as technological, since the people in very wet areas often do not have wood dry enough to use as firesticks, even though the wood will burn when exposed to a direct flame.

The Tasmanians built small huts of branches thatched with grass, covered with bark, and lined them with feathers, which could accommodate up to fifteen people at a time. Because of the bountiful food supply, they lived in settled villages in relatively small areas and did not wander the island. They gathered rolls of bark and reeds to build small boats, much like the reed boats of South America's Lake Titicaca or the ones made by the Marsh Arabs of Iraq. These simple but efficient vessels could hold up to seven people, and were used by the Tasmanians to visit smaller islands up to twenty-five miles from their coast during the seal hunt and the time for gathering muttonbirds. They plastered a small place in the boat with clay in order to keep a fire burning when they traveled.

One of the highest technological achievements of the Tasmanians appears in the small baskets that the women wove from reeds and bark. Some of these carefully woven containers still survive in museums and private collections, and contrast markedly with the other bits of native technology on the island. With their rounded or teardrop shape, the little baskets, which they sometimes wore on strings around their necks, show great precision in their creation, quite unlike the large and poorly shaped stone and wooden tools they manufactured for the work of daily subsistence.

Even though Tasman arrived in 1642, the native people of the island stayed away from him and the other explorers who came by. Perhaps the natives had already had unpleasant encounters with strangers arriving on ships, or perhaps they did not believe that these strange foreigners were even human. Not until exactly a century and a half later, in 1792, did a European make contact with a Tasmanian when a Frenchman, Bruni D'Estrecasteaux, led an expedition into the area and his surgeon, Labillardière, managed to contact the natives and spent several days with them.

The natives seemed as interested in their new visitors as the Europeans were in the natives. The natives repeatedly kidnapped sailors from the visiting party and carried them off to the bush, where they stripped away their clothes and carefully examined their bodies. With their curiosity satisfied, the natives released the horrified men. The natives also enjoyed painting the bodies of the white men with the charcoal and ocher that they wore on their own bodies.

As horrible as life became for the exiled prisoners on Van Dieman's Land, the fate of the natives proved much worse yet. From the beginning, Europeans kidnapped the natives for use as slaves, and they raped and killed them without provocation. When it was found that the aborigines provided no resources or skills that the British settlers could exploit, and that the natives actually posed a threat to the sheep that the settlers brought with them, the Europeans instituted a genocidal war against them. Governor Arthur, for whom Port Arthur was named, ordered that any native should be shot or captured.

When even these severe measures proved inadequate, the governor instituted a notorious "Black Line" by assembling all male convicts and freemen to march slowly across the island in one long military formation. This, too, failed to capture the natives, who fled and hid in places where the whites could not find them.

While the settlers were killing off the native people, they were also killing the island's animals, such as the thylacine, sometimes called the Tasmanian tiger or wolf. This carnivorous marsupial with stripes across its back once ranged over much of Australia and Tasmania, but became extinct in Australia nearly five thousand years ago. The cause of its extinction was quite possibly the introduction of the dingo, which proved to be a much more efficient and vicious hunter than the thylacine, but since the dingo never arrived in Tasmania, the Tasmanian tiger thrived there until the arrival of the Europeans. The Tasmanian tiger, like the Tasmanian aborigines, developed an appetite for the docile and vulnerable sheep brought in by the settlers, and the settlers made war on the animals just as they had on the aborigines. The settlers hunted them, offered bounties for them, and occasionally captured and imprisoned them. In 1936 the government finally declared the Tasmanian tiger a protected species. Three months later the last one died in the Hobart zoo.

After its extinction, the Tasmanian tiger became something of a sacred totem for the new settlers of Tasmania, who use its image as an unofficial mascot. The state proudly displays two of them on its coat of arms, and its picture has been used on various agricultural products from Tasmania.

Societies promoting the introduction of new species worked to adapt a variety of English plants, animals, and even songbirds to the Tasmanian environment, in order to make it similar to the environment they had left behind. They sought to make Tasmania into a different world. The colonists wanted a rolling countryside with meadows, woods, and glens of the same trees, wildflowers, birds, and animals that they had known in their distant homeland. They wanted to see bunnies and hedgehogs scampering through the grass while a nearby robin pulled at a long, juicy worm. They did not want to see naked savages parading around, spearing their sheep and eating the worms before the birds could find them. This re-created, Europeanized world had no place for the native people, who did not make good farm laborers, shepherds, or domestic servants. The native people no longer fit in the rapidly changing environment of the island where they had lived for tens of thousands of years.

The native Tasmanians never raised armies, and had the simplest weapons of any people on earth. Despite their military and technological inferiority to the Europeans, however, the Tasmanians fought vigorously and valiantly against the British encroachment on, and confiscation of, their homeland. One of the earliest Tasmanian leaders was a woman named Wayler, who had been traded to white sealers in exchange for flour and dogs. While living with these sealers she learned the use of firearms, and came to understand the basic culture of the whites. She escaped back to her people in 1828 and led them in resistance against the invaders. Colonists insisted that she stood on the hilltops and shouted orders to the fighting men during the battle, but despite her fierceness, the British authorities captured her again in 1831; despondent and weakened, Wayler died soon after being imprisoned (Clark 1983, 46). Europeans might survive the harsh imprisonment, but Tasmanians certainly could not.

Between 1800 and 1835, the whites killed between three thousand and four thousand natives, while the natives killed 183 whites. Throughout this time, not one white ever faced arrest for the killing or mistreatment of a single aborigine. At the end of the long campaign against the aborigines, colonial authorities rounded up the surviving 135 native Tasmanians and exiled them to remote Flinders Island in the Bass Strait, the passage that connects the Pacific and Indian oceans while dividing Australia from Tasmania. Experienced sailors knew the Bass Strait as one of the least predictable and most dangerous parts of the sea. In

1847 the government relocated the forty-seven surviving Tasmanians yet again, moving them to live on Oyster Cove.

White sealers, fishermen, and convicts divided up the remaining Tasmanian women at Oyster Cove. The men took the aboriginal women to live with them, and used them for sex and for work. As they inevitably became pregnant, many of the captive women killed their infants at birth rather than let them grow up in the captivity that they experienced. But some of the mixed-blood children survived, and their offspring continued to live around the missions and to mate with other whites. A small community of a few thousand mixed-blood descendants of these white men and their aboriginal women survives in the Bass Strait and Tasmania until the present, but the full-bloods and the original Tasmanian culture have been completely destroyed.

The tragedy of Tasmania—the destruction of its environment and the genocide of its native population—is the story of only one of the many native societies to disappear in the past five centuries. The world stage had already seen the rehearsal of the Tasmanian story many times, as the burgeoning world civilization that moved out of Europe killed off the people of the Canary Islands and then most of the natives of the Caribbean Sea. On the mainland they destroyed one native nation after another in North, Central, and South America. At the same time that the people of Tasmania were being destroyed, explorers, conquerors, and colonists were already at work killing off the native societies of Polynesia and New Guinea. The Tasmanians died by the thousands in the nineteenth century, but in the twentieth century, others were to die by the millions.

In a cruel way, Tasmania illustrates the awesome power of governments in modern times. The British government turned all of Tasmania into a prison, and killed off the entire native population. All the ingredients present in Tasmania in the nineteenth century would come back to haunt the world again and again throughout the twentieth.

In the ruins of Port Arthur, on this most isolated speck of land, we see an experiment that was tried, enhanced, and then expanded and used across the globe. The insane and inhuman world of the prison colony appeared again in the concentration camps that the British built to house the Boers of South Africa, in the camps the Germans built in Eastern Europe for the Jews, in the gulags of the Soviet Union and China, and perhaps in many other places whose existence remains unknown to most of the outside world.

The modern world had little tolerance for dissent, variation, or divergence; it demanded a uniform population that fit into a specific social system. Men and women who could not fit into the society found themselves forced into exile, like the British prisoners, or faced extermination like the aboriginal Tasmanians.

PART III

World Culture
and Ethnic Chaos

We think our civilization near its meridian, but we are yet only at the cock-crowing and the morning star.

—RALPH WALDO EMERSON, *Politics*

14

Romancing the Savage

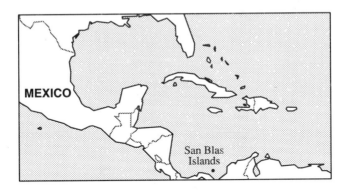

Civilization, for every advantage she imparts, holds a hundred evils in reserve. . . .
—HERMAN MELVILLE

The four hundred San Blas Islands lie scattered along the Atlantic coast of Panama, sixty miles east of Colón and the northern entrance to the great canal. Like a string of broken pearls, some islands abut one another, some lie in a straight line, and still others stand alone. The islands vary from a few miles in circumference to some too small to support a single tree. The Kuna have made these islands their home for unknown centuries. With a population of forty thousand, they have filled many of their islands, and their population overflows onto the adjacent mainland.

The clothes of the Kuna women bear intricate designs of appliquéd materials made into geometric designs connecting various real and mythological beasts and interspersed with random words or letters picked up and copied from such sources as lottery tickets, belt buckles, and cans of beans. With the increased traffic afforded by canal traffic in their area, the pieces of appliquéd material, known as *molas*, became popular with travelers and collectors around the world. Expensive shops in Europe and North America sell jackets, dresses, shirts, and even formal cummerbunds decorated with the colorful *molas*.

The Kuna villages seem to cover every available speck of land on the inhabited islands. Because of low tidal variation and the rarity of hurricanes, the houses go right to the edge of the islands. The Kuna make their houses of bamboo, cane, or wood, which they hammer into a large enclosure over which they erect a thatched roof. These simple abodes have no internal walls, or floors other than dirt, but they are roomy and give ample opportunity for the smoke from the open hearth to escape through the walls and the roof. There seems to be little variation between the walls of the house and the fence around the small garden, other than the roof. In their gardens the Kuna cultivate bananas, breadfruit, and calabash trees, as well as a few vegetables. Some Kuna have tried to grow rice and other crops commercially, but the efforts have usually failed.

The alleys between houses seem little more than narrow paths. An adult walking down such a street can usually touch the thatched roofs on both sides with extended arms. The central plaza is only a small opening in the middle of the village.

Outhouses, built on sticks out over the water, line the edge of the village, while nearby, chickens peck the ground for bugs, and pigs wallow in the mud. Seen from a ship on the ocean, such a village looks as though it stands on stilts. Just such an appearance on the island of Aruba, southeast of the San Blas Islands, led the explorer Amerigo Vespucci to call the islands *Venezuela,* or "Little Venice," a name that was eventually applied to the nearby nation and not to the small islands on its coast.

As soon as a cruise ship appears on the horizon, the Kuna race to their small boats and head out to open water. The boats that they paddle today look little different from the ones they paddled out to meet Rodrigo de Bastidas, their first European visitor, in 1501, and Christopher Columbus in 1502, on his fourth and final voyage to America. The Kuna craftsman makes a canoe by hollowing out a large tree harvested from the Panamanian mainland, and as many as fifty such canoes and small boats paddle out to meet a passing cruise ship. Of the fifty small vessels, not more than four or five might have outboard motors and only a dozen would have a handmade sail of patched and ragged material. Men and young boys, some no more than eight or nine years old, propel the remainder of the canoes with their paddles, just as when they paddled out to meet Columbus.

The small boats race to the sides of the ships, and as soon as it comes within shouting distance, they call out in English for money. Passengers toss small coins in the water, which the boys dive to retrieve as the shiny coins spiral down through the clear Caribbean water. Other boys hold up seashells for sale, and offer model boats crudely carved from balsa wood and covered with string for rigging.

Men operate the boats, but some of them also carry women who sit silently in the middle of the dugout when they come to meet a visiting ship. Each woman decorously wraps herself in a shawl and an ankle-length skirt that gives her the appearance of a veiled woman of North Africa, but unlike the muted blacks and dark blues of the Muslim world, these women wear the brightest combinations of reds, yellows, oranges, and greens. Each of the women smears her cheeks with rouge, and paints a single thin, black stripe down the forehead and nose. The stripe narrows her features and highlights the nose, which is pierced and adorned with a gold ring through the septum. The women adorn their ankles with many strands of beads that pinch the skin and cause it to bulge out. The women, who frequently hold a nursing child, silently lift *molas* in the air and wait for an offer from a passenger on the ship, but they sit with great dignity and never call out to the potential customers.

The men wear small bathing suits and loose, open shirts that give the sun ample opportunity to tan and parch their skin to a dark shade. The women, who usually have much less of a tan than the men, remain covered and frequently hold up umbrellas or sheets of plastic to shield themselves from the sun's powerful rays so close to the equator. Neither men nor women usually surpass five feet in height.

Because no outside army ever conquered the Kuna and no government has completely subdued them, visiting ships must first invite the barefoot chief of the islands and his wife on board to request permission to enter their territory and allow passengers to disembark. The old chief usually receives a meal, a bag of food to take with him, and a gift. From these encounters with visiting ships, the Kuna have acquired a collection of discarded ships' furnishings including old mattresses, towels, stewards' jackets, mirrors, artificial Christmas trees, bathtubs, playing cards, ice coolers, folding deck chairs, and some old stage props, costumes, and wigs from ships' productions of Broadway musicals.

Because the islands have no harbor, the tourists must climb

into small boats to visit the islands. These tenders ferry them to small docks. On days when the cruise ships visit in the mild winter months, the village becomes a giant bazaar, with *molas* and other decorated cloths dangling from the front of every house. Work such as sewing, pounding rice in wooden mortars, and squeezing juice from sugarcane, tasks normally done in the privacy of the compound, are taken into open areas where the tourists might be attracted to photograph them and pay a small fee. To entice more photographers, some women keep lizards or parrots tied to a string and, like Caribbean pirates, wear the lizards on their heads and their shoulders, giving their already exotic appearance a bizarre and even surrealistic dimension. Other women sit silently, smoking their pipes and waiting for a customer.

The San Blas Islands of the Kuna constitute an autonomous entity within Panama. They have elected representation in the National Assembly, and they even have their own treaty with neighboring Colombia. They receive little help from the governments that claim them; yet, because of their poverty, they have faced less exploitation and coercion than have many groups in similar circumstances. Even after Columbus claimed the San Blas Islands for Spain, the Kuna continued to lead their traditional lives, which they preserved while supposedly a part of the Spanish province of Nuevo Granada. In 1819 the name of the whole region changed when it became independent as a part of the new country of Colombia. In 1903 the Kuna were included in the part of Colombia that broke away to become Panama. But whether under Spanish, Colombian, or Panamanian rule, the Kuna have continued as an autonomous group that acknowledges outside powers when it must, but continues to live by its own rules and culture as much as it can.

Because of the autonomy of the Kuna, smugglers between Panama and Colombia use the islands as a refuge and a staging ground for their illegal operations. Often using Kuna men to help them, by night they navigate small boats loaded with marijuana, coca paste, cocaine, and illegal cigarettes, as well as appliances and electronic goods imported from Japan and Korea. A few of the Kuna men sit around for hours smoking marijuana brought in by the smugglers who stop and hide in the islands, waiting for nightfall before they continue on their way with their narcotics for northern markets.

Because of their isolation and their rejection of Western clothes, houses, and culture in general, the Kuna appear to be some of the most primitive people remaining in the Americas, but the Kuna are unique. They are the only Indians visited by Christopher Columbus who are still alive, still living on the same islands where Columbus came to call. The others have been displaced or killed.

Like many tribal people around the world today, the Kuna no longer pose a threat to outsiders, and have now become tourist attractions. Tourists come on ships, or charter excursions from Panama City by small plane or boat. From the highlands of New Guinea to the most remote valleys of Africa, from the Arctic to the tip of Tierra del Fuego, tourists pour in to see the romantic natives, watch a few dances, haggle for some crafts, taste the local specialty, snap a few photographs, and be on their way to visit the next spot. Although no longer featured quite so prominently in literature, the romantic native still holds a major position in world tourism.

During the nineteenth century, as the colonial powers conquered the remaining islands, tribes, and miniature kingdoms of the world, the strength of tribal peoples, and the threat they presented, steadily waned. Confronted with the military arms and technological sophistication of the outside world, the sedate villagers, fishermen, and topical hunters proved virtually powerless. No longer perceived as a danger by the Europeans, native people became objects of curiosity and intrigue. As often happens in history, people tend to despise or else romanticize that which once made them afraid but no longer does so.

The tendency to romanticize ethnic groups and natives can be heard in the European music of the nineteenth century, which focused on virtually the only tribal people left in Europe—the Gypsies. Franz Liszt wrote a series of Hungarian rhapsodies using themes that he based on Hungarian Gypsy music. Similarly, exotic elements came to opera in Bizet's *Carmen*, set among the Gypsies of Seville. Liszt's son-in-law, Richard Wagner, reached back into ancient Germanic tribal history and mythology for his inspiration, resurrecting tribal gods and heroes such as Lohengrin, Brunhilde, Siegfried, and the Valkyries.

By the nineteenth century, however, truly tribal people no longer lived in Europe; they survived only in the more remote places around the globe. Therefore, European writers, artists, and intellectuals set out during the nineteenth century to encounter the primitive, the savage, the truly tribal in its native environment. Some of them went to find only enough to shock their contemporaries in Victorian parlors; some sought sexual as much as artistic fulfillment. Others wanted to escape the law or the confines of bourgeois European life by encountering the Savage.

Some of the earliest descriptions of tribal people did little to romanticize them. Shakespeare's view of Caliban in *The Tempest* uses the native to symbolize everything base, wicked, and savage in humans. Gradually, however, writers began to perceive a slightly more aristocratic side of the native people of America. In 1794, Anne Kemble Hatton wrote the first American opera, called *Tammany*, in which she used American Indian music and a noble portrayal of Chief Tammany of the Delaware.

The nineteenth century opened with a best-selling book set among the savages of North America. The Vicomte François-Auguste-René de Chateaubriand wrote about the Natchez Indian nation of the lower Mississippi River in *Atala*, the novella that brought him to fame in France in 1801. He paints a picture that seems far from idyllic but that assaults the reader with powerful emotions, deep passions, and thrilling adventures many times larger than real life.

Chateaubriand visited America and claimed to have written his story in Indian cabins in the woods. It is doubtful that he ever left the Northeast, but he obviously read extensively about the tribes on the Mississippi. He described the river as it "pours its flood waters around the forest colonnades and the pyramids of Indian tombs; it is the Nile of the wilderness" (Chateaubriand 17).

Chateaubriand set the story at the end of the eighteenth century. The Natchez warrior Chactas, whose name Chateaubriand probably derived from the Choctaw Indians, returns from Florida to his home on the Meschacebe (Mississippi) River, but en route some fierce Muskogee warriors capture him somewhere in Georgia or Alabama. They tie Chactas to a rack and prepare him for torture by tearing the skin from his head and burning out his eyes with hot hatchets. But he sings, in the Natchez style, "I fear no suffering, O Muskogees, I am brave! I defy you and despise you more than women. My father, Outalissi, son of Miscou, drank from the skulls of your most famous warriors. You will not tear a single groan from my breast."

The sweet maiden Atala, an early convert to Christianity who has pledged her virginity to Christ, takes pity on him and frees him. The fleeing Atala and the wounded Chactas find refugee with a maimed French priest in the woods of Kentucky or Tennessee, where they live in frenzied but asexual passion. Her love for Chactas and her vow to Christ drive Atala nearly mad, forcing her to take poison to prevent herself from breaking her vow to God by giving herself carnally to Chactas. As she slowly dies, the pagan Chactas converts to Christianity through his deep love for her.

The great success of *Atala* set off a frenzy of other books about the simple but passionate native people of the Americas. American writers followed with similar stories of great romance and adventure. James Fenimore Cooper published many novels about American characters, from spies to sailors, but his best were in the Leatherstocking series, written from 1823 through 1841, which included *The Deerslayer, The Last of the Mohicans, The Pathfinder, The Pioneers,* and *The Prairie.* Although Cooper wrote mostly about the Indians of the northeastern United States, William Gilmore Simms of South Carolina was writing about the Indians of the Southeast in novels such as *The Yemassee,* which he published in 1835.

Following the literary discovery of the native savage, a variety of artists and intellectuals began searching for their own primitive experiences. Professors of language, theology, literature, and history began studying people around the world. Exoticism became a legitimate academic pursuit in 1896 when Oxford University appointed its first professor of anthropology. Sir Edward Burnett Tylor received the honor as a result of his research and extensive writing on Mexico and in recognition of the importance of *Primitive Culture,* which he published in 1871.

The word *anthropology* first occurred in the writings of Aristotle but did not receive wide usage until the German philosopher Immanuel Kant popularized it at the end of the eighteenth century. The Greek etymology of the term means "the study of people." Such a vague discipline could be applied to many different things, and so it was. It became the study of human culture, of the evolution of the human body, of the collection of human tools and artifacts, of the diffusion of humans around the world, of the archaeology of past civilizations. In time, all of these came to be a part of the discipline of anthropology, the study of the exotic by the eccentric. Anthropology found room for anything that was sufficiently distant from European culture and could be made to appear exotic or at least primitive.

For those people who could not go out and experience the exotic world the way anthropologists, painters, and writers could, the exotic world of savages was brought to them through a variety of traveling shows and exhibits. The world's fairs and expositions that began in the nineteenth century provided a great opportunity for people to see not only the industrial vision of progress for tomorrow but also the frightening and bizarre world of the primitive past. Next to the modern wonder of the Eiffel Tower, the highest steel structure of its time, the French built their exhibit of peoples, which eventually became the Museum of Man.

In 1892, Franz Boas worked to bring Indians and Eskimos, along with all their accouterments of daily life, for exhibition at the World's Fair in Chicago, where he directed the section on North American ethnology. The artifacts and art that he assembled for this exposition formed the beginnings of the ethnographic collection of the Field Museum, which bitterly disappointed Boas when the new museum declined to hire him to manage their anthropology section. Boas later attained prominence at Columbia University and at the Museum of Natural History in New York, but he maintained a strong grudge toward the Field Museum until his death in 1942.

Because most people could not travel to the large cities where the world's fairs took place, entrepreneurs and impresarios brought the exotic shows to the people. Soon, cities were building large museums even if they could not afford a world's fair to go with them. For the more active and less educated public, the American impresario "Buffalo Bill" Cody took his traveling show of Plains Indians throughout the United States and Europe, showing off the exotic and powerful presence of the natives.

The Wild West shows, museum exhibits, and novels set among the American Indians romanticized life greatly, but usually stressed adventure over romance. Even when the Indians were the heroes, the books almost always included numerous scenes of Indians torturing one another or white settlers, and kidnapping women and children. As the remaining Indian nations fell under American and Canadian authority, they lost some of their romance and exotic appeal. They became commonplace, pushing the search for romantic, noble savages ever farther afield, to the South Pacific.

For people of the northern hemisphere in the nineteenth century, the South Pacific offered the quintessentially exotic frontier. The scattered islands from Hawaii to New Zealand were situated as far from Europe as it was possible to go without leaving the planet. The South Pacific was also one of the least understood areas of the world. The islands seemed to represent cultural values in exact opposition to those of Western Europe. In place of rigid sexual codes, the islanders had a relaxed attitude toward sex; rather than working constantly, the climate permitted them the luxury of singing, dancing, and simply enjoying life.

Herman Melville contributed greatly to the world's fascination with the peoples of the South Seas. Although Melville was born, lived most of his life, and died in New York City, he brought the high seas and the exotic locales of the South Pacific to virtually every bookstore. Melville sailed for Tahiti on a whaling ship in 1841. The Marquesas Islands so enchanted him that he jumped ship. Even though the islands offered a kind of paradise, the cannibalism of the natives, or at least the rumors of cannibalism, frightened Melville. He decided to flee on the first available ship, which took him to Tahiti, where French colonial authorities quickly imprisoned him for participating in a ship's mutiny. Finally he made his way to Hawaii and, from there, sailed back to the American mainland aboard the ship *United States.*

Based on these adventures of approximately eighteen months in the South Pacific, Melville wrote several popular books, including *Typee* (1846), about life among the cannibals of the Marquesas; *Omoo* (1847), about Tahiti; and *White-Jacket* (1850), about life at sea on an American frigate. These works enjoyed much more popularity than his masterpiece, *Moby-Dick*, which he published in 1851 and which drew heavily from his whale-hunting days and included as one of the important characters Queequeg, a South Seas islander whom Melville described as trapped between cultures, "neither caterpillar nor butterfly."

Melville provoked a literary sensation with his South Seas books because of his description of great adventures, fierce canni-

balism, and free sexuality, but also because of his honest depic-
tion of missionaries, merchants, and colonial officials. Contrary
to the heroic and self-sacrificing terms in which these groups
portrayed themselves to the home offices and governments that
supported them financially, Melville depicted them as hypocriti-
cal, venal, mean, and lower in morals, cleanliness, and decency
than the people whom they came to convert, teach, and administer. Melville did not portray the expatriates from his own land
as messengers of civilization to the savages. In Melville's opinion,
the interlopers destroyed the native societies, which in many ways
already outranked the supposedly superior civilization of Europe
and America.

The writings of Melville and other visitors to the South Pacific
excited a new migration of artists and misfits of all sorts. For
any creative soul not at home in the culture of his birth, the
South Seas offered the hope that another and more appropriate
home might be waiting somewhere out beyond the horizon.

No artist felt less at home in the north and longed more for
the south than the French painter Paul Gauguin, but like most
romantic searchers, he proved to be equally ill at ease everywhere
he went. He was a permanent misfit alienated from every place
and not just from France, the country of his birth.

Although born in Paris is 1848, Gauguin's maternal roots were
in Peru, where his grandmother, Flora Tristan, was a niece of
one of the last Spanish viceroys. When Paul was less than two
years old, his parents took him on the long voyage from France
to the Peruvian port of Callao, just outside of Lima, but during
this voyage his father died of a heart attack in the Strait of
Magellan and was buried in the icy sea. Young Paul spent the
next five years in the home of his maternal grandmother, surrounded by the strange designs and forms of ancient Peruvian
pots looted by peasants and *huaceros* from the graves of the
Chimu and other ancient Andean peoples.

Gauguin's mother returned with Paul to Paris when it came
time for his education to begin, but she carried with her some
of the images and artifacts of her homeland. The strange but
captivating designs of these objects maintained a lifelong hold
over his imagination, and they appeared repeatedly in his art
throughout his life. In the world around him and within himself,
Gauguin pined after and sought a primitive human nature, one

that was undistorted by modern culture and always seemed to him to be just beyond the horizon.

The mixed-blood heritage from his mother allowed Gauguin to proclaim himself an Indian, a savage, or a man of two races. He spent all his life searching for a way to reconcile that primitive part of himself with the civilization around him. He ran away from home repeatedly, and finally left school and escaped at seventeen years of age to work aboard a ship up and down the Atlantic.

In his early twenties, Gauguin tried to lead the life of the respectable bourgeois husband and father. He married a middle-class Danish woman, fathered five children in ten years, and worked as a banker and stockbroker in Paris. During this time his quest for creativity found a new outlet in art—painting, sculpture, and ceramics. But this new passion only whetted his thirst for creative work without slaking it. Soon he left his office job and took off for Brittany to paint the colorful rustic life of the peasants, but that failed to be primitive enough. By obtaining a job with the French company struggling vainly to build the Panama Canal, Gauguin headed for the Caribbean island of Martinique, the exotic birthplace of Napoleon's wife Josephine. Painting the African descendants of the slaves who worked the sugar plantations still did not offer the primitive society sought by Gauguin. He seems never to have made contact with Indians such as the Kuna, who lived so close to where the French were trying to build their canal in Panama.

After leaving Martinique, Gauguin returned to Brittany, but he yearned for a much more primitive experience than either the African-Caribbean people of Martinique or the Celtic peasants of Brittany. He tried to obtain a government job in the French colony of Indochina or on the African island of Madagascar. Failing in both of those efforts, he decided on Tahiti, France's newly acquired colony in the middle of the South Pacific.

In an interview with the newspaper *Echo de Paris* before leaving on his Pacific foray, Gauguin said, "I wish to live in peace and to avoid being influenced by our civilization. . . . [I]t is necessary for me to steep myself in virgin nature, to see no one but savages."

On April 1, 1891, Gauguin sailed for Tahiti. In Tahiti, his art acquired a new life as he splashed bolder strokes and brighter colors onto his canvases, interspersed with the designs, motifs, and sculptures of his newly adopted home. Ignoring the Old Masters' tradition of working laboriously on flesh and skin tones, Gauguin concentrated on the textures of native cloth and their simple floral and geometric designs.

Gauguin carried with him pictures and drawings of art from around the world. He incorporated into his work the techniques and coloration of Japanese prints, copies of Chinese and Hindu goddesses and Polynesian gods, the designs of Egyptian friezes, and haunting images of the ancient Andean pottery from his grandmother's home. He proved willing, even anxious, to incorporate anything into his art except the models of the Greeks, the symmetrical and super-realistic images that, in his opinion, had started Western art down the wrong path of a near-photographic realism.

The French influence in Tahiti's capital city of Papeete disgusted Gauguin. He particularly disliked the flowing Mother Hubbard dresses introduced by the missionaries and worn by the women in the city. Gauguin turned away from the corruption and change in the city to find the savage of the jungle.

Gauguin explored the interior of the island, searching for the real Tahitian life, but he could never stray too far from the French influence. In his decade in Polynesia, he never learned to speak the Tahitian language beyond a few words, which he used liberally as titles for his paintings. In daily life he continued to speak French, and he always depended on French rations bought in a store. He did not know how to climb a tree or husk a coconut. He depended on the post office to bring him small amounts of money from the sale of paintings that he shipped back to France. He could neither fish nor hunt for himself.

For a while, Gauguin thought that he had found the perfect native in a young girl whom he took as his common-law wife. According to his journal, he was traveling in the interior when he met a woman who asked him, "You seek a wife? You want my daughter?" Within fifteen minutes she returned with "a tall, slender, vigorous child . . . about thirteen years old." Her name was Teha'amana, and his courtship was about as brief as his arrangements with her family.

"You are not afraid of me?"

"No."

"Will you live in my hut for good?"

"Yes."

"Have you ever been ill?"

"No."

Gauguin set out with the young girl, and, to his annoyance, her family followed him for much of the journey home (Danielsson 1988, 7). Of love in Tahiti, Gauguin wrote, "In Europe men and women have intercourse because they love each other. In the South Seas they love each other because they have had intercourse. Who is right?"

Through his young wife, he hoped to be released from his European skin and to emerge as a new and more primitive man. She did enliven his life, but when she became pregnant, she aborted the child. Gauguin deserted her in 1892, when he returned to France and then to Copenhagen for a final visit with his estranged wife and the mother of his children.

During his visit to Paris he contracted syphilis, which helped persuade him to return to Tahiti in 1895 and to resume life with Teha'amana. Unable to bear his deteriorating health, Teha'amana left him, and he formed a liaison with Pau'uru, another beautiful young girl, who eventually bore him more children.

In 1901 Gauguin left Tahiti and sailed seven hundred miles to the northwest of Tahiti to the even more remote Marquesas Islands, the same islands where Herman Melville had jumped ship in order to live among the cannibals whom he described in his novel *Typee*. Gauguin hoped that, far from the French influence of Tahiti, he might find some authentically primitive experience there and perhaps even meet a naked Marquesan cannibal who could still remember and describe for him the forbidden taste of human flesh.

What he found in the Marquesas was stiff opposition from the local priest and from the government officials, with whom he warred for the brief remainder of his life. He took what solace he could in the love of young girls, particularly the fourteen-year-old Marie Rose, whom he enticed away from the Catholic boarding school. The strict and uncompromising nuns who ran the school thereafter bore Gauguin eternal enmity, and they connived unsuccessfully with the French civil authorities to have him removed from the island. Despite the campaign against him, Gauguin's new love bore him a son who lived on in the Marquesas for many years and for a while was himself exploited late in life, as a minor sensation in the international art world of the

1950s. Even the new love and the new son could not improve Gauguin's health or revive his sinking spirits. Alone in his small hut on May 8, 1903, Paul Gauguin, fifty-three years old, died a deranged alcoholic and syphilitic artist still yearning feverishly for the truly primitive experience he had failed to find.

By the time of Gauguin's death, tribal people around the world had been brought into a new world system. From the Sioux in South Dakota to the Zulu in South Africa, from the Maori of New Zealand to the Eskimo of the Arctic, the tribal people had fallen under the administration of some alien nation or state. Defeated and no longer a threat to the national destiny of any government, tribal people became objects of curiosity—romantic novelties from the past, surviving in a rapidly modernizing world.

In the Victorian and early modern period, the exotic peoples of distant islands symbolized leisure and sexual freedom, two things decidedly missing from Western life. As the Western world attained more leisure and greater sexual freedom, tribal people came to have a different type of meaning. In recent decades, tribal people from North Dakota to south Brazil have come to be regarded as possessing greater spiritual qualities and to be more in tune than non-natives with the physical world around them. Rather than representing sexual and artistic freedom, they represent environmentalism and spirituality. Many outsiders still perceive tribal people as somehow closer to the original human nature, of having retained what the larger society has squandered or forgotten.

Because the Western world understood so little about native peoples and their cultures, tribal societies came to symbolize things that proved lacking in that world. Much of the earlier romanticizing of native peoples centered on adventure, but gradually that yielded to a romanticizing of native peoples as great philosophers and stewards of the environment. People see what they want to see in native cultures. They can see vicious barbarism and pagan idolatry, or they can see wise, understanding, noble savages living in harmony with animals and plants as well as other humans.

Our vision of native peoples, no matter whether positive or negative, often reveals more about ourselves than it does about them.

15

Cannibals and Colonials

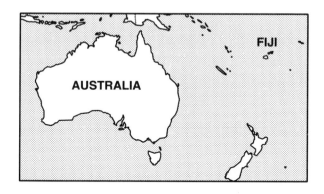

Imperialism is Civilization unadulterated.
—Oswald Spengler, *The Decline of the West*

On most tropical islands, strong colors and pungent smells dominate the senses. The lush green of palm trees and high grasses contrast sharply with the glaring white beaches, which in turn form white ribbons between the vivid blues of the water and the dark greens of the volcanic peaks. But on Sunday mornings, sounds dominate on the tiny Yasawa Islands of Fiji in the South Pacific. The waves lap constantly and rhythmically against the sand and volcanic peaks, birds occasionally shriek, but the native people of the island move slowly and quietly. Sunday is the sacred day of the week, and the native people of Yasawa-i-rara honor it with quiet.

When the time comes for the villagers to gather in the white Methodist church, with its shiny tin roof and green trimming, an elder grabs a large stick in each hand and beats out a tattoo on a log drum. The sound carries to each of the several dozen cane-and-thatch huts, as well as to the concrete-block houses where the two hundred villagers live.

One by one and in small family groups, they leave home and follow the worn paths across the lush grass of the village plaza. The women wear loose, modest dresses with muted prints. The dresses neither reveal much skin nor show anything more than a vague outline of the feminine body beneath it. The dresses fall straight down past their knees, and underneath the dresses they wear matching skirts that cover their legs and ankles down to their bare feet. The men wear white shirts and ties that look like the ones worn to church anywhere on a Sunday morning, but they too go barefoot, and instead of pants they wear sarongs that brush against their calves as they walk. Many of the worshipers carry fans tightly woven from pandanus leaves. Each adult clutches a black Bible printed in the Fijian language. The Bibles are badly worn from daily readings and frequent church attendance; the books no longer have spines but have been reduced to a collection of stitched pages held fragilely between two faded black covers.

The villagers gather outside the church door to sing. They have no musical accompaniment, not even a pitch pipe, but they sing softly, in perfect harmony. A few of them tap their Bibles or beat their fans lightly on the palms of their hands as they sing the lilting Fijian songs. They kneel in the sand to pray, and then go inside for the start of Sunday services. The strong voices of the church members float through the village, as much a part of nature as the rustle of the wind through the thick groves of bananas and plantains on the south of the village, as much as the brushing of the coconut fronds against one another, or the lapping of the waves on the soft white sand of Yasawa-i-rara.

On Sunday in Yasawa-i-rara, people do not stir from their family compounds except to go to church. The family lounges together on mats beneath the trees, and the children play quietly. The small stores make no sales, alcohol is forbidden on the Sabbath as on all other days of the year, and no one smokes in public. Sunday is a day of rest in a decidedly literal way. Lacking electricity to power radios, televisions, or other diversions, and lacking automobiles or motorcycles, the villagers sit quietly and wait through the afternoon until it is time to return to church late in the day.

More people have seen Yasawa-i-rara, at least in pictures, than are aware of it. Because the area looks so perfectly the way people in temperate climates imagine a South Seas island to be, Hollywood producers chose it as the site for the 1940 film *Blue Lagoon*, starring Jean Simmons, and selected it again for the remake of the film in 1980, with actress Brooke Shields. Tourists staying on the Fijian "mainland" of Viti Levu come out on day trips by float plane or on chartered boats from the city of Lautoka, four hours away by boat. The visitors may play in the sand or water, they may snorkel and dive, but the islands offer no hotels, restaurants, or any other facilities to encourage outsiders to linger after dark. During the week, villagers gladly sell shell jewelry and soft drinks, but on Sundays even this minor commercialism ceases.

On weekday mornings the children leave the village at six o'clock for the two-hour walk along an island path to the next village, where they have classes. Each day, two adults accompany them on the five-mile walk, and they prepare the lunch for the children.

After the church, the main building in the village is the chief's house, made of cinder block and rising above the other homes because it it perched on a high stone platform, in the traditional manner of Fijian chiefs' homes. The purple, yellow, and red of the house make it the most colorful in the village, but like the other homes it has no real furniture. People sit on mats and prop themselves on pillows. The kitchens of most of the homes are outside, as are the showers, which depend on rainwater collected in raised tanks from the runoff from the tin roofs.

During my visit in 1992, the chief's house had been empty for a year since the death of the last chief, and the villagers slowly made plans to elect another. Like everything else in Fiji, the selection would come in its own proper time, and it was better for it to develop slowly but properly than for it to come quickly and leave bitterness or division in a community where everyone saw and spoke to everyone else daily.

The movie-perfect image on Yasawa-i-rara of the idyllic life covers up a deeper tension in Fijian social life. Fiji has had a difficult time emerging from the colonial era, but that era has left it with deep social divisions and festering ethnic problems. Fiji had its own problems before the Europeans arrived, and they were perhaps just as deep.

When the first Europeans arrived in the area, over two hundred years earlier, they encountered a scene much different from what we see today on the Yasawa Islands. These islands first came to the attention of the outside world in 1789, when Captain William Bligh encountered them after being put off his ship, HMS *Bounty*, by Fletcher Christian and his gang of mutineers. Without any firearms for defense, Captain Bligh and his eighteen loyal men were cast adrift in a longboat that measured a mere twenty feet, about one foot in length for each man. The mutiny occurred in the waters that now belong to the Polynesian island nation of Tonga. When Bligh called at the first island, seeking food and provisions, he lost his quartermaster to an attack by cannibals. Legend has it that the natives selected the quartermaster because he was the fattest of the party, having spent much of the voyage on the *Bounty* filching the supplies intended for the common seamen. If it is true that he was the largest, this certainly could have slowed his escape and made him the most logical target for the blows of the islanders. The other men escaped by throwing their clothing into the air and water and thus distracting the natives, who had little access to cloth other than the *tapa* that they laboriously pounded from bark.

An expert navigator, Bligh guided his ill-equipped expedition due west into the waters of Fiji, a Melanesian island group. He soon sailed into the maze of reefs and islands known as Yasawa.

The Fijians had an ancient legend about people who drifted up onto their shores. According to this story, the first man and the first woman had three daughters but no sons. Fearing that his family might die out, the father made plans to mate with his own daughters, but before that happened a young man, whom they called Tabua, mysteriously washed up on their island. Despite the father's resistance, Tabua performed a series of heroic deeds and then married the three daughters. Before passing from the scene and surrendering power to the younger outsider, the father decreed that thenceforth any stranger who washed up on their shores should be eaten. This was reinforced by the belief that castaways had been abandoned by the gods on the sea and therefore were fair game for the islanders.

Captain Bligh probably never heard this story of Tabua, but he did know the fierce reputation of the Melanesians for cannibalism. Therefore, when he sailed past the Yasawa Islands and saw large war canoes coming after him, he knew what fate the Fijians had in mind for him and his men. Through desperate rowing and the luck of a short afternoon squall and finally darkness itself, Bligh and his men managed to escape. In recognition of Bligh's experiences, the islands were called the Bligh Islands before officially becoming Fiji, and the passage between Yasawa and the large island of Viti Levu still bears the name Bligh Water on nautical charts.

In addition to eating castaways and strangers who washed up

on their shores, the Fijians also ate one another, or, more precisely, they ate their enemies in intertribal rivalries. Usually these were warriors, but in a raid any victim, including women and children, might suffice. Old vocabulary lists indicate a variety of terms for human flesh, cannibalism, and killing of enemies. Sometimes the captive might be tortured before being cooked. In particularly gruesome episodes, the chief might cut off a digit or other piece of flesh and consume it in front of the still-living victim. The humans were prepared in much the same way that a pig was. The cook wrapped the meat, called *bokola*, in the leaves of *Solanum uporo* and placed it in a pit lined with hot rocks. This form of cooking, common throughout much of the South Pacific, is more commonly known by its Polynesian name of *luau*. While the meat cooked, sexual license prevailed throughout the community.

Only men could eat the meat, and in so doing they acquired the essence or *mana* of the person eaten. Because of the highly charged *mana* of human flesh, the Fijians used a special wooden fork with four prongs at the end. Men could not touch the human flesh with their fingers but had to use the forks, which looked like an enlarged version of the picks used for appetizers.

The chief consumed the most important cuts of meat, such as heart and tongue, liver, and female breasts. The valued shoulders, legs, and arms went to the chief's senior warriors, and the lesser warriors had to make do with hands, feet, and other odd parts. The genitals were frequently hung in a sacred grove, or, in a particularly insulting act, the chief might return the genitals and head to the family of the victim.

Cannibalism in Fiji appears to be many centuries old, but it reached a crescendo in the nineteenth century. During the nineteenth century, the practice grew so common in Fiji that the islands became known around the world as the Cannibal Isles. Under pressure from whalers, traders, and outside colonial powers, rivalries between Fijian chiefs intensified and with them came an increase in fighting, raiding, and cannibalism.

Fijian chiefs encouraged cannibalism and stories of their ferocity as intimidation and propaganda skillfully designed to prevent attacks on their own people. One chief reportedly piled a stone in front of his hut for each victim he had eaten; his pile surpassed 850 before he died. The most infamous of the nineteenth-century chiefs was Cokobau, who made himself into a king, Tui Viti, over most of the islands in the middle of the century. When one chief did not respond quickly enough to him during a ceremony, Cokobau had the unlucky man clubbed to death on the spot. The fate of another captured chief was even worse. Cokobau had his tongue cut out, and then Cokobau ate it raw in front of the bleeding man, who tried in vain to plead for a quicker and more merciful death.

In 1853, Cokobau converted from cannibalism to Methodism. He wisely figured that he had more to gain as a Christian king than as a cannibal king, and with the support of the Wesleyans and their ally, the monarch of Tonga, he increased his authority. His conversion began the gradual decline of cannibalism in Fiji, but his enemies continued the practice. When one missionary, the Reverend Baker, tried to go into the hill country in 1867, the traditional enemies of Cokobau rightly saw him as an ally of their enemy. They consequently killed him and cooked him. As unaccustomed to boots as they were to white men in general, they cooked him with his boots on, and managed with some difficulty to eat part of them. In 1874, Fiji became a crown colony of Great Britain, which made cannibalism illegal.

The colonization of Fiji occurred in the middle of the orgiastic drive for colonies by the European powers. The British ended cannibalism, converted the Fijians to a rather stiff Christianity, and stopped the tribal fighting among Fijians. Instead of the old factionalism, an equally virulent source of ethnic tension developed in a new guise. The British introduced the new ethnic tensions that plague the small nation today.

The British colonizers of Fiji judged the native Fijian workers to be difficult to control; therefore, as they did in many other colonies around the world in the nineteenth century, the colonial authorities imported laborers from India to work in the hot sugarcane fields. Sugarcane grows only in hot, humid climates, and it is probably the most difficult of all crops to harvest. Workers stand in fields of densely growing canes that tower above them and block every breeze. Sweat runs into their eyes and blurs their vision, which needs to be clear if they are to swing with accuracy the large machetes with which they cut the cane. Workers accidentally cut themselves and others with a missed blow of a machete, or they are stuck with the sharp ends of the cut cane, causing them to lose an eye or impair a foot. In the midst of all the dangers, the sweat and sticky canes attract flies and other insects that then stick to the workers' faces and arms.

Despite these dangers in working sugarcane, Indians enlisted in the work gangs recruited by the British government. Because of the near-starvation conditions prevalent in India, many of the Indians gladly submitted to deportation for labor barely above the level of slaves. The British colonial government in India was glad to get rid of as many unemployed young men as possible, and the British business interests in Fiji thereby acquired willing and very cheap workers.

After arriving in Fiji and working for a few years in the fields, many of the Indians found work in the cities, and began to open small enterprises as vendors. As the Indians left the sugarcane fields for these other pursuits, the British brought in more Indian workers to hold the poorly paying jobs. As the men gained some money, they recruited wives from their home districts in India, and soon a full community of Hindu and even Muslim Indians grew up in Fiji.

By the time Fiji became an independent nation, in 1970, the Indian population almost equaled the number of native Fijians. The two groups differed in many ways. The Fijians spoke their native language, and the Indians spoke their own Fijian dialect of Hindi. The Fijians observed a strict form of Christianity, while the Indians professed a rather relaxed Hinduism or Islam. The Indians had generally higher education, and they controlled commerce and the cities. The Fijians controlled the government and countryside, owning 83 percent of the land in Fiji through their communal villages.

As the economic power of the Indians increased after independence from Britain, the tensions between the Indians and the native Fijians escalated. During the democratic election of 1987, the Indians won control of the government and were thus poised to control both the economy and government of the nation. Afraid of Indian domination over them, and particularly of Indian control of the police and the military, Fijian colonels led a sequence of two coups that preserved the power of the native Fijians and removed the Indians from office. Over the next several years, tensions flared repeatedly, but by 1992 both groups had agreed to a new political arrangement that would leave the natives in control of the government and the Indians in control of the economy. The Fijians would continue to own the land, but the Indians would continue to run the island's businesses.

The ethnic rivalries and tensions between the native Fijians and the Indians illustrate problems that have come to plague the twentieth century. The strife between the Fijian natives and the Indian immigrants closely resembles struggles in Asia, Europe, America, and Africa between much larger groups of tens of millions of people.

The British brought Asian Indians to the Caribbean to work on sugar plantations in Trinidad and Tobago and on the South American mainland in the British colony of Guyana. Prior to the arrival of the Asian Indians, the native population had been effectively wiped out and replaced with African slaves. By the time the colonies became independent, their populations were roughly divided between people of African and Asian ancestry in Trinidad and Tobago, but Guyana had more Asians, making it the only country in the Americas with a majority of Asians, and in which Hindu was the major religion.

The British brought Indians to East Africa to build the railroad from Mombasa, on the Indian Ocean, to Kampala, on Lake Victoria. After building the railroad, many of the Indians stayed on to become shopkeepers all along the line but particularly at the end of the line, in Kampala, which became the capital of Uganda after independence in 1962. General Idi Amin seized control of Uganda in 1971, and in the following year he expelled all 45,000 Asian residents, killing many in the process.

The British brought Asian workers to South Africa, but they never reached the numbers of the Africans or the Europeans living there. Approximately three percent of the population, they remained a separate class from the Africans, Europeans, and mixed-blood coloreds. While living and practicing law in South Africa, Gandhi mastered his first lessons in civil disobedience and in confronting the colonial government. He later used this information to achieve independence for his native India.

In many places in the world, the various layers of colonization can still be seen in the population. After the Dutch discovered the uninhabited volcanic island of Mauritius in the south Indian Ocean in 1638, they planted sugarcane but were unable to establish a permanent settlement. In 1721, France took over the island and brought in large numbers of African slaves to ensure a permanent work force for sugar production. The British took over

Mauritius in 1810, at the end of France's disastrous Napoleonic era, and brought in Asian workers from their colony in India. In 1968, the multicultural Mauritius became independent under a government and an economy dominated by Indians, who formed the majority of the population, but who had to deal with tremendous resentment from the less successful African creoles.

Southern Indians, known as Tamils, also crossed over to the island of Ceylon, which was occupied by the Sinhalese, who are primarily Buddhist. Ceylon became independent from Britain in 1948, and changed its name to Sri Lanka in 1972. The Tamils make up less than one-fifth of the total population of Sri Lanka, but they live concentrated in the north. The tensions between the native Sinhalese and the Tamils gradually escalated into a guerrilla war that killed more than ten thousand people, including numerous terrorist attacks against civilians of all types.

Although it is one of the smallest and remotest places on the planet, and one of the last to come into contact with the global culture, Fiji suffers the same tensions and struggles as does any cosmopolitan community with dozens of ethnic groups. No place on earth, no matter how small or remote, seems to be immune from the ethnic tensions of the twentieth century.

The most important historic event of the twentieth century has been the reversal of two thousand years of history and the collapse of the great empires of the world into many smaller countries. Since the origins of the Roman Empire in the Mediterranean and the Han empire in China, the great empires of the world have been steadily expanding and gobbling up smaller countries, eventually reaching tiny outposts such as Fiji.

For a while it appeared that the rise of nationalism, combined with imperialism, might reverse the long-term human pattern of cultural and ethnic diversification. From roughly 1492 until the twentieth century, nationalism brought with it colonialism and a rigid cultural orthodoxy of one language, one religion, and one people. It seemed that the world might be divided into a few major camps of the French sphere, the English sphere, the Russian sphere, and a few odd ones around the edges.

The twentieth century suddenly reversed four centuries of history. As quickly as modern arms and the printing press created a handful of powerful national empires, almost all of them were destroyed and the pent-up cultural aspirations of thousands of newly self-conscious nationalities and ethnic groups, such as the Fijians and the Fijian Indians, were revitalized.

The nationalism that took root in Western Europe and the United States in the eighteenth century spread to Latin America and Eastern Europe in the nineteenth century. Almost all of Spain's American colonies rose in rebellion and attained their independence in the first two decades of the 1800s. Shortly thereafter, from 1821 to 1829, Greece struggled against the Turks for independence, a struggle that elicited great sympathy among Western European romantics, including the poet Lord Byron, who died in Greece in 1824. After the success of the Greeks in freeing themselves from Ottoman rule, Romania formed its own nation in 1861, and Bulgaria followed in 1908.

At this time the speakers of common languages began to form geographic unions. Any people who wanted to be an independent nation had a much stronger case if they could show that their language was different from that of their rulers. Norway became independent in 1905, after nearly five hundred years of rule by Denmark and then another century of rule by Sweden, but part of the drive for its independence was the development of its own language and literature, distinct from both Swedish and Danish. A major part of the Irish struggle for independence against Great Britain included the struggle to keep the formerly outlawed Gaelic language alive, in print, and taught in Irish schools. Catalonia, in northeastern Spain, tried to pursue a similar course of keeping its language alive and separate from Castilian Spanish, as did the Basques in the Spanish northwest. Similar nationalist movements developed among Hungarians, Serbs, Croats, Albanians, Slovaks, Poles, Ukrainians, Lithuanians, Finns, Estonians, Latvians, and Sicilians.

Except for Latin America, Thailand, Liberia, and Ethiopia, the whole world had been divided up among the European powers, the Ottoman Empire, the Japanese empire, and the United States by the opening of the twentieth century. These were approximately forty independent nations and empires, of which a dozen had territory or empires substantial enough to make them truly international players. In the first decade of the twentieth century, it seemed as though the world was being quickly united into one political system with only a handful of major players.

The second decade of this century shattered the imperialist dreams of the global powers and forced the abdication of the

German Kaiser, the Russian Czar, and the Turkish Sultan. The First World War pitted these empires against one another in a mad scramble that reduced the twelve major players to only a few. The war reduced the number of empires but replaced them with dozens of new political entities, each longing and demanding to be a free and independent nation, equal to all others in the world arena.

Following World War I, the conference to write the Treaty of Versailles fanned the flames of micronationalism when President Woodrow Wilson of the United States included as one of his Seventeen Points the right to self-determination for minority nationalities. Even though Wilson intended to apply his doctrine primarily to the smaller nations of Eastern Europe, groups around the world took up the cause as an inalienable right.

So many small ethnic groups lived in Eastern Europe that they had to be lumped together in order to make viable nations. The Czech provinces of Bohemia and Moravia joined with Slovakia to create the artificial nation of Czechoslovakia. In the Balkans, the former Ottoman provinces of Serbia, Croatia, Montenegro, Bosnia-Herzegovina, and Slovenia united with large numbers of Albanians, Macedonians, and Turks to form the new nation of Yugoslavia. While the newly invented nations such as Yugoslavia, Albania, and Czechoslovakia sprang to life, ancient nations such as Poland, Latvia, Lithuania, Finland, and Estonia reemerged from the collapsing empires that had once absorbed them.

Having been liberated from Turkish rule during the First World War, the Arabs wanted independence rather than sustained colonial domination by France and Britain. Within the Arab world, the Kurds, Muslim tribes speaking an Indo-European language, wanted their independence as a separate nation.

Immediately after the war, a few more isolated countries managed to free themselves from foreign rule. Iceland attained independence from Denmark; Mongolia broke away from China; and Ireland managed to free itself from centuries of bloody British rule. The spirit of nationalism, which had been so long joined to imperialism, now became a new union of nationalism with anti-imperialism. The new movement swept the globe, and every ethnic group claimed a right to independence, whether or not it had ever been an independent group or could even claim to be a group aside from some minor variation in language or religion from the people around them.

Following the Second World War, hundreds of new nationalities around the world demanded independence from the colonial powers in a new wave of nationalism and anti-imperialism. Many of these struggles took the form of anticolonial wars, as Vietnam and Algeria fought France for independence or as the Mau Mau rose up in rebellion against British rule in Kenya. Between the end of the Second World War and 1970, almost all the remaining colonies of Britain, France, the Netherlands, Portugal, and the United States received independence.

The Philippines became the first new independent nation when the United States granted them independence on July 4, 1946, shortly after liberation from Japan. The United States began negotiating independence treaties with its holdings in Micronesia, and admitted the territories of Hawaii and Alaska as full members of its union. Puerto Rico moved into an ambiguous category as a commonwealth affiliated with the United States.

Nigeria became Africa's largest and richest independent nation when it left British control on October 1, 1960. Ethnic tensions with the Ibo of the southeast escalated until the Ibos declared the independent nation of Biafra in 1967. At the time of their rebellion, the Ibo, a largely Christian group, claimed the highest literacy and educational level of any African ethnic group. By the time Biafra surrendered in 1970, a million people had been killed, many of them civilians who were starved to death, and even more had been dislocated.

The East African nations of Burundi and Rwanda have long been inhabited by three tribes or ethnic groups. The pygmy Twa probably entered the area first, and lived there for thousands of years. Later came the Hutu, farmers who dominated the foraging Twa. Around the sixteenth century, the tall, thin Tutsi, a cattle-herding people sometimes called the Watusi, migrated down from the north and conquered the farming Hutu. The Tutsi ruled over the other two groups, even though they constituted only about a fifth of the population. Each ethnic group occupied a rank in a three-tier caste system to which the Europeans added a fourth caste when they colonized the area in 1899. The Germans lost the colony to Belgium after World War II.

Even though both Burundi and Rwanda had the same three ethnic groups of Twa, Hutu, and Tutsi, each became an independent nation. In Rwanda, the Hutu rose up in 1959 and overthrew the Tutsi in a bloody revolution. In 1972, the Hutu in Burundi rose against Tutsi domination and slaughtered about 10,000 of their overlords. The Tutsi retaliated against their former vassals with a vengeance, slaughtering 150,000 Hutu, while another 100,000 Hutu fled into neighboring Zaire and Tanzania.

The colonial era created nations around the world, and left behind centralized governments and strong armies. Those two institutions had been the pillars of colonial administration. The colonial powers built railroads and harbors and installed new businesses, but these usually served the needs of the colonial powers. The infrastructure built by those powers served the needs of extracting raw materials rather than stimulating internal commerce to help the native people. Other colonial institutions, such as churches, hospitals, and schools, usually were quite minor compared to the expense and effort that the colonial powers put into their government and military structures. The newly created countries of Africa inherited weak schools, churches, businesses, and hospitals, but very strong administrations and traditions of strong, centralized government supported by military might.

During the early decades of independence, the artificially created nations received high levels of financial and military aid from either the Western capitalist nations or the communist nations. This aid helped the military and ruling elite to remain in power. In many newly emerging countries the ruling authorities tended to the needs of the military and to the profits of a small elite. They allowed foreign governments, religious institutions, and humanitarian aid programs to clothe, feed, nurse, educate, and house the masses. With the death of the Cold War, the aid declined and the stresses pulling the governments apart increased.

Ethnic strife has broken out in at least one African country in virtually every year. Ethnic warfare seems endemic in some countries such as Sudan, Ethiopia, and Somalia. The struggles often focused on religious identity as Muslim struggled against Christian in Sudan and Nigeria, or some appeared to be capitalist versus communist, as in Ethiopia and Angola. Outside powers including France, the Soviet Union, the United States, Libya, Saudi Arabia, Iran, Israel, South Africa, and Cuba often entered the fights with money, weapons, and sometimes even soldiers for one side, and then withdrew or sometimes actually switched sides. No matter what the outside powers did, and no matter who supported which group, the fighting continued along tribal, ethnic, and religious lines.

Many people assumed that the granting of independence to people colonized against their wills would lessen the fighting and violence in the world. The longing for sovereignty seemed to be normal, and once that desire was fulfilled, tensions would evaporate. Indeed, tensions subsided between the newly independent nations and their former colonists, but from Africa to the Pacific, tensions increased among ethnic groups within the newly independent countries.

The slow demise of the colonial era produced even more ethnic divisions and struggles. Rivalries between the Muslims and the Hindus prevented India from making a peaceful transition to independence as a single, whole country; public sentiment and political leaders pushed to create separate Hindu and Muslim nations. When the British withdrew in 1947, they turned the subcontinent into two nations, India and Pakistan. Pakistan was divided into two parts a thousand miles from each other, with India between them. Even though India had gained independence in the nonviolent resistance movement led by Mohandas Gandhi, after victory against Britain, Hindus and Muslims fell upon each other in one of the worst slaughters of history.

Each state persecuted the minorities of the other and tried to expel them. Fighting erupted along the newly emerging borders in northwest India. Muslims left on the Indian side of the border and Hindus left on the Pakistani side faced violent attacks that killed men, women, and children. Vigilantes attacked whole villages, slaying everyone in them; they also attacked trains and even desperate columns of people fleeing on foot. The objective was not to force them to flee or to prevent their fleeing or to rob them, but simply to kill them because they belonged to the other group. In hatred and fear, groups of refugees fleeing in one direction often battled with groups of refugees fleeing in the opposite direction. The death toll will probably never be known. Both Hindus and Muslims exaggerated the number of their people killed by the other side and minimized the numbers they themselves killed. By official accounts the death toll was roughly 200,000, but it may have been many thousands more than that. Another 12 million people became refugees, giving up their homes, communities, farms, and businesses and fleeing into the other country.

Violence in the Indian subcontinent continued after independence as East and West Pakistan went to war and divided into Pakistan and Bangladesh. In the year after independence, the government of Bangladesh showed even less tolerance for its minority and tribal populations than it had under Pakistani rule. The government allowed and even seemed to encourage attacks against tribal people, Buddhists, Hindus, and Christians. The Muslim majority moved into the Chittagong Hills and removed the tribal people.

The Sikhs, the next largest religious group of the Indian subcontinent after the Muslims and the Hindus, combine characteristics of both religions but maintain a strong identity separate from both. The Sikhs can be recognized easily, because the women wear a simple tunic and breeches, and the men wear the distinctive five *kakkas*: uncut hair, covered by a turban; a small ceremonial dagger; a wooden comb; a steel bracelet; and short breeches. The Sikhs first sided with India because of the persecution they experienced from the Muslims of Pakistan. Many of them fled south after the division of Punjab between the two countries in 1947. Since then, they have been advocating for their own country and living in a state of smoldering rebellion that sometimes breaks into brutal violence. In June 1984, President Indira Gandhi sent troops into a bloody fight to take over the Golden Temple, the holiest shrine of the Sikhs. Four months later, two of President Gandhi's Sikh bodyguards assassinated her in revenge for the attack. In the ensuing rioting, thousands of Sikhs died and fifty thousand were driven from their homes.

In Southeast Asia, the series of prolonged wars in Vietnam, Cambodia, and Laos displaced millions of people from the era of the Second World War virtually through the remainder of the century. In the constantly shifting alliances and factions, one ethnic group after another found itself trapped on the cutting edge of the disagreement.

After the Vietnamese successfully drove the French and then the Americans from their land, they began to purify their own nation. Tribal people such as the Hmong, who had sided with the United States in the civil war, became one of the first ethnic groups to flee. When tensions flared between Vietnam and its erstwhile ally, China, thousands of ethnic Chinese who had lived in Vietnam for generations faced expulsion; others fled rather than face new restrictions and persecutions in Vietnam. When Vietnam invaded Cambodia, whose people had often been vassals under Vietnamese rule, millions of Cambodians fled. Throughout the years of warfare, thousands of the refugees fled to camps in Thailand, for eventual placement in the United States, France, and Canada, but many more had to return to an uncertain fate in Cambodia or Vietnam.

At the end of the twentieth century, the globe stands divided into roughly two hundred independent countries or states, but these contain somewhere around five thousand different nations or ethnic groups. The colonialism of the past five hundred years has thoroughly rearranged the ethnic map of the world. The vagaries of government policy, natural disasters, and economic fluctuations have pulled and pushed ethnic groups across the globe. Members of different groups now live cheek-by-jowl with people whose ancestors lived on the other side of the world. The separation and isolation of ethnic groups will never return.

16

Micro-nations

. . . Having come so close to extinction, they had got a keener sense of humility than their benefactors, and paradoxically a greater sense of pride.
—SCOTT MOMADAY, *House Made of Dawn*

The Trans-Siberian Express operates the longest regularly scheduled train trip in the world. A passenger can get on one of five daily trains in Vladivostok on the Pacific coast and, with one ticket, no change of trains, and no stop longer than fifteen minutes, get off in Moscow seven days later and four thousand miles away. A slightly shorter branch of the Trans-Siberian begins in Beijing, passes through Ulan Bator, the capital of Mongolia, and joins the regular line at Ulan Ude, in Russia, for the remainder of the trip to Moscow.

People on the train are not so much passengers as temporary residents. During the week-long trip, the train takes on the character of a long, narrow Russian apartment building. Each compartment becomes a living room, dining room, and kitchen as the residents hang up their clothes, change into pajamas, roll out sleeping mats to go over the benches, and hang bags of fruit, bottles of kefir, whole salamis, onions, and candy from every available hook and screw in their compartment. Neighbors begin long conversations that become marathon life stories of birth, marriage, death, betrayal, suffering, and triumph. A mother braids her daughter's hair and ties it into large, multicolored bows the size of full-grown peonies. Children run up and down the hall in constantly changing games. The women hang up garments to air, and wash their babies' soiled garments, which they hang all over the train to dry.

Soldiers gather to play cards, exchange cigarettes, and share bottles of vodka or bitter beer. The porter brings endless glasses of steaming tea from the samovar that keeps water boiling at the end of each car. Middle-aged men in exercise pants quickly walk the halls and do knee-bends and push-ups outside their compartment doors. A vendor plies the hall, selling sugar-coated berries and hard candies. The same vendor returns later in the day with racks holding metal bowls of soup and hunks of fresh, dense bread. At night, insomniacs talk in the mottled light of the corridor, and lovers meet for a little privacy in the locked toilets at the end of the car or in the vestibule between cars.

At the short stops, the passengers pour off the train to see what might be for sale. Village women with their hair tied up in the traditional babushka sit stoically in front of whatever they have to offer. One sells pickles; another may have a handful of tomatoes from her garden; yet another has cooked two dozen blinys, which she has wrapped individually in old newspaper; the woman next to her has boiled and cubed a pot of potatoes, which she now serves in newspaper cones.

The Trans-Siberian Express represents one of the engineering adventures of the concluding years of the nineteenth century. In a century filled with stories about the building of railroads over impossible terrain, the Trans-Siberian bound together two continents. Even today, only the airplane offers quicker and easier connection between Asia and Europe, and no highways have been built to compete with the railway.

In cutting across the heartland of Eurasia, the Trans-Siberian railway begins at the Pacific Ocean, skirts Manchuria, crosses the Amur River at Khabarovsk, and then parallels the Amur for six hundred miles across the Jewish Autonomous Oblast, through Amuria, into the land of the Russian Mongols, around the shores of Lake Baikal, up the Angara River and across the flat planes of Siberia, through the low-lying Urals, and on into European Russia.

The scenery along the Trans-Siberian seems panoramic and

vast without being dramatic. The mountains show well-worn curves; they are no more than rolling hills that rise only a few thousand feet above sea level. The forests cover great distances, but the individual trees tend to be relatively small. Generations of settlers needing wood for fuel and building have chopped down most of the trees near the railroad. The picturesque villages appear overwhelmed and nearly buried by a century's accumulation of abandoned, rusting junk brought in by the passing trains.

After nearly a week traveling eastward from Moscow toward Vladivostok, the train passes down the Amur River valley, which separates China from Russia. Only two days short of Vladivostok and the Pacific Ocean, the train pauses for a few minutes at the rural town of Birobidzhan. At first there is nothing special about the town; it seems like any of two dozen other such settlements beside the Trans-Siberian Railway. A few women loiter around the platform, selling small snacks in front of an oversized but deteriorated and nearly deserted train station.

The oddity that distinguishes Birobidzhan from the other communities strung up and down the track is that the name of the town is written not only in the Cyrillic letters used in the Russian language, but also in Hebrew. Birobidzhan is the capital city of the former Jewish Autonomous Oblast, set aside by the Soviet government for Jewish colonization in 1928, with Russian and Yiddish as the official languages.

Of course, the clocks in the railway station indicated the real source of power. Like clocks in all airports and train stations across Russia, the one in Birobidzhan shows Moscow time, even though Birobidzhan lies five time zones to the east of Moscow, and when it is midnight in Moscow, the sun is already coming up in Birobidzhan.

Soviet authorities created the Jewish Autonomous Oblast. It is situated on a rather desolate stretch of the Amur River in the Soviet Far East to the northwest of Harbin, China, and due east of Khabarovsk. Later the area became the Evrey Autonomous Oblast, with its capital still in the city of Birobidzhan. The area had no historical connection of significance for Jews, and despite feeble attempts by the Soviet government to foster migration, few Jews ever moved to live there. The region fulfilled the notion that every nation should have its own area. Its existence also gave the Soviet authorities a pretext to prohibit Jewish emigration to

Israel by claiming that Soviet Jews already had their own independent homeland within the Soviet Union and therefore did
not need to leave.

Of all the nations with ethnic problems, the Soviet Union
probably faced the greatest number and variety of any nation
after World War II, but of all the world leaders facing ethnic
problems, Joseph Stalin boasted the most experience and proved
to be the most adept and Machiavellian in dealing with them.
Under Lenin's administration, Stalin, who still ranked as a relatively minor figure, served as the Minister of Nationality Affairs,
which gave him authority over minorities throughout the Soviet
Union. This detailed knowledge of the cultural diversity of the
people gave Stalin a firmer grasp on the population than any
other Soviet leader ever had.

Under Stalin's rule, the government set about creating so-
called republics and autonomous regions for every ethnic group
throughout the Soviet Union. Approximately one hundred different groups made up the Soviet Union. These were divided into
fifteen republics and a constantly changing list of Autonomous
Oblasts and Nationality Okrugs. Even the dominant Slavs were
divided into Russians, Byelorussians, and Ukrainians. Other large
groups included the Turkic peoples, Finno-Ugrics, Jews, and a
variety of Indo-Europeans including Georgians, Armenians, Ro-
manians, and a large population of ethnic Germans. The Soviet
Union even had a small Inuit or Eskimo population living on
the Bering Sea. Stalin distrusted them because of their kinship
and frequent interaction with their relatives in Alaska; so, rather
than giving them an autonomous area, he moved them far away
from their homelands.

The fate of the homelands of different ethnic groups largely
depended on the whim of Stalin. The Crimea, the peninsula
between the Black Sea and the Azov Sea, had been an independent republic from 1918 to 1921, and the headquarters for anticommunist forces of the White Army under Baron Petr
Nikolaevich Wrangel. During World War II, the Germans occupied it for two years, from 1942 to 1944, and even though it
took the Germans nearly 250 days of siege before they captured
the Crimean capital, Sevastopol, Stalin thought that the Tatars
had collaborated with the Germans just as they had with the
anticommunist White Army a generation earlier. Even though

the Tatars had lived there since the thirteenth century, Stalin
uprooted the entire Tatar nation and shipped it to Central Asia.
A decade later, Nikita Khrushchev gave the newly downgraded
oblast of Crimea to the Ukraine to mark three hundred years of
Russian-Ukrainian friendship and unity. When the Soviet Union
dissolved in 1990, Russia and Ukraine quickly fell to arguing
over the peninsula, while thousands of Tatars, who were born in
exile and had never seen the Crimea, began returning to their
ancestral homeland.

The notion that every nationality should have its own homeland was carried to such lengths by the Soviet authorities that
they created new homelands for people who did not have them.
Often the newly created homelands had only a minority of the
people for whom they were intended, while most of them lived
elsewhere. The ethnic Germans did not have a German territory
inside Russia, so they were given one. For a while the ethnic
Germans living in Russia had their own Volga republic, but in
the anti-German sentiment of World War II, Stalin abolished
their republic and sent them to Siberia.

Prior to the Soviet era, most of the Central Asians and many
of the other minorities did not define themselves by nationality.
They more likely defined themselves by religion, usually as
Christians, Jews, or Muslims. Many of the groups in Central Asia
defined themselves by life-style as nomadic people or as farmers.
Within these identifying definitions, they further divided themselves by kinship through a clan or tribe. Stalin's creation of new
nationalities, however, meant that an educated Muslim merchant
of Bukhara was suddenly an Uzbek, and thus belonged to the
same ethnic group as a pagan herder from a distant valley (Hall
1992, 41).

Each republic and autonomous region acquired a history, an
ethnic identity, and all the cultural trappings to show that newly
discovered identity. For each newly created nation, Soviet authorities developed a written language and created official songs
and dances and an official national costume that often seemed to
owe more to Hollywood films than to the ethnic history of the
people themselves. Each republic maintained its own national ballet
company, which wore the costumes and performed the dances for
visitors and at various official functions inside the republic and occasionally even abroad. Local universities worked to establish or in-

vent a national literature, usually complete with an official poet and a great national epic or perhaps even a song cycle.

The Soviet strategy toward its nationalities continued largely as one of divide-and-rule, since the boundaries of the republics seemed to follow no logical divisions. The Soviet authorities split the Turkish tribes of Central Asia into Turkmenistan, Uzbekistan, Kazakhstan, and Kirgizia. Azerbaijan, another republic made up of Turks, lay on the western side of the Caspian Sea, divided into two parts, with Armenia in between. Artificial as some of the Soviet nationalities were, many of them became the basis around which independence movements could coalesce in the 1990s.

Throughout the Cold War era, ethnic problems seemed of minor importance in the great struggle between the socialist nations, led by the Soviet Union, and the capitalist forces, led by the United States. The tensions focused on ideology and power blocs, with each side struggling to gain the allegiance or at least the cooperation of the developing or nonaligned nations. With a series of wars in Korea, Vietnam, and Afghanistan, and with numerous uprisings such as those in Hungary and Czechoslovakia, neither of the major powers had time to look closely at ethnic issues.

The Soviet invasion of Afghanistan in 1979 started one of the greatest dislocations of ethnic groups in the history of that area, which had known many invasions and terrible wars. Since Alexander the Great fought his way through the area in the fourth century B.C., it has been invaded by a succession of armies from the Mongols to the British.

The refugee exodus provoked by the Soviets in the 1980s included large numbers of all the major ethnic groups in Afghanistan—Pushtun, Uzbek, Turkmen, Tadjik, Hazara, Baluch, and Kirghiz. Most of them fled into Pakistan, but large numbers of Afghan Shiites also headed for Iran. The Pushtuns and the Hazara had close tribal and kinship ties with fellow tribe members in Pakistan and could call on them for refuge and assistance. Hazara Shiites, who had no relatives in Pakistan, more likely fled to Iran because of the shared religion and because the Hazara language is more closely related to Farsi, the language of Iran.

A total of 2.7 million Afghan refugees fled to one of 380 official camps in Pakistan, and somewhere over 2 million went to Iran. In addition, several hundred thousand refugees settled in areas outside of the camps, usually as illegal aliens. Seventy-five percent of the Afghan refugees were women and children under the age of fifteen; most of the men remained in Afghanistan to fight, though they occasionally sought refuge or rest and visited with their families in Pakistan.

At the end of the war, with the defeat of the Soviet-installed government in 1992, the different factions of the Afghan nation then began fighting among themselves. They had been able to maintain some degree of cooperation, or at least they had avoided outright war with one another, as long as they had the external foe of the Soviet Union and its regime in Kabul. With the fall of that regime, ethic struggles arose for control of the newly liberated nation.

Prior to the Soviet invasion of Afghanistan, it appeared that ethnic issues were rapidly disappearing in most countries, but they came again to the fore very quickly as soon as the internal restrictions eased. The dramatic and largely unexpected collapse of centralized government and the freeing of ethnic minorities in the Soviet Union came during the political and economic reforms of Mikhail Gorbachev. As soon as the Communist Party and the central government lifted the strict controls that seventy years of communist rule had imposed, ethnicity sprang back to life in multitudinous diversity. The ancient tribal and ethnic affiliations reasserted themselves and tore the weakened nation apart and then fell to fighting over the pieces.

The dissolving of the Soviet Union did not, however, make the political map any more reflective of the ethnic division of people. Instead, it highlighted the variations within the various segments. After the breakup, in 1991, the Russian federation alone still had 150 million people, of whom only about 80 percent were Russian. The remainder belonged to a collection of 130 nationalities and ethnic groups distributed among thirty-one autonomous republics and regions within Russia. To further complicate Russia's plight, another 25 million Russians found themselves living outside Russia in Ukraine, Kazakhstan, Lithuania, Moldova, and other former Soviet republics.

Millions of Russians who had been part of the dominant ethnic group in the Soviet Union now found themselves not only in a distinct minority in many republics, but they were now outside of Russian government or military control. They lived in Lithuania,

Moldova, Georgia, and other countries where they constituted a significant but greatly resented minority that had once been the ruling elite. Even parts of the Russian army found themselves cut off in a new land where they became the object of "cultural purity" efforts. Just as the Russians had tried to impose the Russian language and general Russification on many minorities, those people now tried to make the Russian minority in their independent countries conform to their language and culture.

When Moldova, the small state created by Stalin between Ukraine and Romania, became independent, the Romanian majority reestablished their language as the only official one, and to distance themselves from Russia, they adopted the Latin alphabet used in neighboring Romania rather than the Cyrillic one used by the Russians and imposed on them by Stalin. In Azerbaijan, the majority Azeris wanted to expel Armenians from their territory, while the Armenians wanted to annex Nagorno-Karabakh, a section of Azerbaijan where mostly Armenians lived.

Ethnic issues often overlap with racial ones. At the heart of every racist theory lies the notion that culture is genetic, that people of a certain genetic ancestry, usually referred to as their "race," will by nature have certain cultural, social, psychological, and even moral traits that distinguish them from others. People frequently view their own group as honest, diligent, intelligent, creative, loyal, and loving, the source of human civilization and the true religion of the true god. Other groups are regarded as parasitic, lazy, dishonest, and prone to theft, sexual excess, and other sins associated with their worship of the wrong god or with an inferior state of intellectual and moral development.

Racist theories usually carry the belief that an enemy race bears guilt for some particularly heinous crime in the past. The pattern seems the same, no matter whether it refers to Nazi views of Jews, the Ku Klux Klan's view of Africans, the Japanese imperialist view of Europeans, or the Black Muslim perspective on whites. Under various theories, Africans bore the mark of Cain's murder of his brother Abel or the mark of Noah's son Ham, but in either case the blacks were cursed to be slaves. Supposedly, Jews bore the guilt for the unique crime of deicide, killing the Christian God. Europeans had to bear the collective guilt of the crimes of slavery and colonialism of nonwhite peoples. In each case, subsequent generations of people are punished for the real or supposed actions of their ancestors.

Racism has a long and impressive pedigree in many parts of the world, and it has developed independently at one time or another on every continent. It can be seen in the caste system of India, in the Chinese attitude toward barbarian races, and in the European tradition of global conquest and colonization. People have always divided the world into *us* and *them*, but the division has usually rested on language, religion, or simply area of residence. The notion that this division into *us* and *them* had anything to do with inheritance of race developed rather late in history.

Racist theories became associated with efforts to "purify" a population, as Ferdinand and Isabella began the "purification" of Spain, or as one might purify a strain of pea or a breed of dog. In the eighteenth century a new perspective arose, as evidenced by the British deportation of criminals, the insane, Irish patriots, and religious minorities to America and later to Australia, for punishment in exile. The underlying notion seemed to be that one might cull the defective people from the general population in the same way that one could cull a herd of cattle, sheep, or horses. By the nineteenth century these racist theories began to take on their modern form, which used pseudoscientific garb, cloaking their ideas in terms of genetics, survival of the fittest, and human evolution.

In the latter part of the twentieth century, differences based on language, culture, heritage, religion, or race were increasingly lumped together as *ethnic* issues. The ethnic groups in question might be extremely large, such as the Slavs, who numbered in the hundreds of millions, or comparatively small, such as the Jamaicans living in London. The word acquired the same arbitrary vagueness that *race* had held in earlier generations.

The word *ethnic* comes directly from the Greek *ethnos*, meaning a pagan nation or race of people. When it was incorporated into other languages, the word *ethnic* delineated a group outside of one's own, a foreign group. An ethnic group is a nation, but it is not necessarily an independent country.

The word *nation* derives from the Latin word for "birth," and originally referred primarily to people who were not Romans.

Thus, in origin, *nation* and *ethnos* had essentially the same meaning, but the two words have separate and even opposed histories.

The concept behind the nation-state is that each nationality, or *ethnos* as the Greeks would call them, should have its own state or government. Ideally, for every nation there would be one state and for every state there would be one nation. All Burmese would live in Burma, all French people in France, all Chinese in China, and so forth around the world. For this to work, a nation of people must have its own territory, with no other groups living in it.

National governments are usually antagonistic to ethnic groups because they compete with one another for loyalty and power. The ethnic groups present an alternative definition of public life and culture to that offered, and often insisted upon, by the state. The state has two basic options in dealing with ethnic groups. It can repress them and try to destroy them, or it can try to manage them and balance them against one another while keeping them clearly subordinate to the state.

An ethnic group is a new nation struggling to be born. Eventually it will either be born and become an independent entity, or it will die and be absorbed by the larger nation around it.

For a long time it appeared that ethnic groups were slowly being absorbed into the nations in which they lived. They were viewed as holdovers from another era, and it was thought that gradually as the people modernized, they would naturally abandon their ethnic identity in favor of a national one. Ethnic identities seemed to be a residue of the backward peasant mentality and did not fit in the modern state.

Contrary to this perspective on ethnicity in the modern world, ethnic identities did not dissolve. Instead, ethnic identities have grown stronger in the modern world. Ethnic groups have flourished and become rallying points for opposition to governments. National governments usually seek to subordinate all ethnic groups into sub-units of the government, but ethnic groups usually claim a legitimacy outside of the government, and often claim to be much older and even more important than the government.

When smaller ethnic minorities demanded autonomy or independence in the twentieth century, the large nations imposed a new cultural totalitarianism, with increased persecution of whatever minorities still existed in them. This became particularly acute at the end of World War I. After the collapse and dismemberment of the Ottoman Empire, the German empire, and the Austro-Hungarian kingdom, strong movements for cultural purity arose in their successor states during the 1920s and 1930s.

Ethnic groups that had never been united or independent sought to become sovereign states following World War I, while newly discovered national identities caused some states to begin purges of people not considered to be a part of their nationality. With the collapse of the multiethnic Ottoman Empire, the new nation-state of Turkey arose. The new government disassociated itself from its imperial past in many ways. Women had to discard the veil, and men had to abandon the fez, the distinctive red hat with a black tassel that had symbolized the old empire. The government changed the writing of the Turkish language from Arabic to Latin script.

In order to be a modern nation of Turks, rather than an empire of many ethnic groups, the new government instituted the systematic persecution of anyone who was not Turkish. Large numbers of Armenians, Greeks, and other non-Turks lived in the newly proclaimed Turkish republic, but the new Turkish government persecuted and killed them in great numbers. Many of the Turkish minorities fled to other countries. Those who did not flee had to fight, as in the case of the Kurds. The Kurds and the Turks shared an allegiance to Islam, but the Kurds spoke an Indo-European language rather than a Turkish one. The Kurds have lived in virtual perpetual war with the Turkish government since the founding of the republic.

Despite the bloodshed associated with the formation of the Turkish republic, the new country included only a fraction of the world's Turkish-speaking peoples. Turkish tribes stretched from the Mediterranean across Central Asia and deep into China and Siberia. They also lived in sizable numbers in Europe, particularly in Bulgaria and parts of the old Yugoslavia, as well as increasingly in German cities such as Berlin and Frankfurt.

The ideology of racial purity probably attained its highest expression and greatest political importance under the Nazi regime that came to power in Germany and for a time controlled much of Central and Eastern Europe. Under the Third Reich of Adolph Hitler, Germans sought to bring all German-speaking people into one nation. They annexed Austria and part of Czechoslovakia and Poland into Greater Germany. While it was expanding to include all Germans, the state began the persecution and removal of non-German minorities, including the Poles, Jews, and Gypsies, from all parts of the newly expanded Germany. With German encouragement and leadership, France, Hungary, Croatia, Italy, and Bulgaria began similar purification projects directed primarily against Jews and Gypsies, whom they killed in great numbers or shipped off to German-operated death camps. Countries such as Denmark resisted, at great cost, participation in such murderous enterprises.

The Nazis created the *Lebensborn* project to purify their so-called Aryan race through selective breeding of the best examples of German men and women. The Nazis also began programs of institutionalization, sterilization, and even euthanasia against individuals whom they considered to be mentally and physically defective. The most heinous expression of this racial theory came, however, in its application to other so-called races such as the Slavs, Jews, and Gypsies. The Nazis virtually enslaved the Slavs, particularly the Poles, who were harnessed into the German war effort, working in labor gangs on farms and in factories.

Jews and Gypsies had no place in German society, even to live and work as slaves. Most of the German Jews fled the country during the years before the Second World War, when the Germans enacted a sequence of restrictive laws and launched repeated campaigns of persecution. As the Nazis conquered more lands containing even more Jews, they moved from persecution and imprisonment in concentration camps to the so-called Final Solution, in which masses of Jews and Gypsies were executed in an attempt to exterminate them.

After the collapse of the Axis powers in World War II, overtly racist theories were no longer acceptable in the arena of educated world opinion. The Germans and the Japanese repudiated their racist ideologies. Domestic and international pressures increased on countries such as the United States and even South Africa to end their racist policies of segregation and apartheid.

In place of race, the concept of ethnicity came into vogue, but "ethnic cleansing" turned out to be little different from racial cleansing. With the collapse of Yugoslavia in 1991, the warring states began a process of ethnic cleansing much like the process followed by the Nazis. The Serbs forcefully dislocated Croats from sections of Serbia and Croatia. In 1992 they extended the program to the forceful removal of Muslims and Albanians as well as Croats from Serbia and Serbian-occupied areas in Bosnia-Herzegovina. The ethnic purification of Serbian-controlled territory began with the rounding up of Croatians, Muslim Slavs, and Albanians, who were forced to move or be killed. The Croatians forced Serbs and Muslims from their territory. The Bulgarians forced Muslims to change their Turkish-Muslim names to Bulgarian ones, and to surrender any Turkish identity or face expulsion from their homes in Bulgaria.

Recent decades have seen a great increase in fighting among ethnic groups and factions. Much of the fighting appeared for a while to be regional outbursts in an otherwise cold war, but often the ethnic fighting had very little to do with any outside powers. The United States, China, the former Soviet bloc, the Arabs, and the Israelis all became sources of weapons, money, and supplies, but they were not controlling the wars as much as diplomats in Washington, Moscow, and Beijing may have made it appear.

Fighting in Yemen, Sudan, Angola, Mozambique, Somalia, Peru, Cambodia, Afghanistan, El Salvador, Guatemala, Sri Lanka, Indonesia, Papua New Guinea, New Caledonia, and South Africa centered on local issues of power, not international ones. The demise of the Cold War did not make these issues disappear but only added more such struggles into the global situation.

Ethnic tensions have continued to grow in the twentieth century. In recent decades, older tensions have not only been resurrected but seem stronger than ever. Canada faced a possibility of division along the fault line of language, as French speakers withdrew increasingly from English speakers. After centuries of struggling for Irish independence from Great Britain, Ireland achieved its independence, and then Northern Ireland, Wales, and Scotland began tugging at the fetters that bound them so tightly to London's highly centralized form of government.

Around the world, struggles among ethnic groups seem to be replacing conflicts among nations; no nation seems immune to this modern infection. In Fiji, a tense struggle seems to have found a temporary truce that may turn into a long-term solution with only minimal violence. In sharp contrast, ethnic groups of the Balkans fell into bloody warfare. The Canadians spent years negotiating and discussing the appropriate form for the national government, all the while the federal government steadily lost powers, which flowed into the provinces. Even though the process varies with the cultural and historical circumstances of each country, the direction of movement seems the same. The nation declines in importance, while regional, ethnic, linguistic, cultural, and religious factions increase in power and significance in daily life.

The creation of an ethnic homeland such as the Jewish Autonomous Oblast, or the division of Bosnia-Herzegovina into a series of miniature ethnic homelands, is doomed to failure. The effort derives from an antiquated notion that an ethnic group or a nation is coterminous with a specific piece of land, inhabited by no other such group. Such a notion has never been an accurate reflection of ethnic boundaries, but it has become increasingly irrelevant in recent centuries, as whole groups have moved into new areas. Millions moved involuntarily through the slave trade and the coercion of colonialism. Millions more moved voluntarily as they saw new opportunities in other lands.

There has probably never been a time in human history when the borders of nations or empires have made logical sense, but in the twentieth century, they seem increasingly less rational. Borders separate government territory, but they do not separate nations. National borders do not follow cultural, racial, linguistic, or religious lines.

The development of nationalism occurred concurrently with the concept of *homeland*, according to which each nation had a particular territory that belonged to it, and to it alone. Evidence shows that almost all groups of people have moved fairly frequently in their histories. Changes in climate, soil exhaustion, population growth, diseases, internal strife, external pressure, and mere boredom can all push people toward movement. Often the people may not even realize that they are moving. Expansion by a mere mile a year would place a family's descendants on the other side of a continent in a few thousand years, and humans have been moving around the earth for more than 100,000 years.

Seemingly every parcel of land on earth has had at least two sets of people who have claimed it as part of their homeland. The Bushmen have been in southern Africa longer than the Bantu and the Europeans. The American Indians, Aleuts, and Inuit had been in America for many millennia before the Europeans arrived.

Even Japan, one of the most homogeneous populations in the world, has large minorities of Koreans and Okinawans included within it, as well as the indigenous Ainu people, who lived there for thousands of years before the ancestors of the modern Japanese arrived from the Asian mainland. At the same time, large populations of Japanese live overseas in Brazil, the United States, Bolivia, and Peru.

The Koreans are another of the world's most culturally homogeneous peoples, but even they have spent most of the twentieth century divided into the two countries of North and South Korea. Even should the two unite, Korea has large ethnic communities living in Japan, Russia, China, and Kazakhstan, as well as overseas in the United States, Brazil, and Chile. There will probably never be a time when all people of Korean nationality live in the same country under the same government.

No border in the world coincides precisely with the ethnic divisions of its population. Kurds live in Turkey, Azerbaijan, Iraq, Syria, and Iran, and have emigrated to Germany, the United States, Lebanon, and the United Kingdom. Turks not only live in Turkey and half a dozen Central Asian countries, but their largest community outside of that area is now in Germany. Hungarians, the largest minority in Europe living outside the country bearing their name, live in Slovakia, Slovenia, Romania, Germany, and surrounding nations, and many have emigrated to Australia and the Americas. The Basques are divided between Spain and France. Finland has a large minority of Swedes, while a great number of fellow Finns live across the border in Russia.

The Han Chinese are not only the majority in China, Taiwan, and Singapore, but they constitute major ethnic groups in the Philippines, Southeast Asia, and the islands of the Pacific as well as in Canada, the United States, Mexico, and Peru.

Ojibwa and Mohawks live in Canada and the United States. French Quebecois live not only in Quebec but in other parts of Canada and in New England. Yaquis live in Mexico and the United States. The Maya live in Mexico and Guatemala. The Quechua live divided among Ecuador, Bolivia, Peru, and Argentina.

Because true borders rarely exist in nature, humans go to great expense and effort to create them, and having done so, they go to even greater efforts to make them real and to protect them. Because these borders make so little logical sense, we build great ideological arguments about culture, nationality, race, and ethnicity to support them.

17

Tribal Technology

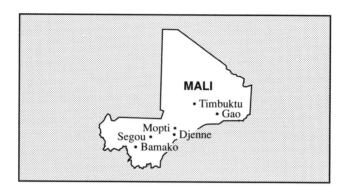

*The new tribalism in the age of the media is not necessarily
the enemy of commercialism; it is a direct outgrowth of com-
mercialization and its ally, perhaps even its instrument.*
—PAULINE KAEL, *Going Steady*

I have seen Segou only at night. Because of the blasting heat
in the West African nation of Mali, the caravans of trucks, bush
taxis, vans, and buses that ply the road usually do so in the cool
of night. Segou stands roughly at the midpoint in the all-night
trip of three hundred miles between Bamako and Mopti. In recent years, Segou offered a special pleasure to travelers because
it gave them the chance to extricate their legs from the com-
pressed mass of flesh, bags, foods, and merchandise jammed into
the back of the truck or from the filled seats, aisles, and floor of
a minibus.

Segou presented a ghostly oasis of shimmering yellow light as
we arrived. The strip along the narrow but paved road that serves
as Mali's major highway had slowly grown through the years into
a combination of truck stop and rest station. A row of dilapidated
buildings offered a small variety of foods and drinks.

In the 1980s, Segou had fewer than 65,000 people. Situated
on the edge of the African Sahel, it was far removed from everywhere. The city was 750 miles east of Dakar, the capital of Senegal, and 585 miles north of Abidjan, the capital of the Ivory

Coast. To the north, the next big metropolis was Algiers, on the other side of the desert, a trek of 1,712 miles. Even though Segou and Cairo both border on the Sahara, 2,650 miles separate them, making Cairo closer to Paris, Warsaw, and even Moscow than to lonely Segou.

Segou has an ancient heritage, but in style it resembles the bureaucratic colonial town that the French built. The rambling colonial buildings persist with new uses. Seen at night, the row of colonial structures resembles an old, abandoned movie set that is now only barely lit. The buildings look dilapidated and useless. Many of the food vendors around them have extension cords running from the buildings out to their small food stands or shacks, giving them a small bit of the weak yellow light of the city.

I had one favorite place to eat in Segou. Like all the other restaurants along the row, it had a dirt floor and was lit by the gallant but incredibly weak efforts of a single naked light bulb hanging from a thin wire tacked to the roof. Crowds lingered through the night, with men sitting on a series of wobbly benches and eating hurriedly before the driver of their truck or bus sounded the horn to leave. Instead of dishes, the restaurant of-fered large plastic washbasins in the bright reds, yellows, greens, and oranges that one finds in only the poorest of countries. With the basin came a large but very light aluminum spoon with which to eat. Each customer picked up the plastic basin and proceeded down the buffet line, which consisted of three men standing be-hind a rickety wooden bench on which were three large pots of food. I always went for the last one, which was a large pot of noodles heavily coated in oil with some tomatoes and a strong aroma of chopped chilies.

Young boys wandered between the rows of customers, carrying buckets of water that they poured into worn plastic beakers. For those who could afford it, the boys also offered cold soft drinks that usually cost more than the meals. The same boys later gath-ered up the plastic basins and beakers and aluminum spoons, which they rinsed in a barrel of dark water and then put out for the next customer.

Aside from the spicy pasta served in this particular enterprise, I and many other passengers liked this place because it had a television, a small black-and-white model with loud though very fuzzy sound. The proprietor had put the television up on a high shelf built especially for it, so that everyone in the throng of men always standing in front of it could see it. At midnight, one never knew what would be showing, but the flickering screen always attracted a large and transfixed audience of travelers, truck drivers, and desert nomads.

I stood one night with a group of desert men as we watched a modern dance by the Stuttgart Ballet. I had no idea what the jerky figures jumping across the stage were supposed to signify, but we all stood there spellbound, watching. There was an occasional commentary in French. The piece featured jagged cuts of people dressed in black leotards making quick, jerky motions against a white background, and suddenly the picture cut to a similar motion by dancers in white leotards against a black background. Sometimes the picture turned upside down and sometimes sideways, and occasionally a silently barking dog appeared on the screen. All of this was accompanied by discordant sounds of various Western musical instruments being abused in assorted malicious ways.

I recognized that the piece probably had inestimable value in last year's art museums and in the homes of the lovers of progressive styles of music. But to me and to the veiled Tuaregs on the edge of the desert, gathered around a television set hooked to a line coming out of an old Foreign Legion fort, the performance had a hypnotic effect. It was like watching the repetitive but meaningless bubbles in a lava lamp. It meant no more to them than did the subsequent broadcast of "Happy Days," a show about adolescents in urban America during the 1950s. Dubbed in French, the show lost much of its meaning for me as well.

Most of the men around me were fierce Tuaregs, desert nomads who spend most of their lives on camel and are unique because their men nearly always go veiled, as they were on this night. They wrapped their heads and faces in long blue cloths that left only their eyes showing. Their headdresses, veils, and matching gowns have earned them the name of the Blue Men of the Sahara. Tuareg women have an equally unique trait, in that they write in Tifinagh, a pre-Arabic script of symmetrical symbols derived from ancient Phoenician and used only by Tuareg women. The Tuareg men stared at the television and, like me, said nothing as they watched the odd figures on the flickering screen.

My visit to Segou showed me the power of the modern world

culture, in which Tuareg camel herders watch the same television programs that suburban Californians and urban Germans watch. The rise of a world culture, however, does not mean the demise of local cultures. This became clearer to me soon after leaving Segou and heading down the Niger River. I saw how the local cultures continued to flourish and how they had found ways to adapt modern technology to help preserve their own cultures.

The great Niger River flows gently out of the highlands along the border between tropical Guinea and Sierra Leone. Even though it begins in the far west of Africa, close to the Atlantic Ocean, it does not seek the easy way to the sea. The Niger pushes toward the Sahara as though it intends to become a second Nile and plow a channel straight through the desert and into the western Mediterranean Sea, but the Sahara defeats it. As the Niger leaves the well-watered jungles of Guinea, it flows into the Sahel of Mali, and even though the river is now much greater in volume and strength, the massive weight of the Sahara ahead causes it to stray eastward from its northerly course. Although it is bent, and even though there are no new tributaries to give it added strength, the river pushes ahead.

The Niger then tries a unique but, in the end, deadly strategy to conquer the desert; it divides into two channels, as though hoping that one might defeat the desert even if the other does not. The two channels then divide into two more, and each of those into two more. One of the great rivers of the world is thus reduced to an unknown number of ever smaller channels that snake through the dry sand along the edge of the Sahara. Channels arise and disappear with various seasons of the year, and change course from year to year. This vast area, known as the inland delta of the Niger, combines the worst characteristics of both swamp and desert. The infinite channels run like a maze, but instead of being surrounded by lush vegetation, there is only mud or sand.

The Niger eventually accepts its defeat by the Sahara, and all of the channels gradually turn southward and form a single mighty river again. As it flows out of Mali, it heads south to Niger and Nigeria, the two countries named for the river. There it gains new strength while swallowing the Kebbi and the Benue, as well as dozens of smaller rivers. Finally the Niger reaches a length of 2,600 miles, and even though it is shorter than the

Nile, it becomes the West African equivalent of the Nile in importance before spilling into the Gulf of Guinea, in the Atlantic Ocean.

I set out to cross the inland delta during January, the driest and coolest part of the year, but the time when the Niger delta is least navigable. By January the water sinks to its lowest level of the year, and during the severe droughts of the 1980s that level dropped ever lower each year. Even in the best of those years steamboats could not pass through the shallow and ever-changing channels of the inland delta; only the native boat called a *pinasse* could do it, but even that became difficult in January.

The pinasse I boarded in the provincial city of Mopti reached about ninety feet in length, but at its widest point in the middle was only about seven feet wide. The pinasse is little more than two large dugout canoes put end to end and joined in the middle. The sides are then built up a little to make it deeper. The boat builders attach a series of arches made from bundles of sticks, over which they drape woven mats to provide a simple roof. This simple yet efficient boat has been the main vessel of the upper Niger for centuries. The one I boarded was filled with large sacks of millet to a depth of about four feet. The captain then took on paying passengers who agreed to sit on top of the millet bags. This particular pinasse took about forty people in addition to its millet cargo.

Passengers sit on the bags of millet, but there is rarely enough room for an adult to sit upright. We all lounged around on top of the bags like diners at a Roman banquet. We sat and slept in the same spot for the five days that it took to wend our way through the inland delta.

The only hint of modernization on the pinasse was the small outboard motor and the occasional strip of plastic added to the woven mat. The primitiveness of the vehicle became painfully clear even before we left Mopti. One of the passengers on the pinasse docked close behind us started to heat water for tea. Suddenly part of the dry mat caught fire, and within seconds the fire raced along the mat framework. Men and women screamed as they gathered their belongings and children to climb into other boats or jump into the water. Our captain shouted to the boys to push us away as quickly as possible. Other pinasses pushed off, but the smaller and less flammable dugouts circled around the burning vessel, rescuing passengers and goods from the water and from the burning ship. From first spark to total conflagration took less than ten minutes.

But it was now too late to have second thoughts about the trip through the inland delta, for in escaping the fire, we were now under way. Once we were away from the environs of Mopti, we did not pass another village for two days. We traveled in the daytime and averaged about five miles an hour. Frequently the pinasse stuck in the low water, and Mamadou, the captain's youngest son, had to jump in the water and search out the channel. Leading the pinasse with a rope, Mamadou guided the way as the other boys pushed and shoved the pinasse. Sometimes the passengers had to jump out and either push or wade to shore to walk for a mile or two until the pinasse found deeper water. Occasionally we met small groups of Bozo fishermen or Fulani herdsmen watering their cattle. The fishermen offered us fresh fish or smoked ones, and the young Fulani girls came forth with gourds of milk in various states of freshness.

The inland delta of the Niger remains one of the least technologically developed places on earth. The shifting channels of the river make the permanent building of villages nearly impossible in all but a few places. Temporary fish and cattle camps dot the banks now as they must have done a thousand years ago, and modern technology seems to have added nothing to these people's lives. Despite billions of dollars spent by the French colonial powers and by international development agencies in recent decades, the Niger has not been tamed.

Drifting day after day through the inland delta proved to be a quiet and repetitive adventure. Occasionally we spotted a group of small hippopotami frolicking in the water, but mostly we watched birds that the captain was trying to shoot but rarely hit. When he did hit a bird, or at least when he claimed he had hit one, he sent Mamadou swimming out to retrieve it and add it to the evening rice dish.

Prayer punctuated the daily routine of the slowly moving boat. The captain would guide the boat over to a muddy bank. All the men would try to walk the long board used as a gangplank, and invariably one would slip off the narrow plank and fall into the mud. The men then lined up on the shore, faced the east, and prayed in unison.

Occasionally, the monotony of the day would be broken by the piercing sound of a portable cassette recorder. One of the passengers proudly carried it among his possessions, and when the mood came over him, he shared it with all of us. He carried only a few tapes, and they sounded like tenth- or eleventh-generation recordings of barely recognizable originals. The tape blasted forth Arabic chanting from the *Qur'an*, interspersed with talking and chanting in Bambara, the common language of communication used along the upper Niger. The first few times I heard the tapes, they seemed quaint and interesting, but after five days they blurred together in one maddening and enigmatic noise. Strangely enough, the other passengers seemed to delight in it. Each playing was like a special treat to them, nearly as exciting as the miniature cup of sugared tea they drank twice a day.

Even though I wanted to spend my time thinking and getting to know the Niger inland delta, my thoughts always shattered when the electronic wailing started again. Of all the possible pieces of technology available from the developed world, I wondered why the cassette recorder was the most popular. Why did I never see a small water-filtration kit, an electronic calculator, or any seemingly more practical bit of technology?

In the past two decades, the cassette recorder has made a profound impact on the poorer communities of the world. It gave them a relatively cheap and easy technology by which they could make audiotapes of whatever they wanted to hear—their native music and singing, stories and myths, chanting and praying, or lessons and preaching. The cassette recorder is technology that they can control. In the case of these Bambara speakers, they wanted to hear the chanting of the *Qur'an*. In the Andes I frequently heard tapes of the high-pitched and unharmonic singing of Quechua women. In Senegal, tapes carried the twanging sounds of Wolof instruments being plucked seemingly at random.

The impact of the cassette tapes has frequently been literally revolutionary. The Islamic revolution of Iran in 1978 and 1979 was probably the first revolution of the world conducted primarily through the cassette recorder. For many years before the revolution, the Ayatollah Khomeini and other exiled religious leaders recorded sermons of revolution in Paris and then distributed them throughout Iran. Each tape player is also a recorder, so that each owner can make new copies as well as play the old ones. In this way the anti-Shah and anti-Western message of the cassette spread throughout Iran from one backwater village to another. Even those beyond the reach of the government-controlled radio found easy access to the ideas of the Ayatollah in France.

Humans seem to be imitators by nature. As soon as they see someone else doing something, they try it. In this light, it is not surprising that technological innovations spread very quickly, whether they be the invention of the sewing needle, spear-thrower, gunpowder, or computers. People constantly adopt the technology of other people, and they invariably change the technology itself by adapting it to meet the needs of their own society, environment, and culture.

Technology creates cultural diversity at one level, even while spreading cultural homogeneity at another. The cassette recorder is not the first piece of technology that allowed for cultural diversity or promoted the florescence of ethnicity. In the woodlands of North America, before the arrival of the Europeans, native women traditionally valued embroidery work on the deer- and elk-skin moccasins, shirts, skirts, and shawls. In coastal areas they embroidered with shells of various colors to make their designs. Farther inland they made their exquisite geometric and floral designs using porcupine quills dyed in an assortment of colors. The introduction of European trade goods such as steel needles and small glass beads allowed this craft to grow and expand far beyond the range and limited number of porcupines. The beadwork of Iroquois wampum belts, which had traditionally been done in shell, could now be done more quickly and easily and in a greater assortment of colors by using steel needles and glass beads. The Ojibwa women around the Great Lakes, and the Dakota women of the plains, used the same technology to create their own individual styles of clothing, moccasins, carrying bags, sacred bags, and other objects. The variations in embroidery styles created a unique expression of woodland and plains cultures, but it also separated one group from another, since they could use the beads to create designs, motifs, and colors particular to one cultural tradition or group. The beadwork of these nations became as important a part of their ethnic identity as did the totem pole for the Haida and Kwakiutl, or the ornate house façades of the Maori. Technology helped give these peoples an international identity that made them stand out and allowed them to be recognized in the world.

For centuries the Kwakiutl, the Haida, and other Indians along the Pacific coast of Canada and the northern United States emphasized carving as an important expression of their culture. They used stone and bone to carve canoes up to fifty feet in length and six feet wide, as well as large wooden chests, ceremonial masks with movable parts, and the fronts of their wooden homes. They copied totemic images of sea mammals, sharks, birds, and land animals to decorate all of these carvings. The introduction of steel tools brought forth the classic flowering of Kwakiutl and Haida art as the carvings became larger and more ornate and numerous. The totemic engravings of the family crests soared to new heights as they became larger and as the carvers added birds with much wider wingspans to the poles. This new object became known to outsiders as the totem pole. The elaborate totem poles of the Pacific coast came about in the nineteenth century through the combination of traditional culture mixed with the new technology of steel axes, improved saws, and other lumbering equipment that could be used for carving. The new objects, created through the new technology, reflected the past but also served as cultural means of emphasizing the Indians' own culture at a time when the loggers, mineral prospectors, and fishermen of Canada and the United States were most threatening them and their traditional society.

Repeatedly we see that almost all native societies that had a tradition of woodwork without metal tools experienced a flowering of their carving once they acquired these tools. Even though the process has been repeated many times in a homogeneous pattern in New Guinea, Canada, Melanesia, and New Zealand, the results are never homogeneous. Instead the new technology emphasizes the cultural ethnicity of the people, rather than homogenizing them into the world culture. The Melanesians and New Guineans used metal tools to carve posts for their ceremonial buildings and to make the masks used in their ceremonies, but they took a form remarkably different from those of the poles and masks of the Americans. Similarly, the Maori of New Zealand carved in their own styles, which are now easily identifiable throughout the world as strictly Maori.

As technology evolves, cultures diversify. The more sophisticated technology becomes, the more it promotes ethnic diversity and allows people to revitalize their cultural traditions as evidenced in the decorative and performance arts. These new creations can, however, be more than merely decorative totem poles or embroidered beadwork. Just as the recordings of the cassette tapes have helped to spread fundamental Islam and to promote new political movements within it, the beaded clothing of the American Indians has become the symbolic focus of new movements in Indian ethnicity within the United States.

In the twentieth century, some of the greatest technological innovations have come with the engineering of new modes of communication and transportation, and these have had a great impact on ethnic groups of all sorts. The new communications technology does much more than revitalize ethnic arts and crafts; it has helped to revitalize and strengthen ethnic identities and social movements.

Some observers initially assumed that the modern communications media would make a homogenized world in which everyone listened to the same Michael Jackson or Madonna songs, interspersed with news from London and Atlanta. To a limited extent this did happen. People became part of an international popular culture, a global culture of international music, television comedies, movies, and news. Arab and Japanese families can watch the same American television shows that Germans and Tongans watch. Young people in all those countries can follow the music fashions through rock, disco, reggae, punk, rap, or whatever happens to be the most recent wave. Similarly, they can dress in local variations of the same international fads. But all of these are fairly superficial levels of conformity compared with some of the deeper changes that communications and transportation technology encourages.

At the same time, the new technology permitted a renaissance of many varieties of local music. The cassette recorder has revitalized native music in the world. The natives who leave a small village in the countryside to work in an urban factory, as a domestic servant, or at an isolated mine, can now take their music with them. Technology made culture more portable.

Communications technology often begins as a highly centralized phenomenon. As late as the 1950s there were relatively few radio and television stations in the world, and they mostly emanated from a few major cities. Steadily, however, stations and channels have proliferated. On a typical day in many international markets, a television viewer can see programs in English, Spanish, Japanese, Farsi, Korean, Vietnamese, Armenian, and Hmong.

The longer a communications technology such as radio, television, video, or cassettes is in operation, the more varied it becomes and the more it caters to the needs and interests of ever smaller audiences. At the same time that it gives people access into an international arena and international culture, it gives them greater opportunities to communicate with their own kind. It allows and even encourages the formation of smaller cultural groups.

Telephone systems that required wiring to connect all the participants meant that the telephone would be an extremely centralized system. Even in the most remote areas of the Amazon, the Sahara, or the Arctic, where access to the world telephone was blocked because it would be prohibitively expensive to string wires into it, the arrival of satellite and wireless telephones opened new possibilities. Each year the systems become more pervasive and a little cheaper, so that ever more people can utilize them.

The same forces that make international communication easier also make intragroup communication easier. The same media that bring the world together can also bring members of an ethnic group together, no matter where they may be in the world. Television and videotapes mean that Kurds in Iran and Ashanti in Ghana can watch the same rock music videos, but it also means that Kurds in Montreal and Ashanti in Edinburgh can watch the traditional marriage ceremony of a cousin even though they live too far away to attend it.

Improved international communications and transportation also foster continued contacts for people, even when they leave their native group to live in a city, or even to travel to the other side of the globe. Students from Eritrea studying in Minneapolis maintain contacts with Eritreans in Washington, Rome, and Nairobi via telephone and fax machines. They have created an international network of Eritreans who shared information and resources among themselves and with their families back in Eritrea throughout the long struggle of Eritrea against Ethiopia.

Technology has helped save parts of traditional cultures that were near the point of extinction. The Tuva of Siberia practiced a type of "throat singing" that was extremely rare. In this singing, the singer sends vibrations from deep down in the throat that sound like an electronic hum or the noise by a large dynamo. It was once a part of singing among Turkic and Mongol nomads, and is related to the women's singing among some Eskimo. Few people remained who could perform this unusual form of singing, but a recording group from the Smithsonian Institution went in and made recordings of it in Siberia. The recordings help to popularize the music among a small but highly interested audience around the globe. More important, the recordings revitalized interest among the younger generation of Tuvans, who had not shown much enthusiasm for learning the difficult and esoteric style of singing.

Throughout the twentieth century, museums have sought to record the music, chants, tales, and ceremonies of tribal people. Early researchers intended to record those events as a way of archiving the culture before a group—or at least its language and culture—died out. As communications technology has become better, cheaper, and more widely distributed, these early recordings and films have found new audiences. Hula teachers in Hawaii can learn from the old masters of several generations ago by listening to the cassettes available from the gift counter of the Bernice Bishop Museum in Honolulu.

Monks in Tibet trade photocopies of pictures of the Dalai Lama. San Blas Indians in Panama copy *mola* designs from photographs of older *molas* on display in museums that the Indians will never visit. In the photographic collections assembled by early anthropologists such as Baldwin Spencer, Australian aborigines can see the designs painted on the bodies of their ancestors over a century ago. In the films made by Franz Boas, Kwakiutl in British Columbia can see how the cannibal dance of their ancestors was done at the end of the nineteenth century. Through the films of Margaret Mead and Gregory Bateson, the modern youths on Bali can see how their grandparents and great-grandparents lived in the first half of the twentieth century.

People driving through the American Southwest sometimes tune their radios to an unusual mixture of country music and Navajo language. The disc jockeys on KNDN radio in Farmington, New Mexico, broadcast only in the Navajo language under the motto "All Navajo, All the Time." Even the advertisements have to be in Navajo, although it is frequently difficult to translate some words, such as *trailer* or *camper shell*. They play country-and-western music as well as classic rock, but they also play a variety of Navajo chants and music, according to the season of the year. *Yai-be-chais*, traditional songs, can be played throughout the year, but others can only be played during the appropriate season.

Because the 5,000-watt signal reaches all parts of the 24,000-square-mile Navajo nation, and most of the Navajos do not have telephones, the station serves as a community bulletin board or as an "electronic trading post." Shepherds listen to it on transistor radios out in the country with the sheep. Ranchers listen while driving in their pickup trucks. The disc jockey announces that a family lost a cow near Four Corners; an older lady wants a ride from Window Rock to Farmington. Someone else is selling sheep, a horse, an old pickup truck, or a portable computer.

The Navajos, like other people around the world, adapt the technology of the radio to their own culture. To facilitate use of the station for announcements, a microphone is kept in the lobby so that anyone needing to make an announcement can come in and do so. Next to the open microphone stands another, solely for the purpose of announcing deaths. Because of Navajo reluctance to be associated with death, the special microphone avoids the onerous purification ceremonies that the disc jockey would have to perform if he made the announcement over his microphone.

By combining popular contemporary music with the Navajo music and commentary, the station attracts younger listeners and helps to ensure the continuation of the language. The station helps to build a strong sense of identity and unity, while keeping outsiders clearly outside the group. Speakers of English, Spanish, and other Indian languages find themselves excluded, if they do not speak the Navajo language and know the area and its culture at a fairly intimate level.

The revival of powwows among Indian groups in recent decades was made possible because of new technology. This revival has depended very much on innovations such as radios that broadcast news of upcoming powwows, microphones to broadcast the drums and singing, and cars that enable participants to follow the powwow circuit over many thousands of miles during a single season.

At most powwows in the United States, the music is provided by a group of men sitting around and beating in unison on one large drum. Today it is often difficult to see these drummers because they are surrounded by a row of people holding up their own cassette recorders, trying to make copies of the music. They then keep or trade these copies of their cassettes. The younger people use the drum songs to practice their dancing and thus increase the likelihood of winning more money at future pow-wows. It also allows drum groups from small communities to become better known over a larger area without having to travel.

Technology helps to make people producers of their own cultural identity rather than mere cultural consumers of someone else's materials. Many ethnic groups are now increasing in size and even expanding their area, aided in part by the new communications and transportation technology.

Computers have also helped in the ethnic resurgence of the twentieth century. In Tahlequah, Oklahoma, stands the former Cherokee national prison, which the Cherokee nation redesigned and made into the Cherokee National Library. One of its primary functions is the teaching of the Cherokee language, which is done by means of computers that write in the Cherokee syllabary, the eighty-six letters developed by the great scholar Sequoyah. For a language with as few speakers as Cherokee, it was too expensive to make typewriters with the Cherokee syllabary, but the computer made it much easier to print in the Cherokee system. The computer can also generate teaching materials for children and adults to be used at many different levels of achievement.

Computers have also made micropublishing possible, so that groups not only have access to writing in their own language, but can also publish materials in it for wider distribution within the group. Prior to that, very small groups wanting to communicate in the published from usually had to do so through a major language such as English, Spanish, or French, and the publishing technology usually rested in a few large cities. As long as the world wrote with typewriters, only a limited number of alphabets were available; with the computer, any literate group of people can write and print their language. The groups still need the major languages for communication with larger national and international audiences, but now they can communicate with much greater ease within their own communities, using their own language and locally available technology.

Technology freed culture from geography. For thousands of years, one had to be surrounded by other members of the same

culture in order to be a part of it. Once removed from the geographic place, one could no longer be a part of the culture.
Technology allows one to take that culture anywhere in the
world and maintain communication with the people back home.
One can still be a Fulani and live in Paris, or be a Hmong and
live in Minneapolis.

Cultural boundaries become less and less related to the national borders of a country. The boundaries now zigzag through
daily life in geographic and nonmaterial ways. Not only do large
communities of immigrants and refugees live in microcommuni-
ties in large cities, the cultural boundary is as close as the remote
control for the television set, the dials of the radio, the monitor
of a computer terminal, or the buttons of a telephone or fax
machine. The communications industry has retribalized the
world.

18

Cultural Castaways

Why have we returned, despite our advances in technology, to the Stone Age picture?
—Margaret Mead

Cochabamba, Bolivia, occupies one of the most beautiful valleys of any city in the world. The valley perches at an altitude of eight thousand feet on the edge of the Andes, near where the mountain valleys suddenly give way to the plains in the south and the jungle in the north. Cochabamba's palm-lined central plaza dates to early Spanish colonial times and still serves as the focal point for community activities. The surrounding snowy peaks of the Andes tower over the city, but also nearby are mountainous mist forests with giant ferns that mark the edge of the Amazon rain forest. Because Cochabamba lies between the high Andes and the jungle, its markets bulge with a great variety of mountain and tropical produce—papayas and potatoes, corn and cassava, pumpkins and pineapples, and the wonderful *locoto*, one of the most flavorful and powerful chilies of the world.

Throughout the 1980s, a new celebration and pilgrimage to the Virgin of Urkupiña gained immense popularity in Bolivia. It became popular with the people who were only one step away from their tribal heritage, the people who were caught between the tribal world and the modern world.

In August of each year, thousands of people leave Cochabamba on foot to make the twenty-mile pilgrimage to the Virgin of Urkupiña, in the small town of Quillacollo. Dance troupes from all over Bolivia gather to dance throughout the day and night in honor of the Virgin. The dancers usually dance for three consecutive years as a votive offering in return for some favor requested of the Virgin of Urkupiña or already granted by her.

Some of the dancers labor under heavy costumes that include large masks of the devil. The brightly painted masks, made from plaster of paris, have grotesquely twisted horns, eyes that bulge out as large as grapefruits, and rows of sharp teeth made from mirrors cut into triangles. The whole contraption can easily weigh forty pounds. Hundreds of dancers in identical devil costumes dance for the Virgin.

La Morenada, the dance of the dark-skinned people, is a dance supposedly derived from those of the African slaves brought to work in Bolivia by the Spaniards, but the costumes show little discernible connection to Africans. The dancers wear elaborate costumes with huge shoulders and bustles, together with hats covered with flowers and tall feathers. Other costumes include some representing the ancient Incas, the Indians of the jungle, and the early Spaniards; there are also bizarre costumes with surreal colors and designs.

Each saint and virgin in the area specializes in particular types of requests. According to Indian tradition, each of the virgins is a sister to each of the other virgins and to the saints. She is even thought to be a sister to the different manifestations of Jesus. One saint cures sickness in humans, while another specializes in animal illnesses. One helps with problems of love; another grants fertility, helps with exams, locates lost objects and animals, corrects errant children or husbands, blesses crops, promises safe journeys, or fulfills any one of the many daily needs of life. Each saint also has a particular fondness for one type of offering. One responds in pity to worshipers who cry; another responds to those who sing songs and write poems or who bring gifts of clothing or decoration for the statue or its home.

The Virgin of Urkupiña responds most to dancing, and as befits a saint in these difficult modern times, she specializes in supplying material wants. She has little to offer in the way of health, love, or good grades in school, but she helps people who want new clothes, a llama, a motorcycle, a car, a truck, a bus, a portable radio, a new house, or simply money. She has even been known to help cocaine traffickers, and perceptive local people think it is much more than coincidence that the Virgin of Urkupiña lives in the Bolivian state that has profited most from the narcotics trade. In some ways her rise as a prominent virgin in the 1970s and 1980s was due to the new cocaine wealth in her district and to support from the right-wing governments of that era. This heightened prestige of a relatively insignificant virgin allowed her to challenge much older and more famous virgins or saints, such as the Virgin of Copacabana, who had been the object of adoration and pilgrimage for many decades.

The festival of Urkupiña climaxes when worshipers take the richly clad and bejeweled statue of the Virgin from the church. Soldiers of the national army of Bolivia form her honor guard, and television cameras broadcast her slow and erratic procession through Quillacollo to viewers throughout the nation. The ceremony has the solemnity of a state funeral, mixed with the boisterous drunkenness of a championship football game. Thousands of grasping hands parade the statue slowly over a mile to a small chapel on a barren, rocky promontory called Urkupiña, a corruption of a Quechua phrase meaning roughly "the mountain over there," supposedly the place where a Quechua-speaking Virgin Mary appeared to some Indian children.

Even though the festival honors the Virgin Mary, and street vendors offer numerous replicas of her for sale wearing a great variety of ball gowns and resplendent robes, the festival has another star who is condemned by the church but who has a role to play nearly as great as the Virgin herself. Replicas of this counter-star are sold by the thousands in far greater numbers than copies of the Virgin. He is an odd and quizzical figure called Ekeko. Plaster-of-paris statues of him come in all sizes, but they all depict a fat, squat man with markedly European features, including pale skin and a painted mustache. He wears a *ch'ulu*, the pointed Andean cap with ear flaps, which someone has carefully knitted in miniature to fit on the statue. Ekeko carries small baskets that have actually been woven and then strapped to his body, each one carrying minute quantities of real commodities— corn, beans, cotton, quinoa, wool, a single coffee bean. He also has miniature sandals, a poncho, and a miniature *chuspa* for carrying coca leaves, and on his back he carries a miniature house. Pilgrims buy the Ekeko, who is also known as the God of Abundance, and carry him home, where he will supposedly bring prosperity to the house for another year. The chances of prosperity increase if periodically the faithful place a new cigarette in his eternally open and greedy mouth.

Ekeko dates back more than a thousand years, to a time long before the Spaniards or even the Incas came to this area. He originated in the Tiwanaku culture, centered on the shores of Lake Titicaca, the world's highest navigable lake. The dwarf of the Tiwanaku has now become a chubby white man; since it is quite apparent to any Indian that the white people now control virtually all commodities, the God of Abundance must be a white man.

Carrying images of both the Virgin of Urkupiña and Ekeko, hundreds of thousands of worshipers spread out over the hills; the total surpasses half a million people and may be as much as ten percent of the total population of Bolivia. The crowd clusters into family groups that gather on the mountain, where each family claims a small stake of land as close to the Virgin's chapel as they can get. The devout worshipers then set about the real business of their pilgrimage. They make the little plot of land into a miniature homestead. The pilgrims carry rented sledgehammers to break the heavy rocks all around them, which they then line up into a fence. They build a small house of rocks and twigs, and plant sprigs of green in the ground to represent orchards and trees planted for shade and firewood. They spread out miniature items specially bought for the day. From vendors throughout the festival, the "homeowners" can buy small animals, sacks of food, miniature televisions, cars, even modern homes made of brightly colored plastic. There is no domestic item so unimportant that it is not offered for sale in miniature at the market. The houses have miniature loaves of bread, cans of food, pots, clocks, and miniature rolls of toilet paper for the miniature bathrooms.

For students who want to go to the university, the vendors sell small diplomas in any discipline; those who want to study abroad can buy the diploma and an exact replica of an airplane ticket on Lloyd Aero Boliviano or an American airline. One can buy miniature bills of Bolivian currency and U.S. dollars. Some of the dollars bear pictures of American presidents; others have the Virgin of Urkupiña or even the devil's portrait instead. After arranging all of the items they want inside their little homestead, the worshipers throw confetti and streamers all over it and one another.

After the pilgrims complete construction of their small homesteads on the hill, they bring out drinks for the Virgin. They offer her colas or perhaps a few bottles of beer, but mostly they pour out chicha, the local homemade beer made from fermented corn. They pour the drinks on the ground for the Virgin, tell her their woes, and then drink the remainder of their alcoholic offering. The family picnics, drinks, and plays music for the Virgin. The tinny brass music of hundreds of bands constantly cuts through the air, and with their ponchos twirling in the air, the Indians dance around and around for hour after hour.

In acts of incredibly positive thinking and visioning, the worshipers who have built the small, rocky homesteads sit at their homes and imagine themselves already having all the things that they requested and that now surround them in miniature. They invite their friends over and entertain them on their fantasy estates. Only the alcohol and food are real, but if they believe hard enough and pretend convincingly that the little plastic home and toy truck are a real home and truck, then it must come true. The ceremony emphasizes belief, and the more strongly the worshiper holds to a belief that is obviously contrary to fact, then the more the Virgin will be moved to help make the unreality into reality.

As a reminder of the material goods they are to receive in the future, the pilgrims carry home rocks from the hills, usually a rock that they have personally broken off from a larger boulder by hitting it with a sledgehammer. Lloyd Aero Boliviano, the national airline, has to limit the size of the rocks so that they will fit under the seats of the airplane, but otherwise there is little control on the size or weight of the rock carried away. The following year the pilgrim must return and carry the same rock back to the hill.

The relationship between the pilgrim and the Virgin of Urkupiña is supposed to be long-term. Once the supplicant gets what was requested, that item has to be brought and shown to the Virgin at the next pilgrimage. A long parade of freshly cleaned cars and trucks always passes in front of the Virgin. Alpaca blankets drape the hoods of the vehicles on which the proud owners spread a variety of their acquisitions—sewing machines, radios, silver dishes, candelabras, pots, and every manner of goods. Such displays of material goods may appear ostentatious, but the worshipers insist that they display these goods in the spirit of thanksgiving rather than in venal pride.

The festival of Urkupiña combines elements and characteristics from cultures of many times and places. It combines the medieval Catholicism brought to Bolivia during Spanish colonial rule with the older religion of the Incas and the pre-Inca civilizations of the Andes. It is not merely a Christian ritual overlaying a more ancient religious ritual; it combines religion with the quest for modern technology, the capitalist system, and the acquisition of manufactured goods.

The festival clearly belongs to the Indians and the poor mestizos of Bolivia, not to the wealthier white people. In this festival the different dances show all the different groups of the nation— the Indians of the jungle, the Indians of the highlands, and the Africans. Even though few white people, aside from church, military, and some civic leaders, attend the ceremonies, their place is clearly represented at the festival in two contrasting ways. The power of white society, its government and religion, is clearly represented by the beautiful white Virgin who reigns over the peasants like a queen and represents the most idealistic and church-approved version of reality. The whites are also represented in the unofficial, disapproved native god Ekeko, the greedy white dwarf with the rosy cheeks and black mustache who loves alcohol and cigarettes and hoards all material goods and dispenses them to Indians very grudgingly after great acts of subservience and propitiation.

The festival of Urkupiña has attained particular popularity among *cholos*, people who are Indian by birth but have lost their traditional native culture. The *cholos* are trapped between two worlds; they have lost their Indian identity but have not been admitted into the white Hispanic world. In bringing their miniature trucks and money to the festival, they rely on a type of traditional magic; yet they seek the material goods of the modern society, not the traditional goods of their tribal culture.

The *cholos* of Latin America are cultural castaways, forced out of the old, but not admitted into the new. In Bolivia, Peru, Brazil, and Colombia, they have proven to be good recruits into the narcotics industry and commerce. They work in the jungle kitchens making coca paste, they transport it across international borders, and they serve in the armies of the coca barons.

The festival of Urkupiña gives the *cholos* and Indians a chance to express their longings in a dramatic and somewhat pathetic religious ceremony. As cultural castaways, they then return to their lives in the city, where they have only a marginal place.

In Cochabamba, life centers around the ancient market, called *koncha* in Quechua. Surrounding the great market of Cochabamba are a series of large warehouses for storing goods and equipment. I usually saw the warehouses during the day, when they were crowded with Indian farmers anxious to sell their produce and escape from the city. One night I lingered at the market until after dark, and I saw a change in a warehouse. Two young Catholic priests arrived and began sweeping the potato dust into a large cloud, in a vain effort to clean out part of it. They then unloaded their equipment and supplies and, using donated and discarded food, began to prepare a meal in a large pot.

As the streets grew quiet and the sun quickly went down soon after six o'clock, as it always does in the tropics near the Equator, small boys began to appear. The oldest ones were only about eleven or twelve years old, and the youngest seemed no more than perhaps four. They wore torn and ragged clothes. Barely out of diapers, some of the youngest boys had no pants at all. They all seemed to have runny noses, but the mucus dripping from them cleared away enough of the grime on their faces to let their skin show through. Their hair lay caked in greasy, matted piles on their heads.

The collarless priests ushered the skinny boys into the deserted warehouse, where they undressed and took a cold shower. The men then gave them large T-shirts to wear while they washed out the ragged clothes. The T-shirts had been donated through the Partners of the Americas from the United States, and many of them carried advertisements or slogans for a variety of causes: a North Carolina bank, a marathon, or a regatta. Once the boys passed their cleanliness inspection, the priests gave each one a large bowl of the thick soup they had prepared.

This was only a small group of the street children, called *polillas*, or "moths," who live on the streets of Cochabamba. Like their namesakes they dart in and out of the life of the city, and as one man explained to me, if you crush one of them, then like the moth they leave behind only a finger smudged with dust. During the day they shine shoes, wash cars, scrounge for food, beg, steal, and sell drugs.

Sometimes they live in small gangs with a young Indian

woman as their leader. She serves as a sort of mother to them. In turn they protect her and bring her whatever food or money they have gleaned during the day. They sleep in doorways, in alleys, in sewers, along the riverbank, or anyplace where they can find some shelter and be out of the way of traffic, police, and the townspeople, whom they fear.

Cochabamba ranks as only a small city compared with the metropolises of South America, and its urban problems seem quite manageable by the standards of Lima, São Paulo, or Bogotá. Cochabamba has relatively few abandoned children. The children become so numerous and pesky in cities like Rio de Janeiro that gangs of men conduct organized hunts to kill them. Reportedly in the pay of the shopkeepers and residents of neighborhoods where the children live in the streets, armed hunters stalk the homeless children like rats, and kill them and leave them in ditches and gutters along the road.

In the larger cities, the cultural castaways present an increasingly grave problem. Lima, on the Peruvian coast, attracted millions of Indians from the mountains and other rural areas in the 1970s and 1980s. A profound change comes over the Indians as they migrate into the cities. They soon abandon their traditional Indian clothes, the multicolored textiles that the women weave on backstrap looms and that identify the wearers by region and village. On the hot coastal plain of Peru, their woolen mountain clothes become too uncomfortable, and they mark the wearer as a recent urban arrival or as a poor Indian away from home. The migrants quickly adopt jeans and simple T-shirts and shifts. They exchange their leather sandals for rubber thongs, sandals made of old tires, or plastic shoes. The women cut off their long braids and switch from their native Quechua or other Indian language to Spanish, no matter how poorly they might speak it.

Instead of living in tightly connected rural communities, the migrants now live in *pueblos jovenes,* the new towns that spring up around Lima. These are not towns in the traditional sense, however, but collections of shacks made from cardboard and other waste materials in jumbled communities without electricity, running water, or other urban amenities. Pushed out of the countryside by terrorism, famine, and extreme poverty, the Indians have overwhelmed the capacity of the city to absorb and enculturate them.

In the city, the immigrants become mere laborers. Their rural skills in agriculture and animal husbandry become useless. If they have experience in selling or bartering their produce in the rural markets, sometimes the newcomers can apply that knowledge in the streets of Lima, where long lines of vendors sell an array of merchandise from shoe polish and safety pins to feathered masquerade masks and artificial flowers. The major problem with such work derives from the tradition that in the rural areas women traditionally handle selling and marketing, but in the mestizo environment of the city, such work belongs to males. The women who have the experience have fewer chances to use it, and the men who have the opportunity have almost no experience.

In addition to being called *cholos*, Indians huddled around Lima are referred to as *desclasados*, people without class. They are no longer farmers, but they are not yet workers. The culture that they learned proves useless to them in the city, where they must acquire a new culture. Their kinship, religious, and economic institutions and networks become less relevant in the city. The Indians have lost their native culture but have not acquired the culture of the urbanized Peruvian middle class. They are no longer classified as Indians, but they are not classified as white. They live in a social and cultural paradox, but they are not alone. The *desclasados* of Lima number in the millions.

The desperate lives of the de-Indianized masses of Lima result in epidemics, crime, and insanity. Some men find their situations so unbearable that they suffer a complete social breakdown. No longer knowing whether they are Indian or mestizo, they refuse to wear the clothes of either group. They strip off all clothing and wander naked through the streets. They refuse to shave or wash. They sleep in the open, protected from the weather and the dangers of city life only by a piece of cardboard or a few old bags. Frequently they live along major roads and dash in and out among cars, sometimes causing traffic accidents or even being killed. Their bodies quickly become covered with so much soot, grease, mud, feces, and other filth that it becomes difficult to tell whether they are clothed or naked, male or female.

Like characters who flourish in the background of the Peruvian novels of Mario Vargas Llosa, the wild men on the streets of Lima fight dogs over scraps of food, or accept what is given to them, but they are too antisocial even to beg. Stripping away their clothes as well as all social identity and gender, ultimately living with animals, these wild men are no longer fully human. In such conditions, living exposed to the elements and without human relations, the men rarely survive for more than six months. If dogs and scavenging birds do not find their bodies first, sanitation workers or highway-repair teams stumble upon the corpses in ditches or on the dusty medians in the road.

The wild men of Lima represent one of the extremest social and psychological responses displaced people have made to the harsh demands of contemporary urban life. The shantytowns of the *pueblos jovenes* represent a second response that appears less dramatic but is no less devastating.

Throughout the 1980s and into the 1990s, time bombs exploded in Peru on a daily basis. Electricity pylons were blown up, and urban neighborhoods went without electricity for hours or weeks. During much of President Alan García's term, the government sustained a curfew for many of these years with roadblocks and tanks parked on main thoroughfares to prevent violence. Despite the precautions, assassinations, kidnappings, bombings, and arson continued as virtually commonplace events. García's successor, President Fujimori, suspended the democratic government in a move called an *auto golpe*, a "self-coup." He imposed virtual military rule, but still the bombs continued.

Terrorists of the Sendero Luminoso movement specialize in car bombs. They steal a common, unremarkable car, pack it with dynamite, rig it as a giant bomb, and park it in a place where it might do maximum real or at least symbolic damage. Sometimes the car bombs are placed to target soldiers, policemen, foreign diplomats, or judges, or to destroy key installations such as banks, embassies, military schools, or police stations. At other times the terrorists place the bombs near a busy intersection, a bus stop, a school, or in the middle of the affluent Miraflores district. The bombs can kill more than a dozen people when they explode, but they cause much more terror because of the apparent random nature of the killings. The bombs kill motorists, bus passengers, shoppers, workers, or children who have no connection to the government, to politics, or to any positions of power. The terror of the bombs lies not so much in their force as in the capricious randomness of their targets.

Although founded in 1970 by a small group of intellectuals from the University of Ayacucho, the Sendero Luminoso chose to become a guerrilla terrorist organization relying almost exclusively on displaced Indian peasants, the so-called *desclasados*, as its soldiers and operatives. The willingness of so many tens of thousands of these displaced Indians to follow such a deranged philosophy as that presented by the Sendero Luminoso indicates just how hopeless these people perceive their situation to be in modern Peru. The Indians have always been on the bottom socially and economically, but in the twentieth century they have often lost the ability even to feed themselves and their families. In desperation they follow a movement as radical and alien to their traditional culture as Sendero Luminoso.

Terrorist groups in many parts of the world have found recruiting grounds among the detribalized masses of the countryside and the urban area. The Miskito, Sumu, and Rama Indians of Nicaragua were uprooted from their homelands by the Sandinista government, then became easy prey as recruits for the Contras, the antigovernment army along the Honduran-Nicaraguan border. The refugee camps became recruitment pens for the military.

Throughout most of this century the government of Nicaragua worked to make the Miskito Indians into Nicaraguans who spoke Spanish and followed the dictates of the government in Managua. But the Miskito have a long history of resistance to Spanish colonial authority and to the Nicaraguan government. Mosquitia, the homeland of the Miskito, on the eastern coast of Nicaragua, operated as a separate nation under British protection during the nineteenth century, and the native people absorbed many parts of British culture. Many Miskito learned to speak English and became Protestants, although Moravians rather than Anglicans. They adopted British names such as Steadman Fagoth and Brooklyn Rivera, two of their leaders. The Miskito resisted Spanish and Nicaraguan power and culture by maintaining their own language, continuing to be Protestants in a Catholic country, giving their children English names rather than Spanish ones, speaking English as their second language and Spanish as their third.

Tribal lines and ethnic boundaries represent major fault lines in the cultural terrain. As long as there is little disruption or pressure from outside, the faults lie dormant and may even seem to disappear. As soon as pressure builds up, however, the fault lines begin to bulge and stretch. The fault lines form the route along which the society will buckle, move, and perhaps even break.

The split between the Indians of the Atlantic and the central Nicaraguan government of Managua started long before the Sandinistas or the Somoza family came to power in Nicaragua, and it seemed destined to last long after the Sandinistas and their successors in the government of Violeta Chamorro have gone from power. During the warfare of the leftist Sandinista era in Nicaragua, the cultural fault lines between the Indians and the majority mestizos ruptured. The fissure deepened between the mestizos and the Indians and, in turn, a fissure deepened between the Miskito Indians and the Sumu Indians.

While visiting the zone of refugee camps and Contra forces on the Nicaraguan-Honduran border in the mid-1980s, I had an unexpected jungle encounter with the commander of the Contra army, Enrique Bermudez. In an odd misunderstanding, his black, unmarked helicopter landed in a remote field where I was traveling with two companions in a jeep. Commander Bermudez and his guards jumped out and raced over to us; only later did I find out that they had mistaken us for representatives from the CIA, sent to pick him up.

Bermudez was on his way to Danlí for a gathering of military and political leaders of the Contra forces to meet with the CIA, the agency entrusted by the United States government with the distribution of the hundred million dollars appropriated for the Contras. The gathering in Danlí was the first planning session of that distribution.

Bermudez and his guards climbed in our jeep and ordered us to take him to Danlí, a town about an hour's drive over mud roads. Unsure whether we had picked up a hitchhiker or had been hijacked, we complied. I sat in the back of the jeep, face to scared face and knee to knee with Bermudez, who was flanked by his silent young Indian guards. The boys sat with their arms poised to shoot. They never looked me in the face, yet they watched me and the driver constantly. I tried to talk to them, but they refused to answer any of my questions or give any sign that they even understood anything that I said to them.

Wearing a Giants baseball cap, the affable Bermudez wanted to talk, so, while we were together in our involuntary companionship, I asked him about the Indian refugees from Nicaragua—the

Miskito, Sumu, and Rama. Bermudez took up the responsibility
of answering by telling me that there were no Indians anywhere
near this area where we were. All the Indians, he assured me,
were much farther down the Río Coco. The Indians were not
involved in this struggle he said. They had fled the oppression
of the Sandinistas and now they lived peacefully along the Hon-
duran border waiting for the liberation of Nicaragua when they
could return to their ancestral homes.

When we arrived in Danlí, Bermudez suddenly ordered our
driver to stop, and then he and his bodyguards crouched low as
they jumped from the back of the jeep and ran to another waiting
vehicle. They bent over and held their weapons ready, as though
they expected someone to open fire on them at any moment.

Within a few years the Sandinistas were out of power in Nicaragua, and the Contras had been demobilized. Soon after Violeta
Chamorro took over as president of the country, the former
Contra commander Enrique Bermudez was assassinated by unknown agents.

I often wondered what had happened to the Indian boys. I
doubt that the young soldiers had any more of a place in the
new society than in the old. Cultural castaways such as they serve
for fodder in everyone's war. The boys were not the oppressed
peasants and workers in whose name the Sandinistas claimed to
act, nor were they freedom fighters searching for democracy, as
proclaimed by the Contras. They were willing to fight for the
government, for the rebels, for drug traffickers, for anyone who
gave them food, a place, a home, and a mission in a hostile world
that they did not understand.

From Vietnam to Angola, from Nicaragua to Ethiopia, many
of the civil wars between the fall of the German Nazis in 1945
and the fall of the Russian communists in 1991 were explained
in Cold War terms of East versus West, of capitalism versus
communism. But many of the people fighting on both sides were
cultural castaways who had no place in the modern world other
than that given them by outsiders. They proved as willing to
fight for local warlords, capitalism, or communism as for Islam
or for drug traffickers.

Across the world, these castaways are piling up in refugee
camps and in the armies of drug workers used for the heroin
trade from Southeast Asia or the cocaine trade from South

America. They represent vast resources waiting to be organized, activated, and directed by anyone with the money and the interest to do so.

In Liberia I saw much the same kind of situation I had seen in Central America. The declining years of the Samuel Doe regime, in the 1980s, gave rise to some of the worst abuse and naked corruption that I have experienced in any city. Liberia had not been an official colony of another nation, but it had been ruled by an elite class of former American slaves with strong backing from United States business and government. At the end of this long period of rule, the ethnic tensions of Liberia flared with vicious violence. The police brutalized the poor and jailed them at will, threatening them and extorting fines for nonexistent crimes and infractions of the rules. Everyone seemed to know that the government was collapsing, and each government official with even the lowest job wanted to use that job to extort as much as he could of money, jewelry, or anything else of value before the final demise of the government. Such officials preyed upon the tribal people of the countryside, the urban poor and middle class, and occasional visitors into their country. Rebels finally seized Samuel Doe, stripped off his clothes, and then sliced off his ears and methodically tortured the screaming tyrant to death, while they recorded the whole event on videotape.

The loss of ethnic and social identity represented by the roving armies of Liberia, the rebels of Nicaragua, or the displaced Indians of Latin America can be found on every continent. The large cities of Africa have their millions of detribalized natives who no longer fit in their traditional communities but have not mastered urban life. Their anomalous status evidences itself in various ways. The poorest cities of the world have often been the most victimized by the detribalized rural people. In countries such as Somalia and Liberia, they have nearly wrecked their capital cities and crippled the national economy.

The cultural castaways pour into cities such as Nairobi and Lagos in Africa, or Rio de Janeiro and Bogotá in South America. In recent decades, however, they have also been flooding into the cities of the richer nations. Large numbers of Senegalese tribal people have taken over communities of Paris and Marseilles. People from the West Indies and Asia crowd into the poor sections of London and Liverpool. Hmong from the highlands of Southeast Asia live in Minneapolis, and South Pacific islanders make their homes in Los Angeles and Honolulu. Displaced people are no longer the exclusive problem of distant cities such as Cochabamba, Calcutta, and Nairobi; they have become a problem throughout the world.

19

Survival of the Savage

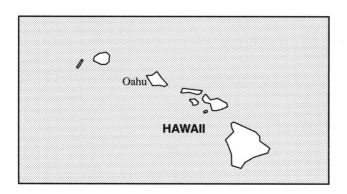

Let Rome in Tiber melt, and the wide arch of the
ranged empire fall. . . . The jungle is still the jungle be
it composed of trees or skyscrapers, and the law of the
jungle is bite or be bitten.
—GEORGE LESTER JACKSON, in a letter written in
    Soledad Prison to his mother, March 1967

A ferocious warrior with an intricately tattooed face stood at
the entrance of a small circle of thatched buildings. He wore a
short skirt, had feathers dangling from his ear, and carried a war
club. The warrior drew back his club as though poised to strike
the approaching visitor. He rolled his eyes down low in their
sockets to show the whites of his eyes and thrust out his tongue
almost to touch his chin.

The warrior guarded the entrance of Aotearoa, the New
Zealand exhibit at the Polynesian Cultural Center on the northern side of Hawaii's Oahu Island. The exhibit contains several
authentically reproduced Maori buildings including the *whare*
puni, the family house, together with the *whare waka* for keeping
the canoe, and the *pataka* for storing food. The buildings faced
onto an open plaza at the head of which rose the *whare runanga*,
the main meeting house of the miniature community. Maori
craftsmen had been brought from New Zealand to carve the
buildings and a large adjacent canoe in the traditional styles.

In the warm Hawaiian afternoon, hundreds of visitors shuffle through the exhibit. Parents come dragging their children who would rather be at the beach. Groups of giggling Japanese honeymooners come through, led by their interpreter-guide, who carries a large umbrella so that his charges can always see him.

Moving through the Polynesian village from Samoa to New Zealand to Hawaii to the Marquesas, the visitor must cross over a boundary, such as a bridge over a canal. The exit from one culture and the entrance to another is clearly marked by signs in several languages. At each pavilion, the visitor learns the appropriate greeting in the language of that area—*talofa* for Samoans, *ka oha* for the Marquesans, *iaorana* for the Tahitians, *malo o lelei* for the Tongans, and *bula vinaka* for the Fijians.

Most of the actors in the Polynesian village come from the society being portrayed in the exhibit, and as a part of their work, they make conversation with the visitors and try to answer a variety of questions ranging from serious or curious to merely stupid.

"Do you still cook pigs in a pit at your home?"

"Only on special occasions."

"Then how do you usually cook your food?"

"My mom uses a stove, but I usually pop it in the microwave."

Such rounds of questions usually produce a mixture of puzzlement and laughter in the audience. The visitors seem unsure whether the answer was meant as a joke or whether the native people in New Zealand and Tonga really do use microwave ovens today.

Scattered among the buildings of the exhibits, Maoris perform songs, dances, and games, and make a variety of crafts. The Maori women, wearing black lipstick, twirl *poi* balls—soft, white balls attached to long strings, which they twirl in various patterned ways. They also teach young children how to twirl them. The young warriors show the visitors the art of Maori warfare with the *tewhatewha* and other weapons. Following the demonstrations, the Maori men and women gather together for a series of songs and dances in which the women twirl the *poi* balls; the couples also play games with *ti raku*, sticks that they hit together in elaborate games of skill and playful dances.

At different exhibits over the forty-one-acre site, the performers teach the visitors to dance the hula, to beat the drum, to weave palm fronds, to make coconut-fiber mats, to grow taro, and to make floral leis. The performers offer visitors an opportunity to taste freshly cooked taro and green bananas, coconut milk, Tongan pigs baked in an earth oven, and Hawaiian poi, a nearly tasteless paste pounded from the starchy taro root.

As the visitors leave the Maori village, they can pause for an ice cream before following the small canal to any one of seven other islands representing Samoa, Fiji, Hawaii, the Marquesas, Tahiti, Tonga, and the early Christian mission to the South Pacific. Each village has its own show of culture and artifacts native to it. In Tonga they make *tapa*, the traditional bark cloth, and weave coconut leaves. In Fiji the men play the drum and dig a pit to roast a pig wrapped in banana leaves. In Samoa one learns how to husk a coconut and grind its meat, how to make coconut cream, and even how to make fire, while listening to an outrageous comic making jokes about himself and about the tourists gathered around him. In each of the exhibits, the hosts welcome the visitors warmly in their native language and try to teach something of their native culture.

Contrary to first impressions, the Polynesian Cultural Center, which attracts over a million visitors a year, is not an amusement park. It operates as a nonprofit center opened on the northern side of Oahu in 1963 by the Mormons, officially known as the Church of Jesus Christ of Latter-Day Saints. They built the center adjacent to the Hawaiian campus of Brigham Young University, where students from throughout the United States and other Pacific nations attend classes during the morning and work in the cultural center in the afternoon. The students from the islands represent the crafts, dances, and languages of their own cultures. Other students work in the ticket booths, concession stands, gift shop, and theater; they push the canoes and visitors in wheelchairs, and guide tour groups speaking Japanese, Spanish, Korean, German, or French.

The actors complete their performances with all the precision and excellence that one expects form Mormons. The young people have wide smiles, carefully coiffured hair, smooth faces, perfect teeth, and no apparent facial hair. As befits the environment of a cultural center attached to a university, the costumes, crafts, dances, ornaments, foods, and games correspond in great detail to the real places portrayed. Some of the performers have traditional tattoos, but most of them apply thick makeup to create the elaborate Polynesian tattoos anew each day. The center even has the trees, flowering shrubs, and other plants typical of each island portrayed. The organizers have gone to great trouble to portray the culture as accurately and precisely as possible in such a limited setting.

With no alcohol allowed on the premises, and virtually no smoking or coffee drinking permitted, the walkways, exhibits, eating areas, and even bathrooms stay sparkling clean, despite the thousands of daily visitors and hundreds of young employees. The stores even refrain from selling chewing gum because someone might spit it on the ground or stick it to the underside of a cafeteria table.

Each night, just after dark, a convoy of buses drives up the dark leeward highway on the one-hour drive from Honolulu and Waikiki, bringing hundreds more visitors for the grand evening performance called "Mana! The Spirit of Our People." For almost two hours of youthful exuberance and energy, each of the Pacific nationalities presents a pageant of chanting, drum beating, juggling, *poi* ball twirling, kava serving, and hula and war dancing, climaxing in a grand entry of all the nations united.

The grandchildren of people whom the missionaries punished for wearing their traditional clothes and for participating in their traditional songs, dances, and ceremonies now perform those same songs, dances, and ceremonies for large paying audiences. The young people can now parade themselves in the clothes that the missionaries once condemned as too revealing and savage. Fierce young men fight in choreographed battles and lunge at the audience in mock attack. Images of the gods that were burned and hacked apart by zealous Christian converts have been carved anew for display in Hawaii, but now they have carefully placed loudspeakers hidden in their gaping mouths or nestled into their protruding bellies.

The Polynesian Cultural Center presents a cleaned-up, wholesome, inviting, and even cute version of cultural variety, ethnic groups, and the environment of the South Pacific today. The exhibits concentrate on the arts and the clever skills of each culture. The center shows us the way we want to see the savages of the past, but it probably says much more about modern American culture and ideals than about the Polynesian people depicted there.

The tribal people of the world have now been confined to reservations, tribal reserves, and tourist parks. They pose no threat to anyone, and remain within easy visiting range of tourists who find tantalizing entertainment in seeing their modern descendants dance, make crafts, and reenact the savage horrors of primitive cultures.

When we look to places such as the Polynesian Cultural Center in Hawaii to find the savage or even the merely primitive, we are looking in the wrong direction. To find the savage in the modern world, we need not look to romantic Polynesia, darkest Africa, the mysterious East, or the feral Amazon. We must turn our gaze back into our own societies, into the cities that form the heart of the civilized world. In the nineteenth century, Polynesia may still have had fierce warriors and even cannibals, but today such people and practices belong in the large cities of the modern world. Rather than looking in Polynesia, we need to look in Los Angeles, Paris, New York, Rome, Chicago, Frankfurt, and Montreal.

For the second half of the twentieth century, Washington, D.C., presided as virtually the political capital of the world. Images of the Capitol and the White House bounce around the airwaves as reporters broadcast news from the front steps of the city's major monuments. Broadcasts carry the speeches of the President and the proceedings of the Senate and the House of Representatives around the world. Washington seems to be a city of momentous events, great decisions, and grave seriousness, as politicians, lobbyists, and reporters attend to the business of running the United States and formulating economic and foreign policy for all corners of the globe.

Central Washington, the area encircling the White House, the Mall, and Congress, is arguably one of the most important and powerful places in the world. By day, office workers fill the streets and buildings as the workers scramble to and from their jobs in the Treasury Department, the Office of Management and Budget, the Federal Bureau of Investigation, and the ranks of lobbying organizations, all interspersed with office-supply shops, photocopiers, travel agents, and a great array of fast-food franchises purveying burgers, tacos, fried chicken, and deli sandwiches.

At night, the offices and shops close, and caravans of cars pull out of their underground parking garage and crowd the streets, while the less affluent workers head underground into the subway and line up to wait for their trains. The government workers head for their homes in the surrounding suburbs, but the fast-food restaurants in the center city remain open into the night and cater to a different clientele.

The district around the White House gives way to the business of the night. Pushers sell heroin, cocaine, speed, and crack in every darkened corner. Women line the streets in a gauntlet, offering themselves to the drivers of the caravan of cars that come out every night and to the men who walk the streets from one nude bar to another. In cars parked with the motors still running but the lights switched off, women in skimpy dresses crawl in through the passenger's door and kneel on the floorboards to perform oral sex on the drivers. The usually overweight drivers wear wrinkled jackets and loose ties and sometimes even have their government building passes dangling from a pocket clip or a chain around their necks.

Teenage boys hawk what they claimed to be genuine designer watches, diamond rings, gold chains, and bracelets, which they dangle in the air before the faces of passersby. They offer cheap prices on car stereos, televisions, computers, and other goods that they cart around in cardboard boxes. Unshaven and wearing urine-drenched clothes, derelicts line up at the mission for a free meal and, for the fortunate first ones, a place to sleep. Others sleep in the alleys or in abandoned and boarded-up hotels, which they enter through a pried-open door and where they warm themselves with open fires in the middle of their rooms. Runaway boys and girls hang around the hamburger restaurants, dabbling in drugs, petty theft, and opportunistic prostitution or any other activity that produces quick returns for minimal effort.

Within shouting distance of the White House bedrooms, pimps fight constantly with other pimps and with their prostitutes for control of the sex trade. Competing street gangs fight over control of the drug trade; organized crime factions struggle to maintain control over the clubs and houses of prostitution. No matter what the business, the competition is fierce, violent, and frequently deadly. Pimps beat errant prostitutes to death; rival drug dealers shoot one another in the streets. A mysterious serial murderer preys on gay men, and people kill for control of the pornography industry and even over rival video-game arcades.

Throughout the time that I worked there, competing gangs fought over the bookstore where I worked. The clerk who worked in the store before me was shot in the head and killed.

The clerk who replaced me was beaten with a metal pipe and left for dead; although he survived, he never fully recovered. During my research, the store was robbed and trashed, and later the headquarters was burned out, killing yet another person who worked for the company that employed me.

At night, the streets of Washington belonged to the strongest who preyed upon the weakest. The police picked at the edges of crime, arresting a steady but inconsequential flow of prostitutes, pimps, drug pushers, delinquent youths, and petty criminals, but they did little to limit or interfere with the operation of the system. As long as the police kept the criminal activity confined to specific neighborhoods, the city government and electorate seemed satisfied and little concerned with how much crime there was, or how violent it became, within those enclosed zones. The city by night belonged to gangs, criminals, whores, drug pushers, pimps, and their customers and clients. The city's authorities surrendered control of the city by night, and the people who illegally managed the city by night organized themselves into tribal gangs.

Nowhere in the world had I ever witnessed as much savagery, brutality, crime, and cruelty as I saw on the streets of the capital city of the United States. The Tuareg warriors of the Sahara and the Muslim militants of Egypt seemed peaceful compared with the people who ran the sex trade of Washington. Work in the Amazon jungle, among people whose ancestors shrank heads, or among the descendants of cannibals in Melanesia, ranked lower in stress and fear than work among the gangs of Washington. Even research into the cocaine trade in South America, with its coca farms, drug kitchens, and private armies of drug lords' thugs, ranked far lower in danger and capricious violence than research among the drug sellers of Washington.

On the streets of Washington I saw forms of social organization and culture that I had never seen among any tribal people. Everywhere in the world, tribal life centers on the family and on family units, but in the center cities of America the family has broken down. In Washington's crime district, young males pursue lives and interests increasingly separate from the females with whom they beget children. Much of the male activity in these gangs varies between idle boredom and fierce violence. Females lead separate lives in their own world, socializing with other females and maintaining their kinship and friendship groups as a way of coping with and providing for their children.

The young people, particularly males, coalesce into gangs that control much of the legal and illegal activity of the area. Many of the young men die from injecting drugs or sniffing chemicals, or from accidents, sexually transmitted diseases, and murder. Young men and, increasingly, young women spend a significant portion of their youth in jail or prison, where their tribal gangs and culture continue with much the same activities, violence, and murder as in the community outside. Those who survive youth in these center-city areas often themselves become victims for a new generation of young people growing up behind them.

Sometimes the cultural castaways of the city organize their gangs along ethnic lines, but regardless of ethnicity, the gangs operate with the common values of male toughness, bravado, and materialism, values that do not grow out of any ethnic segment of the larger society. Even when they come from a common cultural background, the gangs have more in common with one another than with any particular ethnic group.

The cultural castaways have not stayed in the rural areas of the world; instead they have flooded the cities of the world. They are the descendants of people who were ripped out of their traditional societies and either forced or enticed into a world where they find scant welcome. They have been forced to make a place for themselves in a society that rejects them and does not share their values.

Throughout the urban world, from Hong Kong to Berlin, we find the growth of new gangs organized around almost tribal principles of organization but warped into a new urban format. The gang members wear distinctive clothes, hairstyles, and body adornments. They have their own tribal culture, music, emblems, dances, and speech that clearly separate them from the greater society, even though private companies and the news media may occasionally pick up some part of the gang music, dress, dance, or style and commercialize it to the mainstream culture. The gangs claim a particular territory, which they defend against other territories. The gangs live in a state of continual warfare with one another and with any outside force. They control territory and the flow of some goods, particularly illegal ones, and they tend to be heavily armed.

The twentieth century produced a new form of urban violence among the cultural castaways of society. In Peru the violence takes the form of leftist terrorism and attacks on the power structure. In Germany the violence takes the form of attacks against the refugees and foreigners themselves. In Colombia the violence takes the form of a drug cartel built on an army of thugs who view the whole world as their potential prey. In Britain the violence takes the form of soccer hooligans terrorizing the streets and of Irish terrorists planting bombs in subways, pubs, and department stores. In the United States the violence takes the form of a low-intensity street war of crime that periodically flares into a full-scale riot that lasts for several days.

In the twentieth century, affluent people began to abandon the central cities, or to retreat into fortified high-rise buildings protected by iron bars, security guards, video cameras, razor wire, and electronic doors. In Lima and Paris, New York and London, the affluent class began moving to the outer areas, protected suburban rings of homes, shopping centers, schools, and clubs with manicured green lawns and high, protective walls topped with broken glass set in cement. After first moving to the outer areas, office workers commuted back into the city for work. As communications systems improved, however, more people began working in the outlying areas as well as living there. Using telephones, computers, and fax machines, they could maintain the commercial connections they needed from anywhere. As workers and jobs flowed to the suburban areas and into the edge cities, the department stores, restaurants, and other businesses that had catered to their affluent clientele followed them away from downtown.

Once the jobs began following the commuters out of the city and into the suburbs, the central cities increasingly became the areas of the poor and less educated, the people most likely to be involved with drugs and other forms of criminal behavior. Once-exclusive shopping districts now offer the services of pawn shops that ask for no proof of ownership; convenience stores with iron bars over the windows and an armed policeman at the checkout counter; stores that sell T-shirts with the names of rock groups and various expletives emblazoned on them; fast-food stores that no longer allow the public into their bathrooms; and check-cashing businesses that charge customers a large percentage for a cashier from behind a bulletproof window to cash welfare checks made out to people without bank accounts.

Where neighborhoods used to be, people now live in miles of high-rise warrens covered with graffiti and fence wire, and ripe with the stench of urine and rotting food. Aside from a few exclusive and heavily guarded enclaves, the central city is home to the lost. Cheap hotels offer rooms to rent by the week, the night, or the hour. There are halfway houses for the mentally retarded, the handicapped, and the criminals. Other houses take in abused women, runaway teenagers, and prostitutes fleeing their pimps. Civic and religious groups maintain shelters for the homeless and soup kitchens for the poor of all kinds, but increasing numbers of people simply live on the streets, in abandoned buildings, wrecked cars, and dumpsters.

Civic authorities around the world must go to increasingly greater lengths to ward off the plague of modern crime. One night in the Chinese city of Xian, I witnessed the extent to which Chinese authorities proved willing to go to limit crime in their cities. I saw a major public spectacle near the center of town as a noisy but nervous crowd gathered around a dozen young men with shaved heads. The young men stood with terrified eyes on the back of a truck before the crowd. Signs on the side of the truck proclaimed their various crimes, which they had to confess in public.

At the end of the ceremony of public confession and shame, the police drove the young men to the edge of town and shot them, each one with a single bullet to the back of the head. The family of each executed criminal then had to pay a token fine of a few cents to pay for the bullet. The fine did not cover the cost of the bullet, but it demonstrated symbolically yet clearly that the family must bear part of the blame for what happened.

In countries where authorities have far less civic and martial power than in the totalitarian system of China, citizens increasingly take justice into their own hands. In many parts of the world, justice is rapidly becoming a private affair as the strong use hired protectors to correct any wrongs against them. Increasingly, criminals are kidnapped, beaten, and even killed outside the justice system. Citizens who cannot afford the special services of hired defenders arm themselves to protect their own homes, families, businesses, cars, and other property.

Wherever gangs and uncontrolled crime rise, vigilantes soon follow. Soon it becomes difficult to distinguish one group from the other as the criminals and vigilantes both operate outside the law and employ similar tactics and weapons in their struggle against each other for control of the streets and neighborhoods.

In the twentieth century we have seen the cultural distinctions between city and rural begin to break down as urban blended into suburban, and suburban blended into rural. The city as we have known it in the past few thousand years, since its invention during the agricultural revolution, seems to be changing from the center outward. It no longer holds the death grip on economic and political power that it once had, and it no longer monopolizes the communications and transportation networks.

The city is not dying for lack of people. Around the world, the poor still flock to the city, but the era of the city, as a dynamic institution and as the center of civilization, seems finished. The need for such extreme concentration of social, political, religious, and economic institutions has passed. New forms of communication, transportation, and manufacturing make the traditional form of the city increasingly obsolete in the most developed nations.

Despite the etymology of *civilization* from *city* and the development of the word *savage* from the Latin word for "forest," the most savage way of life is now found in the centers of our most modern cities. Civilization has produced a savagery far worse than that which we once imputed to primitive tribes. Civilization has made its worst fear come true; it has created the very savagery that it feared and projected onto others for thousands of years. The savages have become internal to civilization. Civilization creates and nourishes them. The center city has become the new frontier.

20

The Crisis of Civilization

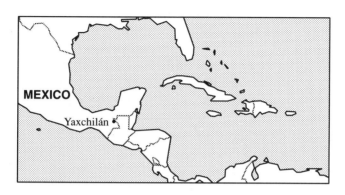

The times combined civilization and savagery.
—HELEN HILL MILLER

Water seems to float in the air of the Lacandon jungle along the Usumacinta River, which divides Guatemala from the state of Chiapas, Mexico. The humidity hangs so heavy that it becomes difficult to tell whether it is actually raining or only dripping. The rain falls in shapeless blobs that hit the large, outstretched leaves of the trees and bushes. The drops of rain glide over one leaf and fall down to the next as though descending a stairway from the towering tops of the trees to the permanent puddles of water on the mossy ground. I step carefully, trying to avoid the puddles and the marshy bogs; yet, even when I step on what I think is dry ground, it gives way and water squeezes out of the ground as though it were a wet sponge.

The rains nourish but do not refresh. They seem merely to add steam to the already oppressive heat. Rain and sweat drip off my head, run into my eyes, and fill my ears. My clothes sag and cling to my skin, but if I roll up a sleeve, the thick swarms of mosquitoes descend on my arms and cover them like the black sand on a volcanic beach.

Today this jungle still serves as home to the Lacandon Maya. Barefoot and dressed in simple white tunics that come down to their knees and make them look like ancient Greeks with long black hair hanging to their shoulders, the Lacandon Maya still wander the rain forest that has been their home for millennia. They visit the ruins of the great cities where their ancestors once lived, and they still hold ceremonies and smoke their sacred cigars among the broken walls and vegetation-covered pyramids. The Lacandon Maya have managed to live in greater harmony with their environment than did the ancient city dwellers, but now new city dwellers are invading their forest home and pushing out the Lacandon as their trees are harvested for wood and their land is drilled for oil.

Photographs and films of the rain forest usually appear so beautiful because of the dense greens and the beautiful colors of the blossoms, fruits, birds, and butterflies, but the rain forest rarely feels even minimally comfortable. Despite all this, people have not only lived in the jungle for thousands of years, but have even built cities in it.

The rain forest of Guatemala, Chiapas, and Campeche once thrived as the social and cultural heartland for some of the most mysterious cities of the world. Why did the Maya build their cities in such inhospitable surroundings, and why, after many centuries, did they then desert them and go elsewhere?

Mystery clings to the Lacandon rain forest like the great vines that dangle from the trees. To get to the ruins of Yaxchilán, it is necessary to follow a long path up from the river and then find the way through a long, dark tunnel. The passageway wends through the rock foundations of a large complex of once official and important buildings that must have overflowed with nobles, priests, servants, petitioners, and worshipers.

To enter the tunnel, I walk through dirty water and slippery mud while insects dart through the air and attack everything that enters their subterranean lair. Slime clings to the walls, and I must stoop low to pass, at times almost crawling through the moist darkness. Stepping at last out of the passageway and through the last corbeled arch, I see a long, large plaza opening out between the buildings and trees before me. From its sides, a sequence of temples and sacred staircases rise up to exquisitely carved temples and more public buildings, looking almost like giant bleachers arranged around an open football field.

The massive scale of the ruins distorts perspective. To regain the human dimension, one needs to examine the detail on the carved archways and the memorial stones the Maya erected in the plaza for unknown religious or political purposes. One of the most important stelae found at Yaxchilán shows a kneeling woman passing a long, knotted cord through her tongue in order to make a blood sacrifice from one of her most sacred body parts. Aristocratic men made similar sacrifices, but they often made them from the genitals. Even though we can easily recognize the human dimensions of these illustrations, we find it difficult to pass the cultural barrier into understanding and full appreciation.

Fear and foreboding hangs as heavy and thick as the moisture in the air around Yaxchilán. The fear does not emanate from the jungle or from the poisonous snakes, stinging insects, killer bees, or fierce jaguars. The fear does not come from the solitary Indians who can be seen slipping behind a tree or watching from a great distance. It does not even come from the whine of low-flying planes bringing in petroleum prospectors and loggers to photograph and map the jungle, or from the armed smugglers who sometimes wander into this deserted area as they ferry contraband and people across the river.

The fear of Yaxchilán does not grow out of anything in nature. Nor is it personal fear of attack or individual harm; it strikes more deeply and spreads more broadly than that. The fear of Yaxchilán is not mortal fear for oneself, it is fear for civilization, or perhaps even a fear *of* civilization.

The fear comes from the cool, damp stones of Yaxchilán itself. It comes from the words and pictures carved into the walls and onto the stelae. It is perhaps the same fear that the early conquistadors and friars felt when they denounced Mayan ruins as places of evil, as the home of the devil. Perhaps it is the same fear that led the early missionaries to destroy the stelae, to bury the stones with their pagan images carved on them, and to burn the Mayan books with their strange inscriptions.

Perhaps the early visitors were right to fear the stones and ruins of the Maya, for in the Maya we see another civilization. We see their written words, their calendar, their astronomy. We see all that knowledge; yet the people of Yaxchilán disappeared. Their civilization crumbled. In Yaxchilán we encounter the fragile and transient nature of civilization, of something that we normally feel is concrete, solid, permanent. Yet, even when built in stone and concrete, it can disappear back into the jungle with hardly a whimper from nature. Yaxchilán reminds us just how ephemeral our civilization really is.

As it was told in the *Popol Vuh*, the creation story of the Quiche Maya, the forces of nature came together to create humans. In their first attempt, the spirits mixed earth with water, and this created people of mud. But the mud people had no substance to hold them together, and when the first rains came, the mud people melted back into the earth from which they came.

On the second creation, the forces of nature came together once again, and this time they made humans of wood. The wooden people were greedy, and they abused the world around them. One day the animals and plants rose up against the wooden people. The animals bit them, the rocks hit them, and the fire burned them, and even their own knives and tools turned against them and cut them. The wooden people disappeared back into the forest from which they came, but their descendants live on in the trees as monkeys to remind us of what greed does to the world.

The third time the powers of nature came together to create people, they made humans of flesh, bone, and blood. The powers of nature gave these humans spirits with which to care and minds with which to think. Nature put these new people on the earth to allow them to make their own life amid the animals and plants. The spirits gave them the power to hunt animals and to grow crops, to make tools and to build cities. The ruins of Yaxchilán warn us that this tale may not have a happy ending unless we do things differently than in the past.

Like the ancient ruins of Angkor Wat in Cambodia, Tiwanaku in Bolivia, Stonehenge in Britain, or Great Zimbabwe in Africa, the deserted city of Yaxchilán holds up a strange and misty mirror in which we can see something that looks very much like ourselves; yet it remains beyond our grasp. Its full meaning eludes us. We recognize the traits of a similar civilization, but we do not understand it much better than we would if it had been found on a small planet in a distant universe. Yaxchilán makes us know that other people have walked this civilized road before us. We did not carve this road from the wilderness, and Yaxchilán reminds us that we too may disappear as completely as did its ancient residents.

We see in Yaxchilán a human experiment that extended over hundreds of generations and thousands of years. It absorbed the work and genius of repeated generations working year after year to build and improve, to grow the food, erect the buildings, train the children, make the feathered headdresses, weave the textiles, sew the clothing, write the books, carve the stones, gather the taxes, make the weapons, fight the wars, worship their gods, and do all the other mundane and spectacular acts of human life. Then suddenly it died, and the whole civilization disappeared except for a few ruined buildings and whatever may have been left buried in an old grave or a trash heap.

For me, the quest that began at the sky burial in the Tibetan Himalayas ended in the jungles of Chiapas, but it ended with its own set of questions and new concerns. At Yaxchilán I can see so much of human history at once. From the temple ruins, I look over the trees at the single-engine airplane that brought me into the jungle. I see the mysterious Lacandon Indians wandering among the trees with purposes I do not comprehend. All around me I see the ruins of the great city of Yaxchilán. Each of these vistas is an important part of the scene. They all live intertwined with one another in a strange way—the tribal past and the civilized present, or perhaps the civilized past and the tribal future. At Yaxchilán I see more than I understand, and I wonder whether I am looking at our past or our future.

Across history, one civilization after another has collapsed. These civilizations rarely fade away; rather, they often collapse relatively suddenly and spectacularly in war, civil unrest, pestilence, environmental disruption, or some combination of all of those things. When they collapse, such civilizations take the surrounding towns and even other cities with them.

When a local city such as Yaxchilán collapsed or when a regional center such as Rome fell, the damage devastated large areas. The collapse of a city usually meant the collapse of a nation or an empire, but civilization continued to flourish somewhere else on the globe. While Rome fell, China and Persia flourished. While Yaxchilán collapsed, the Andean civilizations of South America thrived.

Today we have no local and regional civilizations. The world now stands united in a single, global civilization. Collapse in one part could trigger a chain reaction that may well sweep away cities across the globe.

Will the fate of Yaxchilán be the fate of all cities, of all civilization? Are they doomed to rise, flourish, and then fall back into the earth from which they came?

*   *   *

Civilization began ten thousand years ago with the development of agriculture, the rise of towns and cities. Although at first glance ten thousand years may seem like a long time over which to test and refine a strategy and a way of life, it is a brief span in the millions of years of human history and even less in the scale of billions of years of natural history. Perhaps these ten thousand years mark only a brief experiment in human history; if so, it falls far short of the duration of the experiment in big-game hunting in the last Ice Age. The last ten thousand years of history may prove to have been a mistake that nature will force us to rectify in the millennia ahead.

Conversely, perhaps these ten thousand years have been a mere transition from foraging to some vastly superior way of life. Perhaps we stand on the verge of a great breakthrough in human culture that will lift us to a level as high above today's world as we stand above the humans who lived in caves.

Whether we take an optimistic view or a pessimistic one, it seems clear that we stand now at the conclusion of a great age of human history. This ten-thousand-year episode seems to be coming to an end, winding down.

For now, it appears that civilization has won out over all other ways of life. Civilized people have defeated the tribal people of the world who have been killed or scattered. But just at the moment when victory seems in the air for civilization, just at the moment when it has defeated all external foes and made itself master of the world, without any competing system to rival it, civilization seems to be in worse danger than ever before. No longer in fear of enemies from outside, civilization seems more vulnerable than ever to enemies from within. It has become a victim of its own success.

In its quest for dominance, civilization chewed up the forest, leeched the soil, stripped the plains, clogged the rivers, mined the mountains, polluted the oceans, and fouled the air. In the process of progress, civilization destroyed one species of plant and animal after another. Propelled by the gospel of agriculture, civilization moved forcefully across the globe, but it soon began to die of exhaustion, leaving millions of humans to starve. Some of the oldest places in the agricultural world became some of the first to collapse.

Just as it seems to have completed its victory over tribal people, the nation-state has begun to dissolve. Breaking apart into ethnic chunks and cultural enclaves, the number of states has multiplied in the twentieth century to the point that the concept of a nation-state itself starts to deteriorate.

The nation-state absorbed the remaining tribal people but has proven incapable of incorporating them fully into the national society as equal members. The state swallowed them but could not digest them. The state could destroy the old languages and cultures, and it easily divided and even relocated whole nations. But the state proved far less effective at incorporating the detribalized people into the new national culture. Even though the state expanded across the frontier, it could not make the frontier disappear. The frontier moved into the urban areas with the detribalized masses of defeated nations, emancipated slaves, and exploited laborers.

After ten thousand years of struggle, humans may have been left with a Pyrrhic victory whose cost may be much greater than its benefits. Now that the victory has been won, we stoop under the burdensome costs and damages to a world that we may not be able to heal or repair. Unable to cope with the rapidly changing natural, social, and cultural environment that civilization made, we see the collapse of the social institutions of the city and the state that brought us this far.

The cities and institutions of civilization have now become social dinosaurs. Even though we may look back with pride over the last ten thousand years of evolution and cite the massive number of humans and the ability of human society and the city to feed and care for all of them, one major fluctuation in the world might easily end all of that. The civilization we have built stretches like a delicate and fragile membrane on this Earth. It will not require anything as dramatic as a collision with a giant asteroid to destroy civilization. Civilization seems perfectly capable of creating its own Armageddon.

During the twentieth century, civilization experienced a number of major scares, a series of warning shots. Civilization proved capable of waging world war on itself. Toward that end, we developed nuclear energy and came close to provoking a nuclear holocaust, and we may well do so yet. When we survived World War I, then World War II, and finally the nuclear threat of the Cold War, we felt safe. When catastrophe did not follow the warning, we felt relief, as though the danger had passed, but danger still approaches us.

Civilization experienced several "super plagues" ranging from the devastating world influenza epidemic early in the century to AIDS at the close of the century. These may be only weak harbingers of the epidemics and plagues to come. Even as life expectancy in most countries has continued to climb throughout the twentieth century, diseases from cancer to syphilis have grown stronger and more deadly.

If war or new plagues do not bring down civilization, it might easily collapse as a result of environmental degradation and the disruption of productive agricultural lands. If the great collapse comes, it might well come from something that we do not yet suspect. Perhaps war, disease, famine, and environmental degradation will be only parts of the process and not the causes.

Today all of us are unquestionably part of a global society, but that common membership does not produce cultural uniformity around the globe. The challenge now facing us is to live in harmony without living in uniformity, to be united by some forces such as worldwide commerce, pop culture, and communications, but to remain peacefully different in other areas such as religion and ethnicity. We need to share some values such as a commitment to fundamental human rights and basic rules of interaction, but we can be wildly different in other areas such as life-styles, spirituality, musical tastes, and community life.

We need to find a way for all of us to walk in two worlds at once, to be a part of the world culture without sacrificing the cultural heritage of our own families and traditions. At the same time we need to find ways to allow other people to walk in two worlds, or perhaps even to walk in four or five worlds at once.

We cannot go backwards in history and change one hour or one moment, but we do have the power to change the present and thus alter the future. The first step in that process should come by respecting the mutual right of all people to survive with dignity and to control their own destinies without surrendering their cultures. The aborigines of Australia, the Tibetans of China, the Lacandon of Mexico, the Tuareg of Mali, the Aleuts of Alaska, the Ainu of Japan, the Maori of New Zealand, the Aymara of Bolivia, and the millions of other ethnic groups around the world deserve the same human rights and cultural dignity as suburbanites in Los Angeles, bureaucrats in London, bankers in Paris, reporters in Atlanta, marketing executives in

Vancouver, artists in Berlin, surfers in Sydney, or industrialists in Tokyo.

In recent centuries, Western civilization has played the leading role on the stage of human history. We should not mistake this one act for the whole drama of human history, nor should we assume that the present act is the final one just because it is before us at this moment. Much came before us, and much remains yet to be enacted.

We must recognize the value of all people not merely out of nostalgic sentiment for the oppressed or merely to keep them like exhibits in a nature park. We must recognize their rights and value because we may need the combined knowledge of all cultures if we are to overcome the problems that now threaten to overwhelm us.

At first glance, the Aleuts who hunt seals on isolated islands in the Bering Sea may seem like unimportant actors on the world stage of today, but their ancestors once played a vital role in human survival of the Ice Age. The Quechua woman sitting in the dusty market of Cochabamba may seem backward and insignificant, but her ancestors led the way into an agricultural revolution from which we still benefit. Because we do not know the problems that lie ahead of us, we do not know which set of human skills or which cultural perspective we will need.

The coming age of human history threatens to be one of cultural conflicts between and within countries, conflicts that rip cities apart. If we continue down the same path that we now tread, the problems visible today in Tibet or Mexico may seem trifling compared with the conflicts yet to come. If we cannot change our course, then our civilization too may become as dead as the stones of Yaxchilán, and one day the descendants of some alien civilization will stare at our ruined cities and wonder why we disappeared.

Selected Bibliography

1. The End of the Modern World

(epigraph quotation) Murdoch, Iris. *A Severed Head*, Harmondsworth, England: Penguin, 1976.

Ekvall, Robert B. *Fields on the Hoof: Nexus of Tibetan Nomadic Pastoralism*. Prospect Heights, Ill.: Waveland Press, 1968.

Twedell, Colin E. and Linda Amy Kimball. *Introduction to the Peoples and Cultures of Asia*. Englewood Cliffs, N.J.: Prentice-Hall, 1985.

2. The Red Heart of the Desert

Blainey, Geoffrey. *Triumph of the Nomads: A History of Ancient Australia*. Rev. ed. Chippendale, New South Wales: Macmillan of Australia, 1975.

Chatwin, Bruce. *The Songlines*. London: Picador, 1988.

——. *What Am I Doing Here*. London: Picador, 1990.

Daniel, Glyn. *The Idea of Prehistory*. Middlesex, England: Penguin, 1962.

Dawson, Sarah, ed. *The Penguin Australian Encyclopaedia*. Victoria, Australia: Penguin, 1990.

Hart, C. W. M., Arnold Pilling, and Jane Goodale. *The Tiwi of North Australia*. New York: Holt, Rinehart and Winston, 1988.

Hughes, Robert. *The Fatal Shore*. New York: Vintage, 1986.

Morgan, Sally. *My Place*. New York: Arcade Publishing, 1990.

Tonkinson, Robert. *The Mardudjara Aborigines: Living the Dream in Australia's Desert.* New York: Holt, Rinehart and Winston, 1978.

3. The Ice Age Revolution

Fagan, Brian M. *The Great Journey.* London: Thames and Hudson, 1989.
————. *The Journey from Eden.* London: Thames and Hudson, 1990.
Fisher, Raymond H. *Bering's Voyages.* Seattle: University of Washington Press, 1977.
Lantis, Margaret. "Aleut," in *Handbook of North American Indians,* vol. 5. Washington, D.C.: Smithsonian Institution, 1984.
Laughlin, William S. *Aleuts.* New York: Holt, Rinehart and Winston, 1980.
McEwen, Edward, Robert L. Miller, and Christopher A. Bergman. "Early Bow Design and Construction." *Scientific American,* June 1991.
Smith, Barbara Sweetland and Redmond J. Barnett, eds. *Russian America: The Forgotten Frontier.* Tacoma: Washington State Historical Society, 1990.
Swartz, Marc J. and David K. Jordan. *Anthropology: Perspective on Humanity.* New York: John Wiley and Sons, 1976.

4. Crops, Animals, and Diseases

Champion, Timothy, Clive Gamble, Stephen Shennan, and Alasdair Whittle. *Prehistoric Europe.* London: Academic Press, 1984.
Fairservis, Walter, Jr. *The Threshold of Civilization.* New York: Charles Scribner's Sons, 1975.
Flon, Christine, ed. *The World Atlas of Archaeology.* New York: Portland House, 1988.
McNeill, William H. *Plagues and People.* New York: Anchor Press, 1976.
Martin, Calvin Luther. *In the Spirit of the Earth.* Baltimore: Johns Hopkins University Press, 1992.
Reader, John. *Man on Earth.* New York: Harper & Row, 1988.
Sauer, Carl O. *Seeds, Spades, Hearths and Herds.* Cambridge, Mass.: MIT Press, 1969.

5. Nomads Across the Heartland

Anthony, David, Dimitri Y. Telegin, and Dorcas Brown. "The Origin of Horseback Riding." *Scientific American*, December 1991.

Basilov, Vladimir N., ed. *Nomads of Eurasia*. Los Angeles Natural History Museum, 1989.

Belt, Don. "The World's Great Lake," *National Geographic* 181, no. 6 (June 1992).

Humble, Richard. *The Fall of Saxon England*. New York: St. Martin's Press, 1975.

Jagchid, Sechin and Paul Hyer. *Mongolia's Culture and Society*, Boulder, Col.: Westview Press, 1979.

Legg, Stuart. *The Barbarians of Asia*. New York: Dorset Press, 1970.

McNeill, William H. *The Pursuit of Power*. Chicago: University of Chicago Press, 1982.

Popple, Nicholas. *Mongolian Language Handbook*. Washington, D.C.: Center for Applied Linguistics, 1970.

Twedell, Colin E. and Linda Amy Kimball. *Introduction to the Peoples and Cultures of Asia*. Englewood Cliffs, N.J.: Prentice-Hall, 1985.

6. The Camel and the Quest for Contact

Bulliet, Richard W. *The Camel and the Wheel*. New York: Columbia University Press, 1990.

Davidson, Basil. *The Lost Cities of Africa*. Boston: Little, Brown, 1959.

Langewiesche, William. "The World in Its Extreme." *The Atlantic Monthly*, November 1991.

McIntosh, Roderick J. "Historical View of the Semiarid Tropics." Paper delivered in the Carter Lecture Series at the Center for African Studies of the University of Florida (Gainesville), 1992.

7. Civilization and Slavery

(epigraph quotation) Rand, Ayn. *The Fountainhead*. New York: Bobbs-Merrill, 1943.

Anti-Slavery Society. "Slavery in Sudan." *Cultural Survival Quarterly* 12, no. 3 (1988).

Stearns, Peter N., Michael Adas, and Stuart B. Schwartz. *World Civilizations*, New York: HarperCollins, 1992.

Thernstrom, Stephan, ed. *Harvard Encyclopedia of American Ethnic Groups*. Cambridge, Mass.: Harvard University Press, 1980.

Turnbull, Colin. *Man in Africa*. Garden City, N.Y.: Doubleday, 1977.

Wittfogel, Karl A. *Oriental Despotism*. New York: Vintage, 1981.

8. Tribe Versus City

Davidson, Basil. *The Lost Cities of Africa*. Boston: Little, Brown, 1959.

Fischer-Fabian, S. *Die ersten Deutschen*. Ludwigsburg, Germany: Droemer Knaur, 1975.

Flon, Christine, ed. *The World Atlas of Archaeology*. New York: Portland House, 1988.

Langewiesche, William. "The World in Its Extreme." *The Atlantic Monthly*, November 1991.

Stearns, Peter N., Michael Adas, and Stuart B. Schwartz. *World Civilizations*. New York: HarperCollins, 1992.

Oliver, Roland and J. D. Fage. *A Short History of Africa*. New York: Penguin, 1990.

Sandars, N. K., trans. *The Epic of Gilgamesh*. Middlesex, England: Penguin Books, 1960.

Service, Elman. *Origins of the State and Civilization*. New York: W. W. Norton, 1975.

Tapper, Joan, ed. *Peoples and Places of the Past*. Washington, D.C.: National Geographic Society, 1983.

9. Alexandria and the Gift of Knowledge

Durrell, Lawrence. *Justine*. New York: E. P. Dutton, 1957.
———. *Balthazar*. New York: E. P. Dutton, 1958.
———. *Mountolive*. New York: E. P. Dutton, 1959.
———. *Clea*. New York: E. P. Dutton, 1960.

Forster, E. M. *Alexandria*. Alexandria, Egypt: Whitehead Morris Ltd., 1922.

Grant, Michael. *From Alexander to Cleopatra*. New York: Collier, 1982.

Jean, Georges. *Writing: The Story of Alphabets and Scripts*. Translated by Jenny Oates. New York: Harry N. Abrams, 1992.

Kitto, H. D. *The Greeks*. New York: Penguin, 1951.

10. The Technology of Nationalism

Abercrombie, Thomas J. "When the Moors Ruled Spain," *National Geographic* 174, no. 1 (July 1988).
Braudel, Fernand. *The Structures of Everyday Life*, translated by Sian Reynolds. 3 vols. New York: Harper & Row, 1979–84.
Meisler, Stanley. "The Golden Age of Andalusia Under the Muslim Sultans." *Smithsonian*, August 1992.
Van Doren, Charles. *A History of Knowledge*. New York: Ballantine, 1991.

11. The Silver Ship Across the Pacific

Helms, Mary W. *Ulysses' Sail*. Princeton: Princeton University Press, 1988.
Kandell, Jonathan. *La Capital*. New York: Henry Holt, 1988.
Wolf, Eric R. *Europe and the People Without History*, Berkeley: University of California Press, 1982.

12. Civilization and Its Environment

Crosby, Alfred W. *Ecological Imperialism*. Cambridge, England: Cambridge University Press, 1986.
Hall, Sam. *The Fourth World*. New York: Vintage, 1988.
McGaa, Ed. *Mother Earth Spirituality*. San Francisco: Harper & Row, 1990.
Vivian, Cassandra, ed. *Cairo*. Cairo, Egypt: American University in Cairo Press, 1988.
Wolf, Eric R. *Europe and the People Without History*, Berkeley: University of California Press, 1982.
Wright, Ronald. *Stolen Continents: The Americas Through Indian Eyes Since 1492*. Boston: Houghton Mifflin, 1992.

13. The Lonely Tasmanian

(epigraph quotation) Fairservis, Walter Jr. *The Threshold of Civilization*. New York: Charles Scribner's Sons, 1975, 5.
Clark, Julia. *The Aboriginal People of Tasmania*. Hobart, New Zealand: Tasmanian Museum and Art Gallery, 1983.
Diamond, Jared. "Ten Thousand Years of Solitude."*Discover*, March 1993.

Fagan, Brian M. *Clash of Cultures*. New York: W. H. Freeman, 1984.

Weidenhofer, Maggie. *Port Arthur: A Place of Misery*. Oxford, England: Oxford University Press, 1981.

14. Romancing the Savage

(epigraph quotation) Melville, Herman. *Typee*, from *The Portable Melville*. New York: Penguin, 1952, 171.

Berlin, Isaiah. *The Crooked Timber of Humanity*. New York: Vintage, 1992.

Chateaubriand, François-Auguste René de. *Atala/Rene*. Translated by Irving Potter. Berkeley: University of California Press, 1952.

Danielsson, M-T. and Bengt. *Gauguin in Tahiti*. Paris: Museum of Man, 1988.

Huyghe, René. *Gauguin*. New York: Crown, 1928.

Pearce, Roy H. *Savagism and Civilization*. Berkeley: University of California Press, 1988.

15. Cannibals and Colonials

(epigraph quotation) Spengler, Oswald. *The Decline of the West*. Translated by Charles Francis Atkinson. Oxford, England: Oxford University Press, 1932, 28.

Oliver, Douglas L. *The Pacific Island*. Garden City, N.Y.: Doubleday, 1961.

Smith, Anthony D. *The Ethnic Origins of Nations*. Oxford, England: Basil Blackwell, 1986.

Vayda, Andrew P., ed. *Peoples and Cultures of the Pacific*. Garden City, N.Y.: Doubleday–Natural History Press, 1968.

16. Micro-nations

(epigraph quotation) Momaday, Scott. *House Made of Dawn*. New York: Harper & Row, 1968, 16.

Cohen, Abner. *Two-Dimensional Man*. Berkeley: University of California Press, 1976.

Hall, Michael. "From Marx to Muhammad." *Cultural Survival*, Winter 1992, 41–44.

Kinnedy, Michael and David Kertzer, eds. *Urban Life in Mediterranean Europe*. Urbana: University of Illinois Press, 1983.

17. Tribal Technology

(epigraph quote) Kael, Pauline. *Going Steady*. Boston: Little, Brown, 1970.

Linthicum, Leslie. "All Navajo All the Time." *Albuquerque Journal*, 21 June 1992.

Mokyr, Joel. *The Levers of Riches: Technological Creativity and Economic Progress*. New York: Oxford University Press, 1990.

18. Cultural Castaways

(epigraph quotation) Mead, Margaret. "American Women." *Saturday Evening Post*, 3 March 1962.

Burger, Julian. *The Gaia Atlas of First Peoples*. New York: Doubleday, 1990.

Thernstrom, Stephan, ed. *Harvard Encyclopedia of American Ethnic Groups*. Cambridge, Mass.: Harvard University Press, 1980.

Toland, Judith D., ed. *Ethnicity and the State*. New Brunswick: Transaction Publishers, 1993.

Wallace, Scott. "The Guns Fall Silent on the Miskito Coast." *Grand Street*, Spring 1988.

Weil, Jim. "From Ekeko to Scrooge McDuck: Commodity fetishism and ideological change in a Bolivian fiesta," *Ideologies & Literature*, 4:1 (Spring 1989).

19. Survival of the Savage

(epigraph quotation) Jackson, George Lester. *Soledad Brother: The Prison Letters of George Jackson*. New York: Coward-McCann, 1970, 107.

Moorehead, Alan. *The Fatal Impact*. Honolulu: Mutual Publishing Paperback Series, 1966.

Oliver, Douglas O. *Native Cultures of the Pacific Islands*. Honolulu: University of Hawaii Press, 1989.

Tainter, Joseph A. *The Collapse of Complex Societies*. New York: Cambridge University Press, 1990.

20. The Crisis of Civilization

(epigraph quotation) Miller, Helen Hill. *Sicily and the Western Colonies of Greece*. New York: Charles Scribner's Sons, 1965.

Quinn, Daniel. *Ishmael.* New York: Bantam/Turner, 1992.

Schele, Linda and David Freidel. *A Forest of Kings.* New York: Quill, 1990.

Tedlock, Dennis, trans. *Popol Vuh.* New York: Simon & Schuster, 1985.

Weaver, Muriel Porter. *The Aztecs, Maya, and Their Predecessors.* Orlando, Fla.: Academic Press, 1981.

INDEX